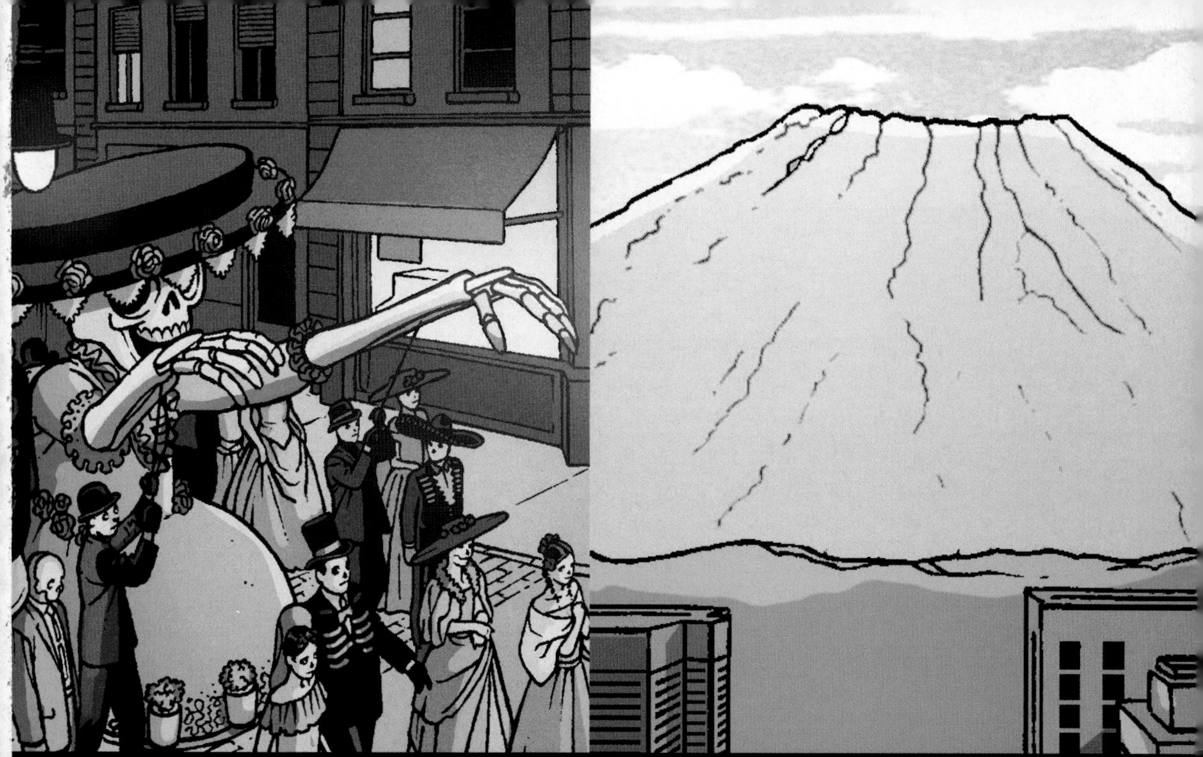

AWA UPSHOT PRESENTS

YEAR ZERO

BENJAMIN PERCY
WRITER

RAMON ROSANAS
ARTIST

LEE LOUGHRIDGE
COLORIST

SAL CIPRIANO
LETTERER

KAARE ANDREWS
COVER ARTIST

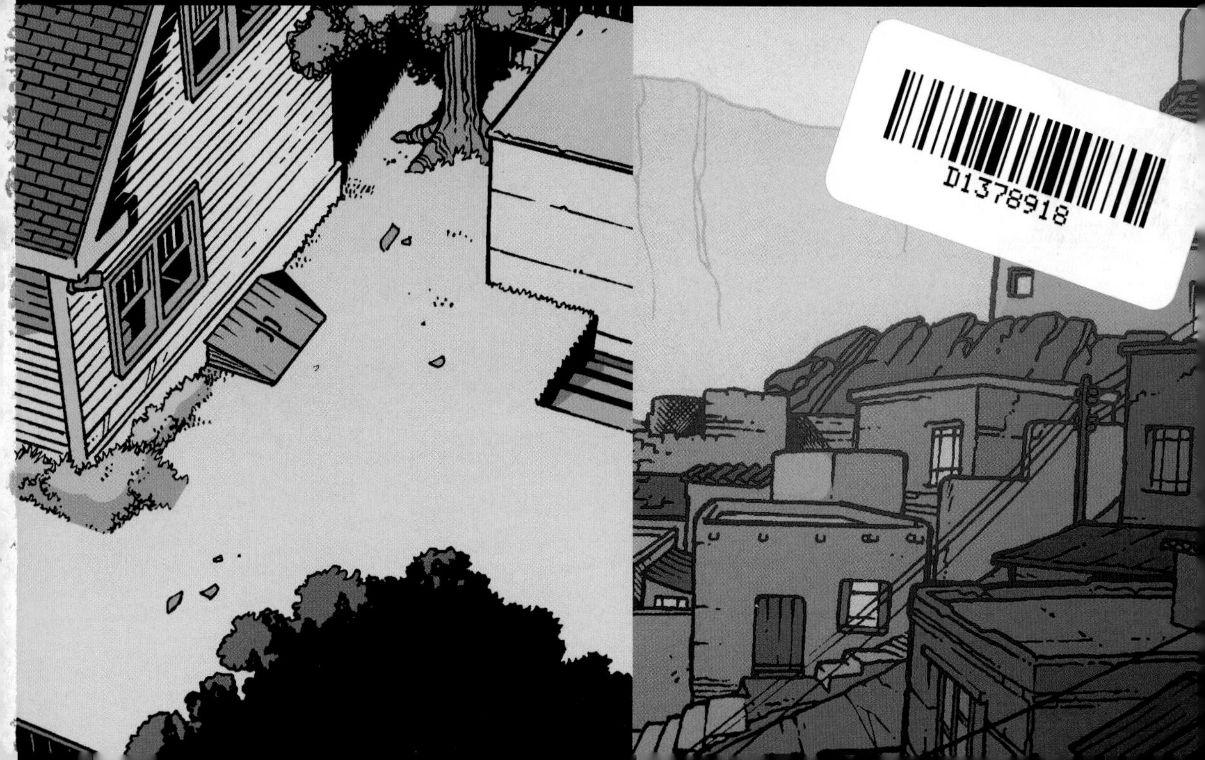

 UPSHOT  @AWA_studios  AWAstudiosofficial  UPSHOT_studios  UPSHOTstudiosofficial

Axel Alonso Chief Creative Officer
Chris Burns Production Editor
Stan Chou Art Director, Logo Designer
Michael Coast Senior Editor
Jaime Coyne Associate Editor
Frank Fochetta Senior Consultant, Sales & Distribution
William Graves Managing Editor
Bill Jemas CEO & Publisher

Amy Kim Events & Sales Associate
Bosung Kim Production & Design Assistant
Allison Mase Executive Assistant
Dulce Montoya Associate Editor
Kevin Park Associate General Counsel
Maureen Sullivan Controller
Lisa Y. Wu Marketing Manager

YEAR ZERO, VOLUME 1. October 2020. Published by Artists Writers & Artisans, Inc. Office of publication: 1359 Broadway, Suite 800, New York, NY 10018. © 2020 Artists Writers & Artisans, Inc. or their respective owners. All Rights Reserved. No similarity between any of the names, characters, persons, and/or institutions in this magazine with those of any living or dead person or institution is intended, and any such similarity which may exist is purely coincidental.

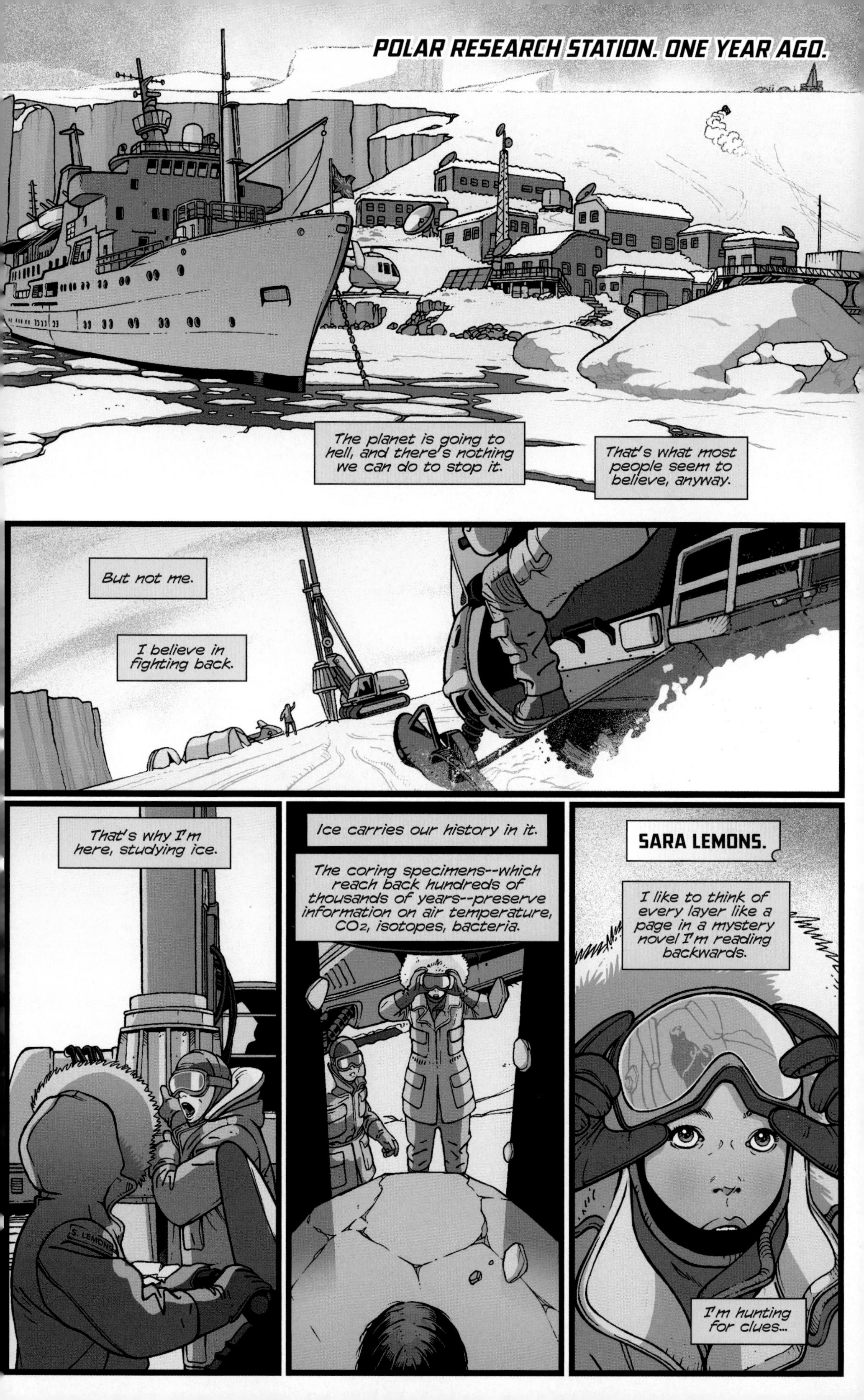
POLAR RESEARCH STATION. ONE YEAR AGO.
The planet is going to hell, and there's nothing we can do to stop it.
That's what most people seem to believe, anyway.
But not me.
I believe in fighting back.
That's why I'm here, studying ice.
S. LEMONS
Ice carries our history in it.
The coring specimens--which reach back hundreds of thousands of years--preserve information on air temperature, CO2, isotopes, bacteria.
SARA LEMONS.
I like to think of every layer like a page in a mystery novel I'm reading backwards.
I'm hunting for clues...

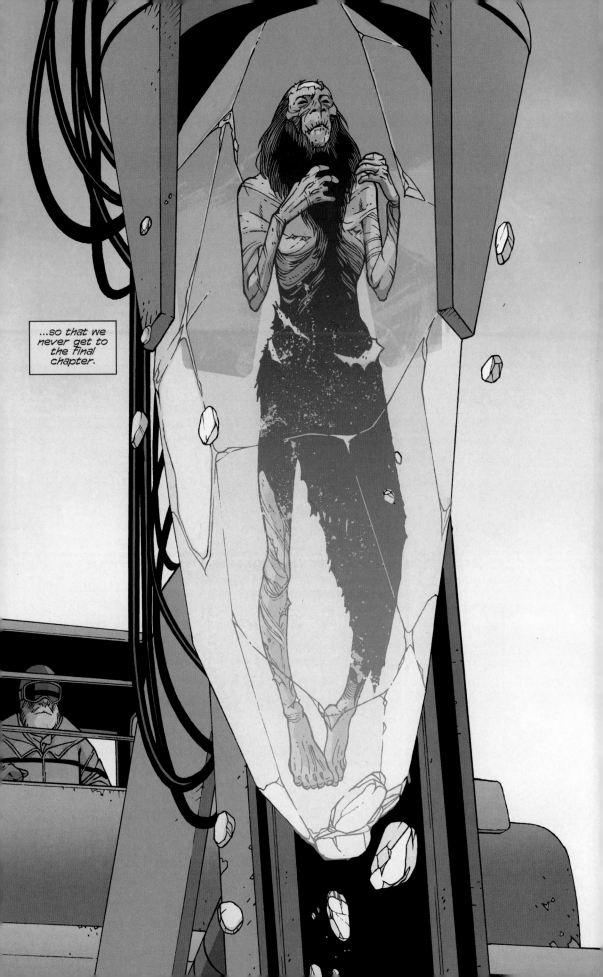

...so that we never get to the final chapter.

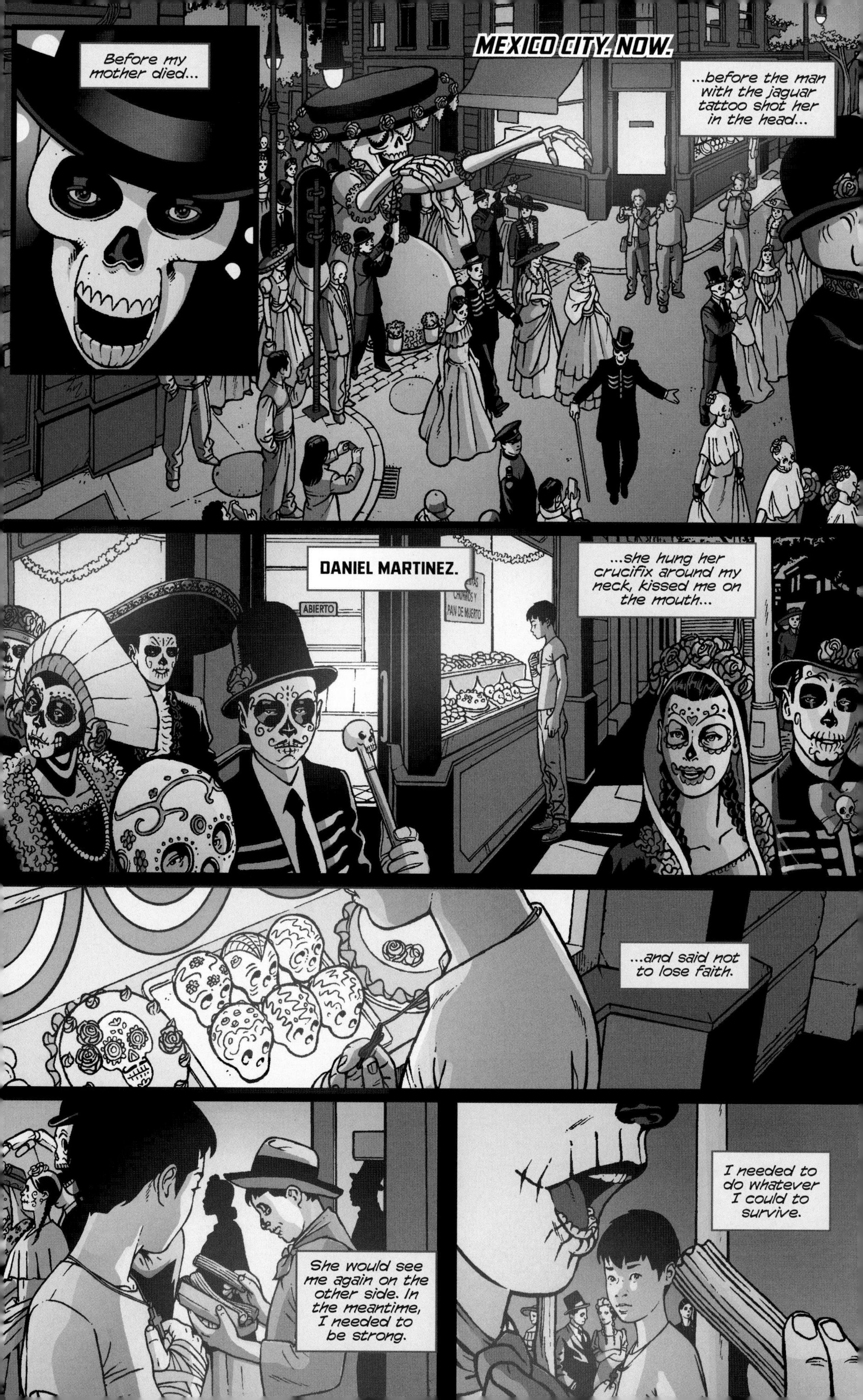
MEXICO CITY. NOW.
Before my mother died...
...before the man with the jaguar tattoo shot her in the head...
DANIEL MARTINEZ.
ABIERTO
PAN DE MUERTO
...she hung her crucifix around my neck, kissed me on the mouth...
...and said not to lose faith.
She would see me again on the other side. In the meantime, I needed to be strong.
I needed to do whatever I could to survive.

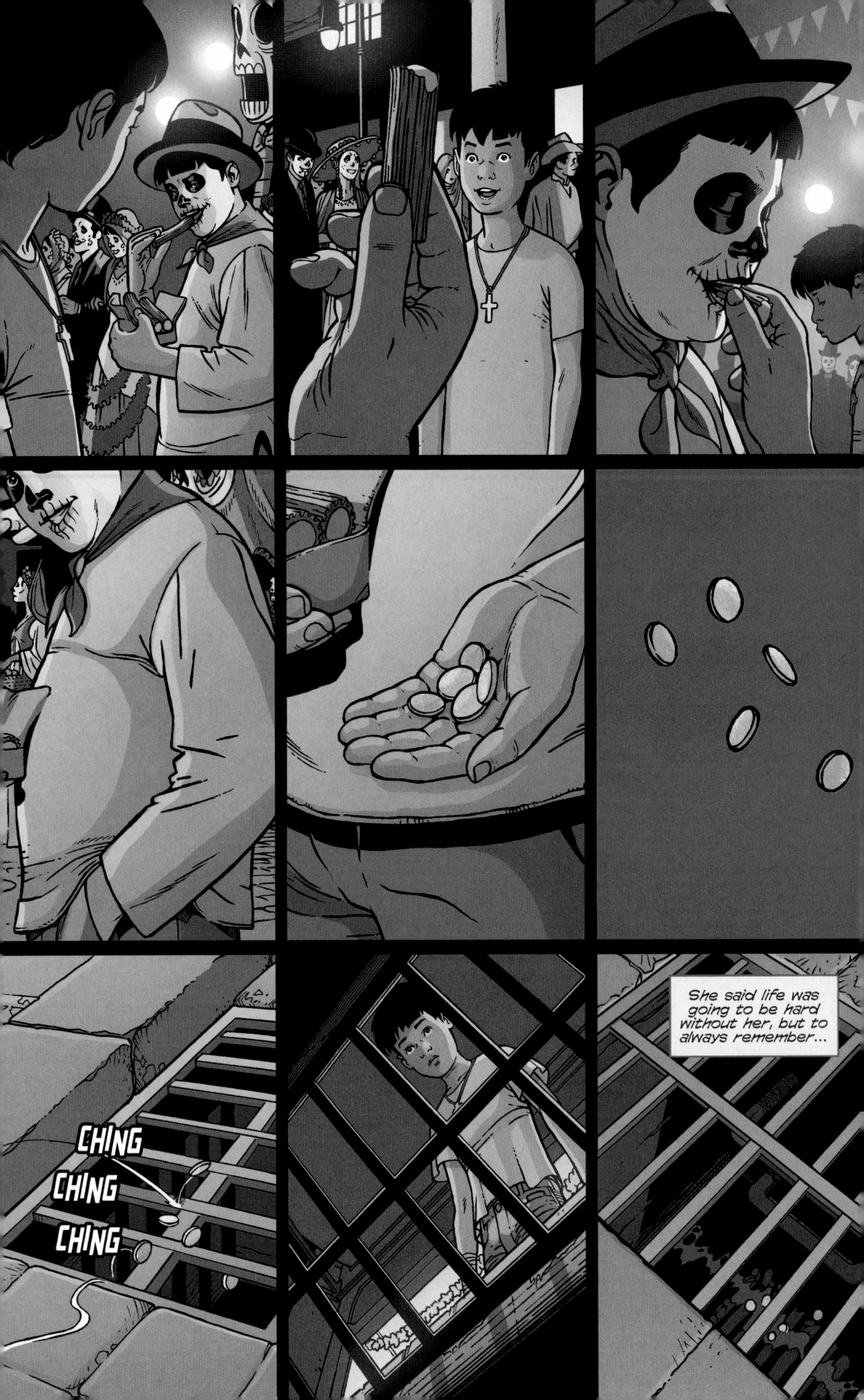
CHING
CHING
CHING
She said life was going to be hard without her, but to always remember...

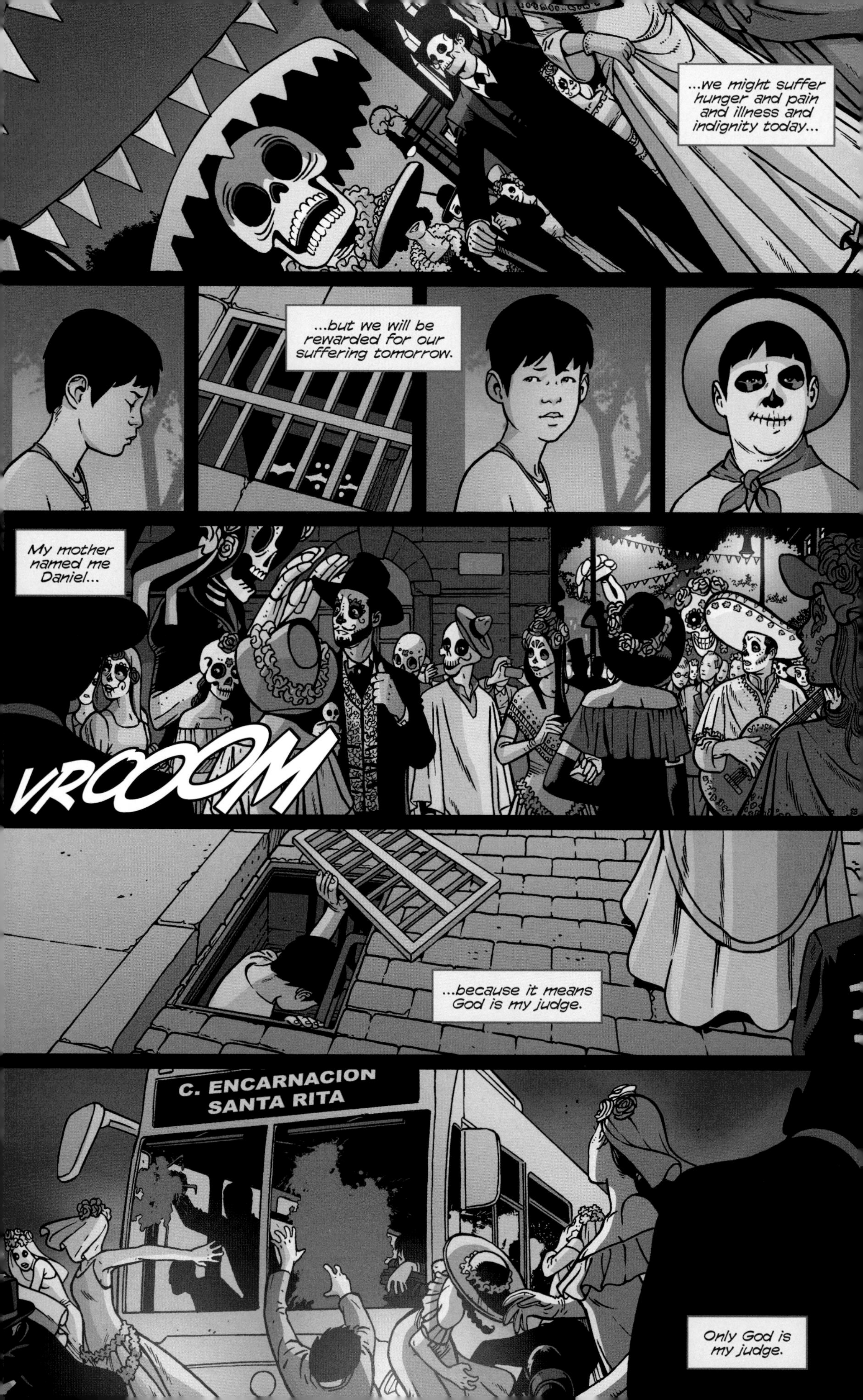
...we might suffer hunger and pain and illness and indignity today...
...but we will be rewarded for our suffering tomorrow.
My mother named me Daniel...
VROOOM
...because it means God is my judge.
C. ENCARNACION SANTA RITA
Only God is my judge.

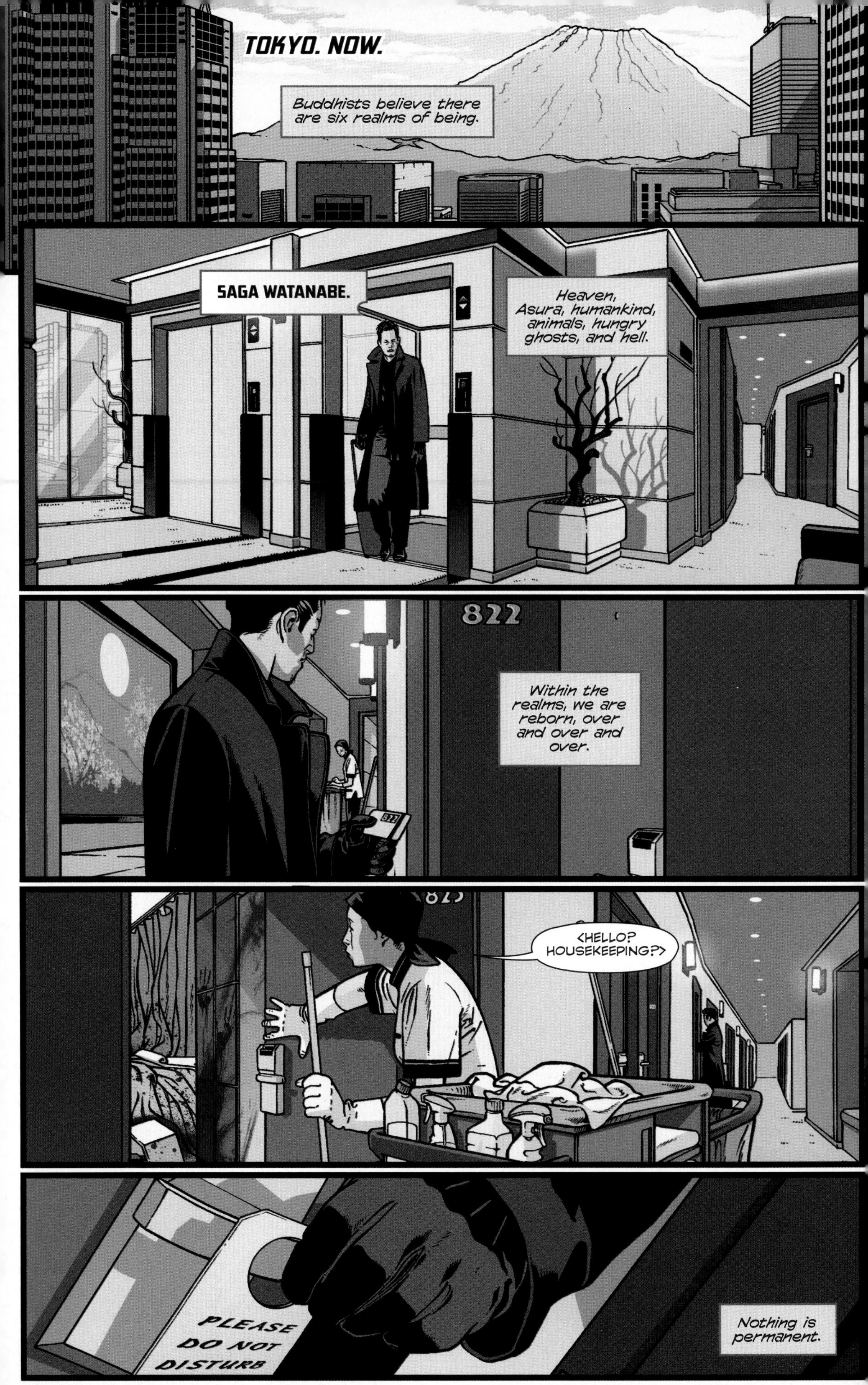
TOKYO. NOW.
Buddhists believe there are six realms of being.
SAGA WATANABE.
Heaven, Asura, humankind, animals, hungry ghosts, and hell.
822
Within the realms, we are reborn, over and over and over.
<HELLO? HOUSEKEEPING?>
PLEASE DO NOT DISTURB
Nothing is permanent.

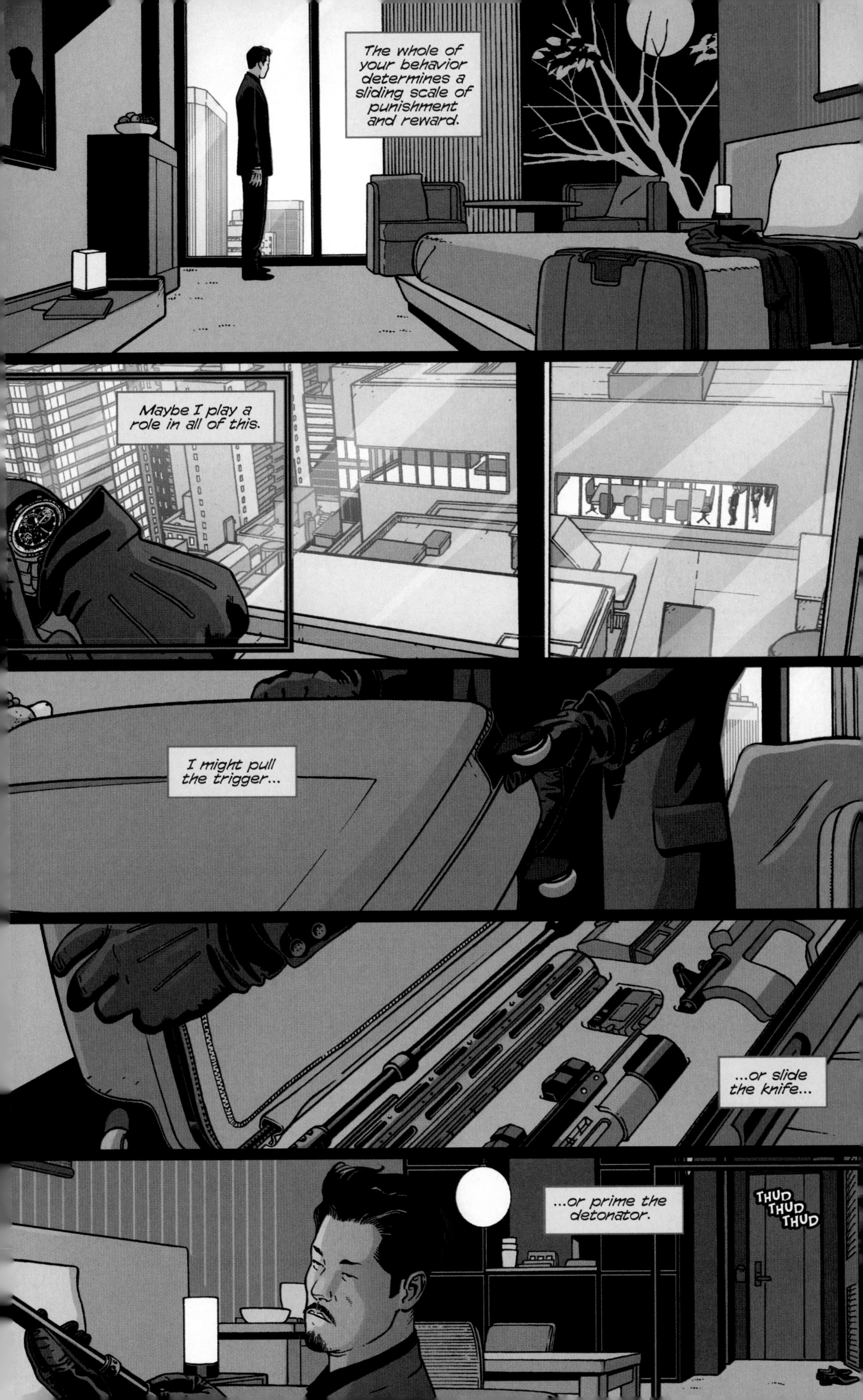
The whole of your behavior determines a sliding scale of punishment and reward.
Maybe I play a role in all of this.
I might pull the trigger...
...or slide the knife...
...or prime the detonator.
THUD THUD THUD

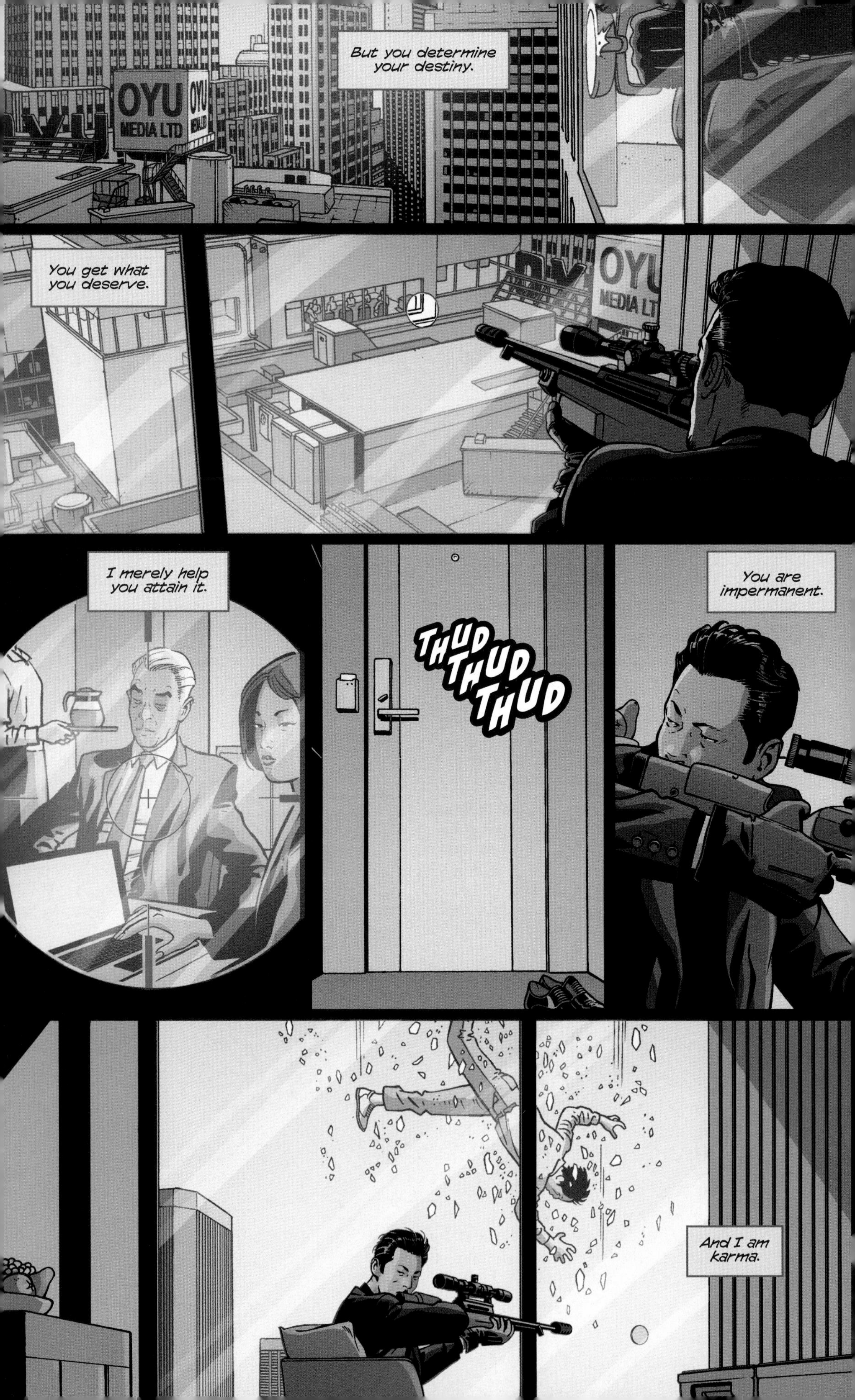
OYU MEDIA LTD
But you determine your destiny.
You get what you deserve.
OYU MEDIA LT
I merely help you attain it.
THUD THUD THUD
You are impermanent.
And I am karma.

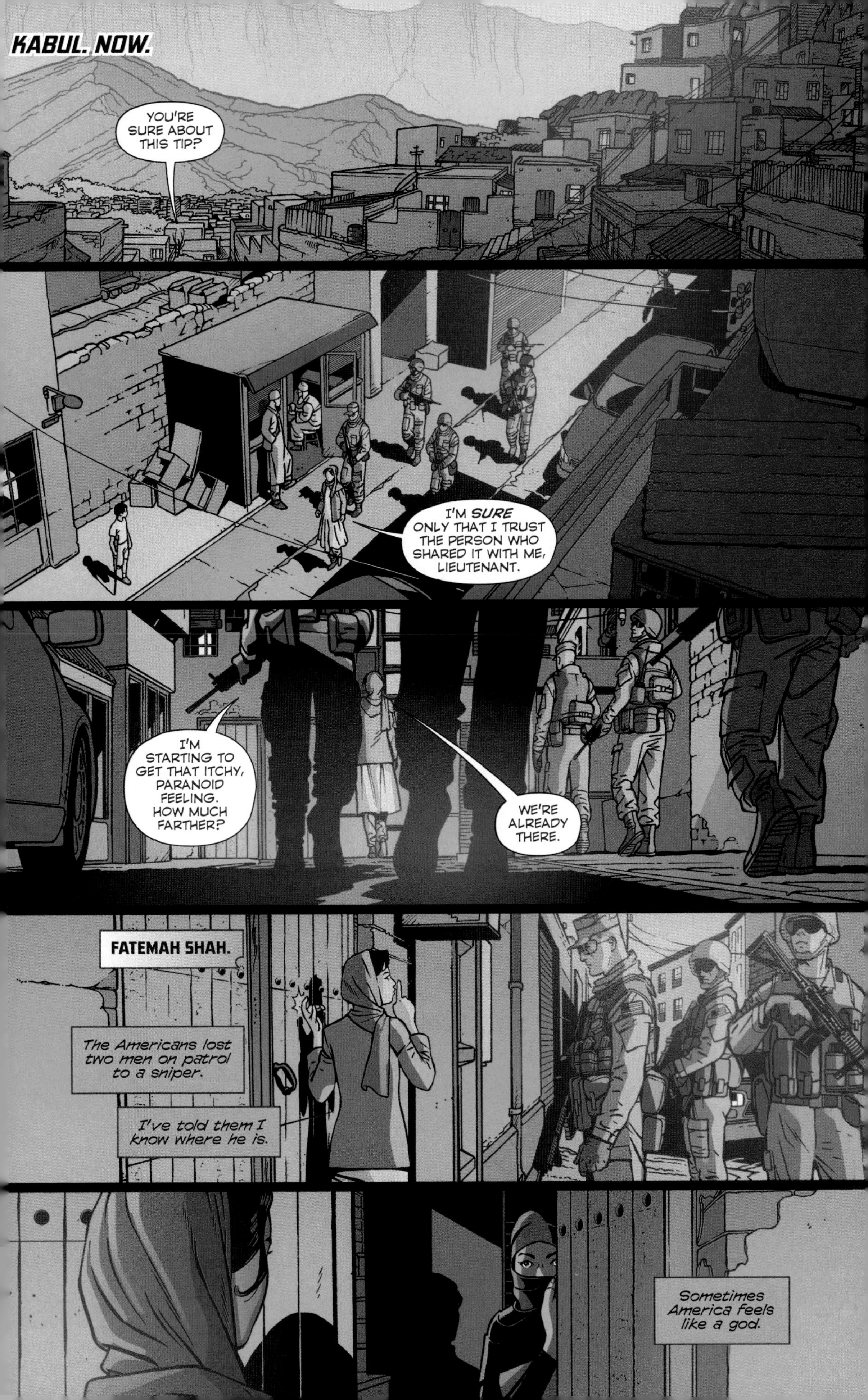
KABUL. NOW.
YOU'RE SURE ABOUT THIS TIP?
I'M *SURE* ONLY THAT I TRUST THE PERSON WHO SHARED IT WITH ME, LIEUTENANT.
I'M STARTING TO GET THAT ITCHY, PARANOID FEELING. HOW MUCH FARTHER?
WE'RE ALREADY THERE.
FATEMAH SHAH.
The Americans lost two men on patrol to a sniper.
I've told them I know where he is.
Sometimes America feels like a god.

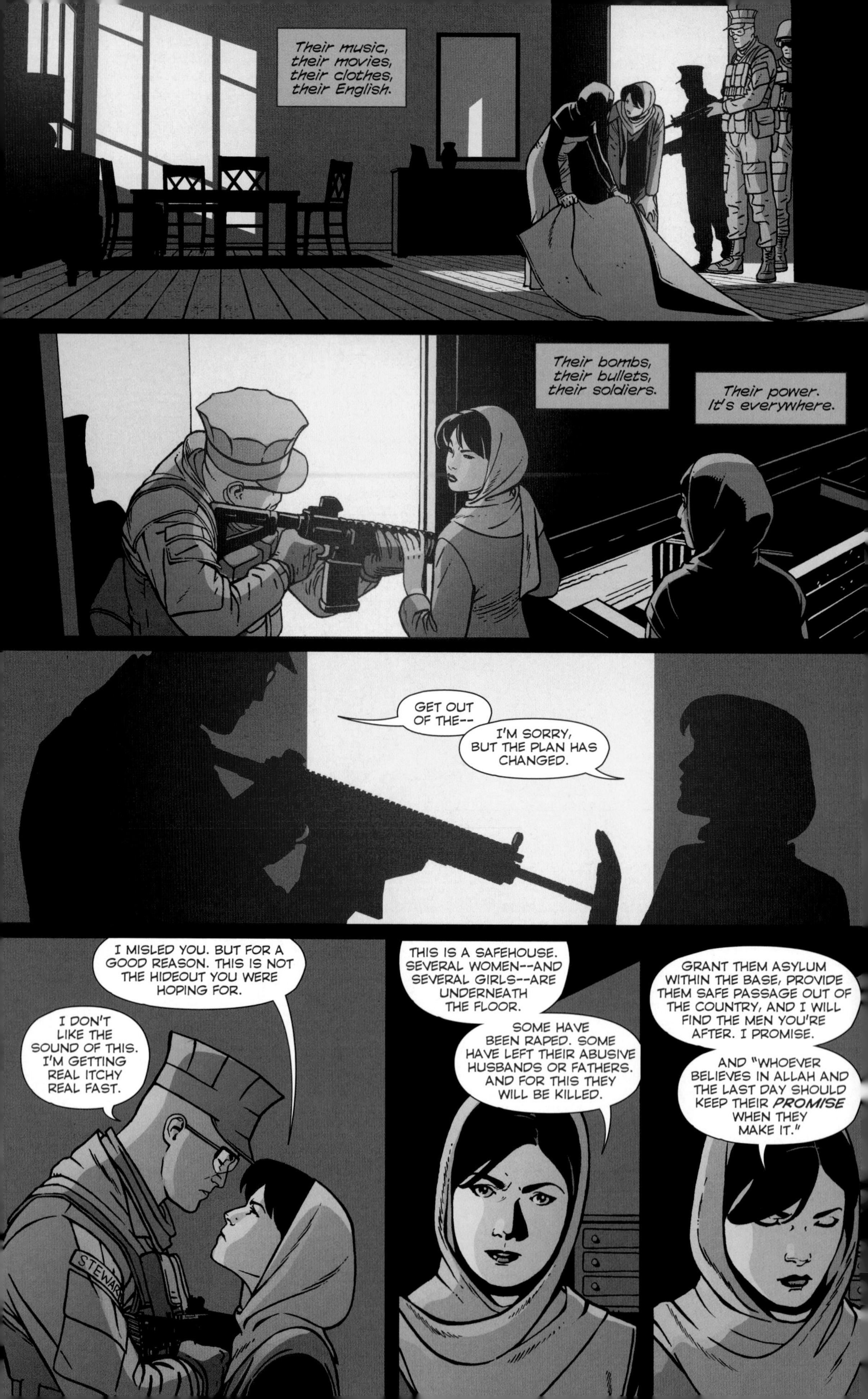
Their music, their movies, their clothes, their English.
Their bombs, their bullets, their soldiers.
Their power. It's everywhere.
GET OUT OF THE--
I'M SORRY, BUT THE PLAN HAS CHANGED.
I MISLED YOU. BUT FOR A GOOD REASON. THIS IS NOT THE HIDEOUT YOU WERE HOPING FOR.
I DON'T LIKE THE SOUND OF THIS. I'M GETTING REAL ITCHY REAL FAST.
STEWAR
THIS IS A SAFEHOUSE. SEVERAL WOMEN--AND SEVERAL GIRLS--ARE UNDERNEATH THE FLOOR.
SOME HAVE BEEN RAPED. SOME HAVE LEFT THEIR ABUSIVE HUSBANDS OR FATHERS. AND FOR THIS THEY WILL BE KILLED.
GRANT THEM ASYLUM WITHIN THE BASE, PROVIDE THEM SAFE PASSAGE OUT OF THE COUNTRY, AND I WILL FIND THE MEN YOU'RE AFTER. I PROMISE.
AND "WHOEVER BELIEVES IN ALLAH AND THE LAST DAY SHOULD KEEP THEIR *PROMISE* WHEN THEY MAKE IT."

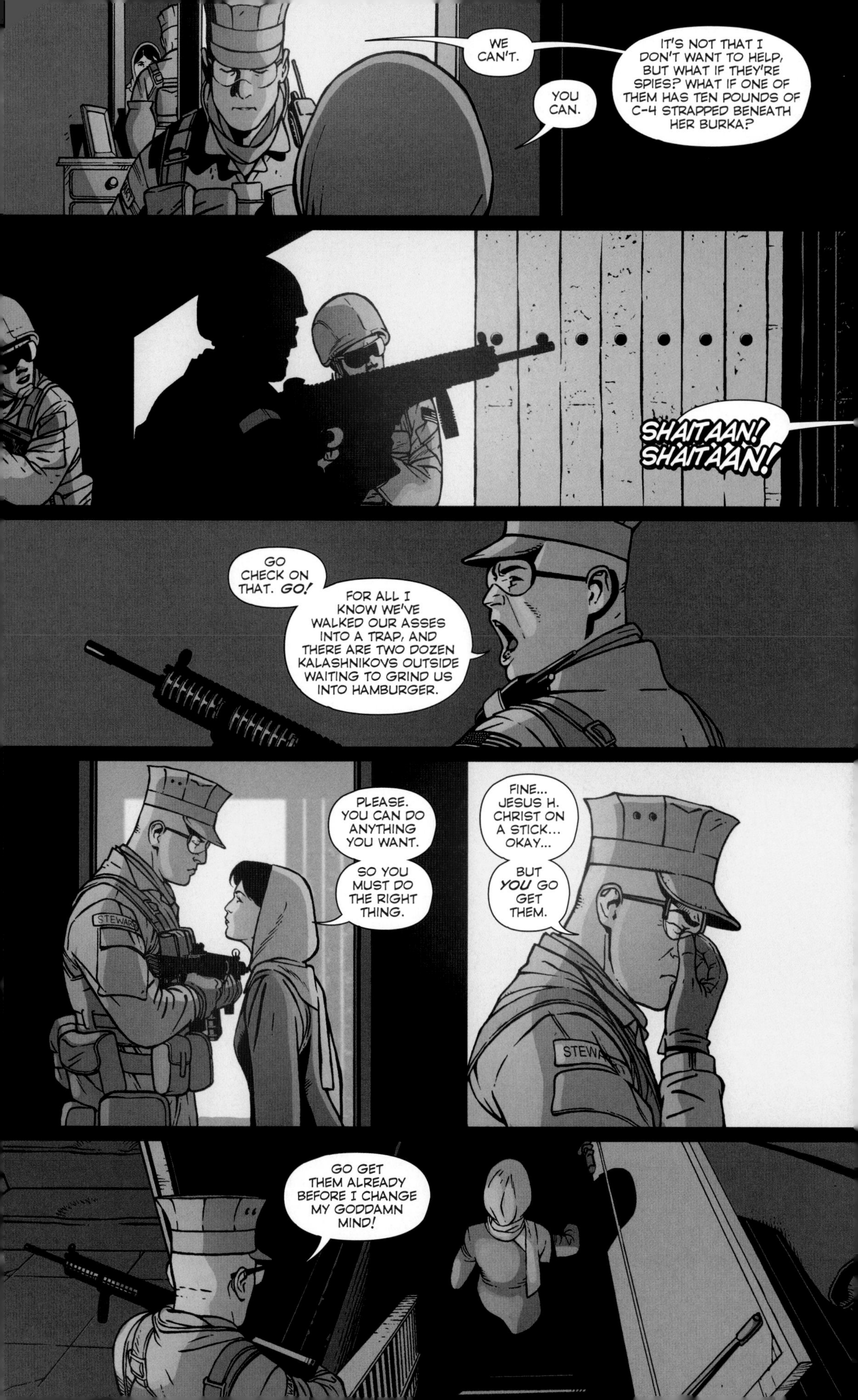
WE CAN'T.
IT'S NOT THAT I DON'T WANT TO HELP, BUT WHAT IF THEY'RE SPIES? WHAT IF ONE OF THEM HAS TEN POUNDS OF C-4 STRAPPED BENEATH HER BURKA?
YOU CAN.
SHAITAAN! SHAITAAN!
GO CHECK ON THAT. GO!
FOR ALL I KNOW WE'VE WALKED OUR ASSES INTO A TRAP, AND THERE ARE TWO DOZEN KALASHNIKOVS OUTSIDE WAITING TO GRIND US INTO HAMBURGER.
STEWARD
PLEASE. YOU CAN DO ANYTHING YOU WANT.
SO YOU MUST DO THE RIGHT THING.
FINE... JESUS H. CHRIST ON A STICK... OKAY...
BUT YOU GO GET THEM.
GO GET THEM ALREADY BEFORE I CHANGE MY GODDAMN MIND!

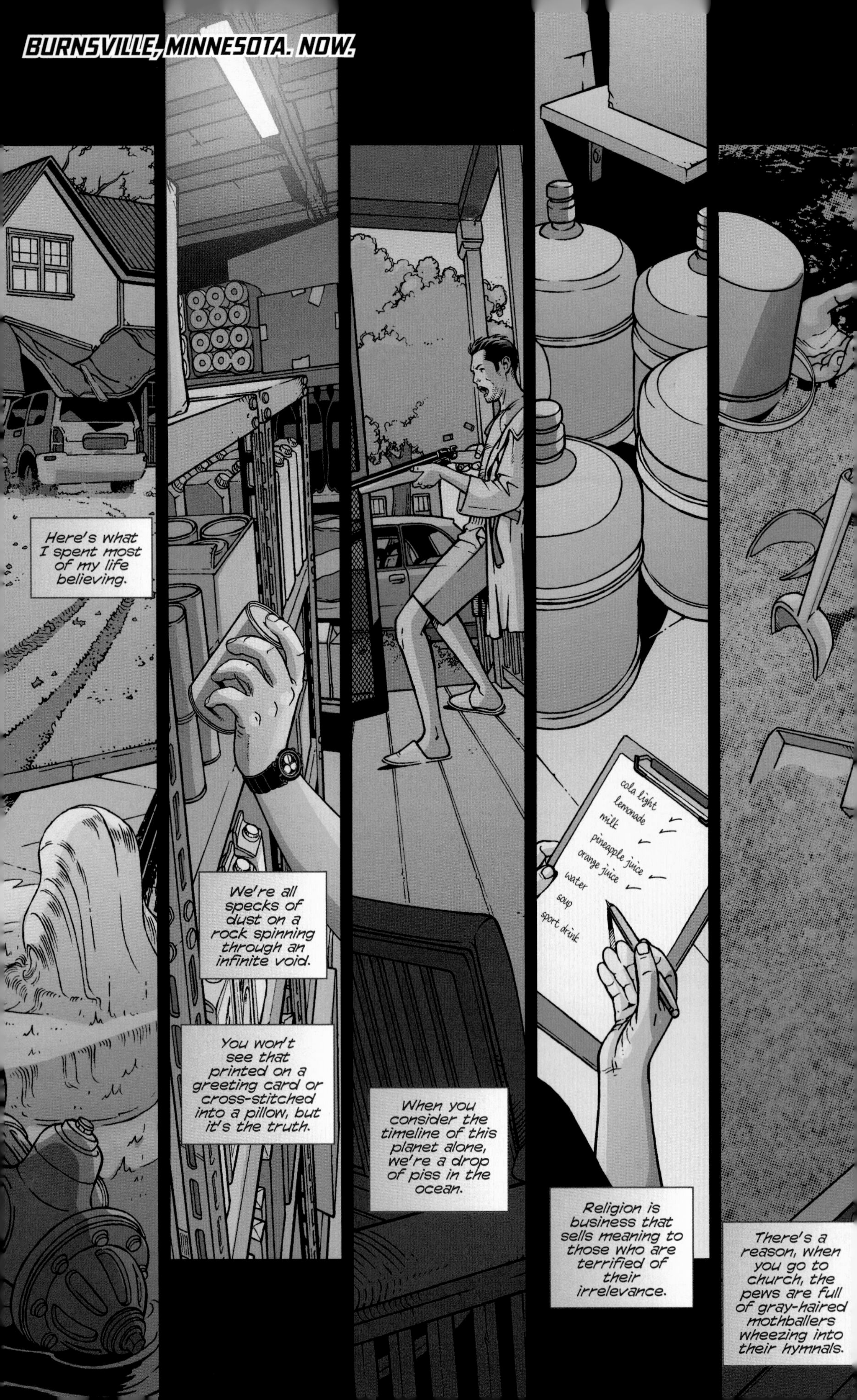
BURNSVILLE, MINNESOTA. NOW.
Here's what I spent most of my life believing.
We're all specks of dust on a rock spinning through an infinite void.
You won't see that printed on a greeting card or cross-stitched into a pillow, but it's the truth.
When you consider the timeline of this planet alone, we're a drop of piss in the ocean.
cola light
lemonade
milk
pineapple juice
orange juice
water
soup
sport drink
Religion is business that sells meaning to those who are terrified of their irrelevance.
There's a reason, when you go to church, the pews are full of gray-haired mothballers wheezing into their hymnals.

Because they're at the end. They've got coffin breath. They're facing the void.

And that's when people panic.

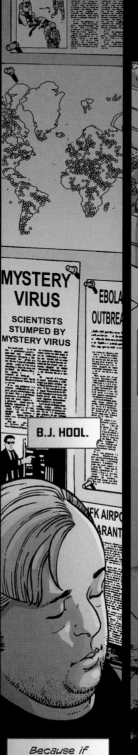

MYSTERY VIRUS

SCIENTISTS STUMPED BY MYSTERY VIRUS

EBOLA OUTBREA

B.J. HOOL.

JFK AIRPO RANT

Because if there's nothing but worms and darkness waiting for you...

...then why did you spend all that time cranking a lever on the factory floor...

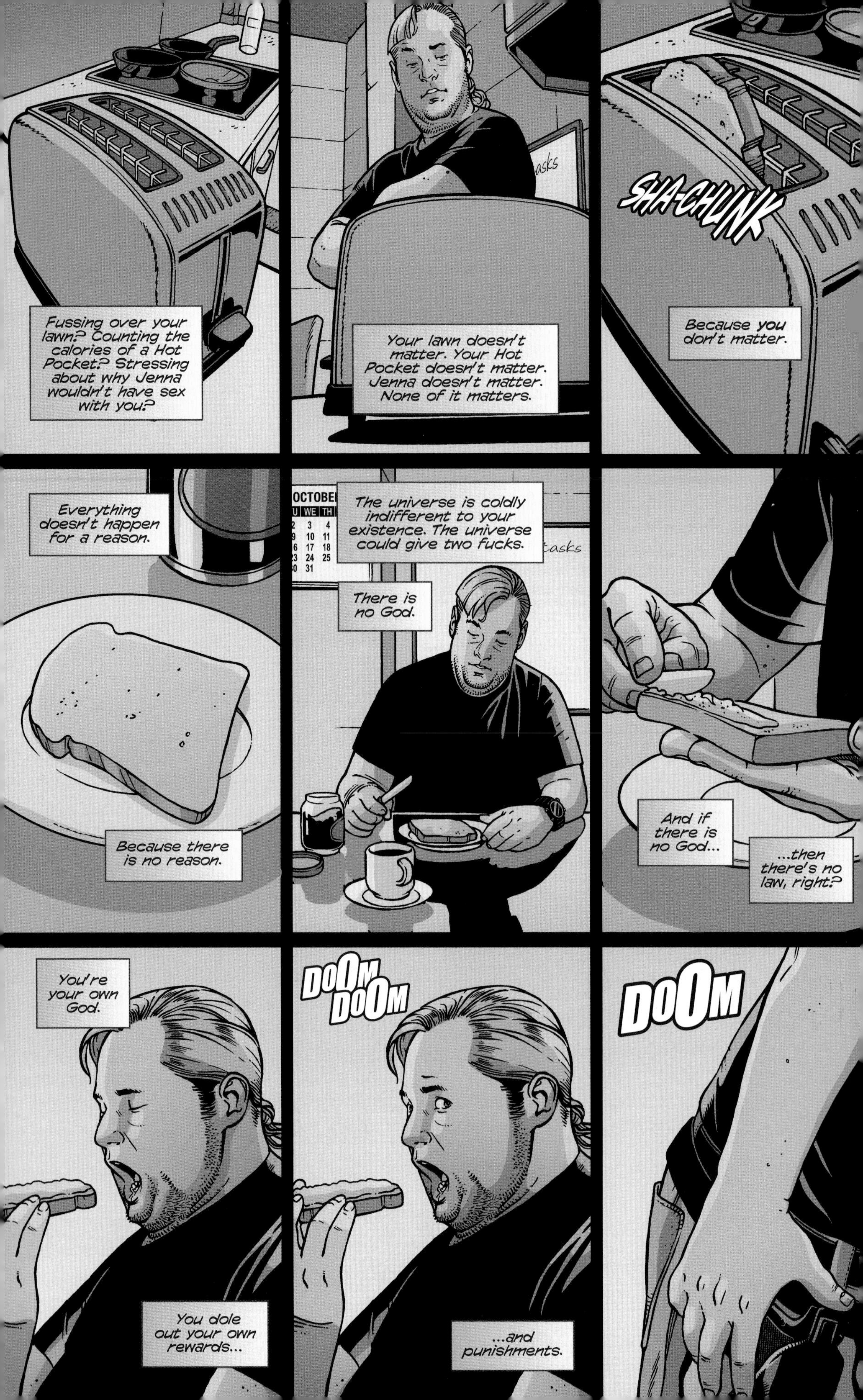
Fussing over your lawn? Counting the calories of a Hot Pocket? Stressing about why Jenna wouldn't have sex with you?
Tasks
Your lawn doesn't matter. Your Hot Pocket doesn't matter. Jenna doesn't matter. None of it matters.
SHA-CHUNK
Because you don't matter.
Everything doesn't happen for a reason.
Because there is no reason.
OCTOBER
The universe is coldly indifferent to your existence. The universe could give two fucks.
Tasks
There is no God.
And if there is no God...
...then there's no law, right?
You're your own God.
You dole out your own rewards...
DOOM DOOM
...and punishments.
DOOM

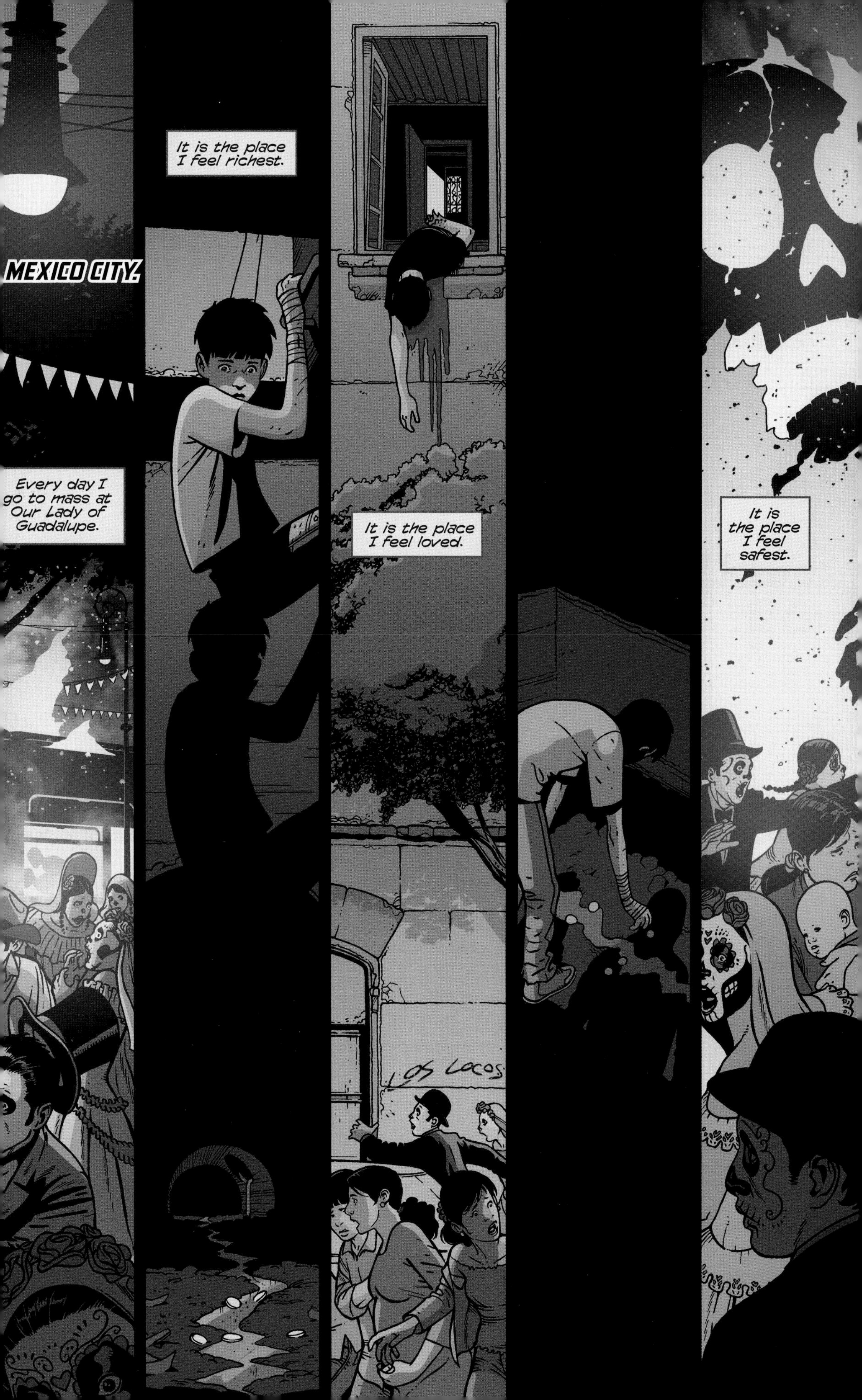
MEXICO CITY.
Every day I go to mass at Our Lady of Guadalupe.
It is the place I feel richest.
It is the place I feel loved.
LOS LOCOS
It is the place I feel safest.

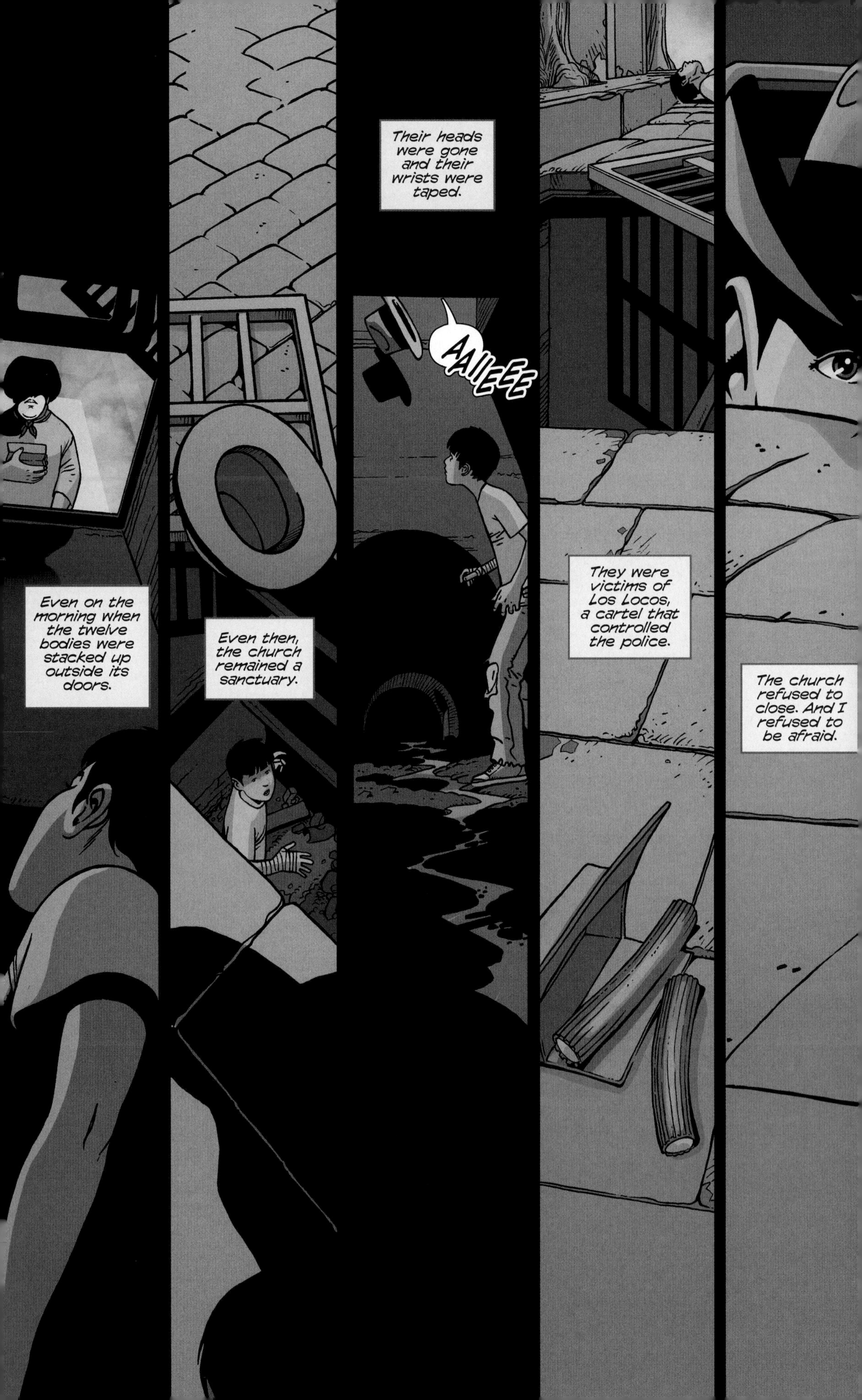
Even on the morning when the twelve bodies were stacked up outside its doors.
Even then, the church remained a sanctuary.
Their heads were gone and their wrists were taped.
AAIIEEE
They were victims of Los Locos, a cartel that controlled the police.
The church refused to close. And I refused to be afraid.

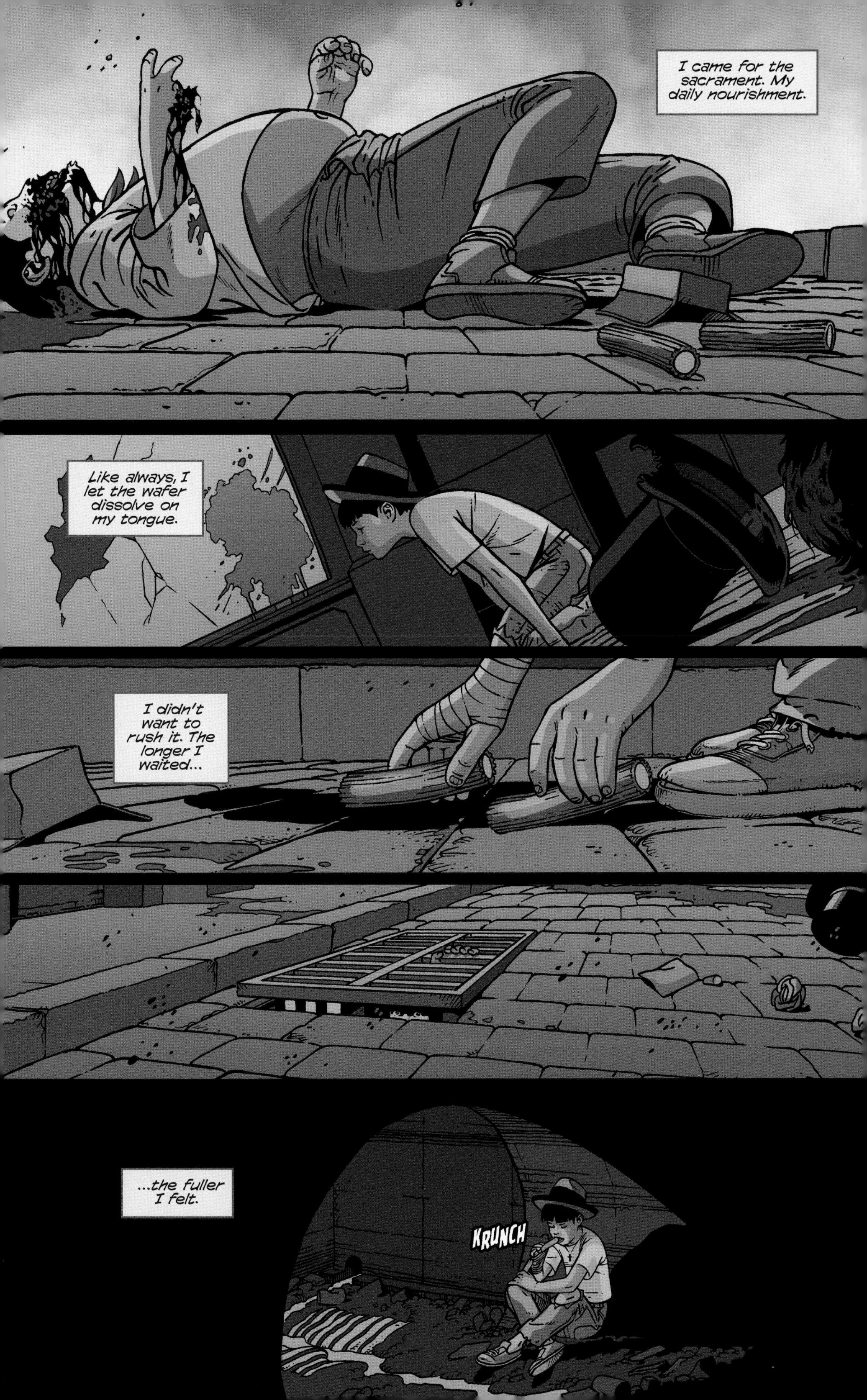
I came for the sacrament. My daily nourishment.
Like always, I let the wafer dissolve on my tongue.
I didn't want to rush it. The longer I waited...
...the fuller I felt.
KRUNCH

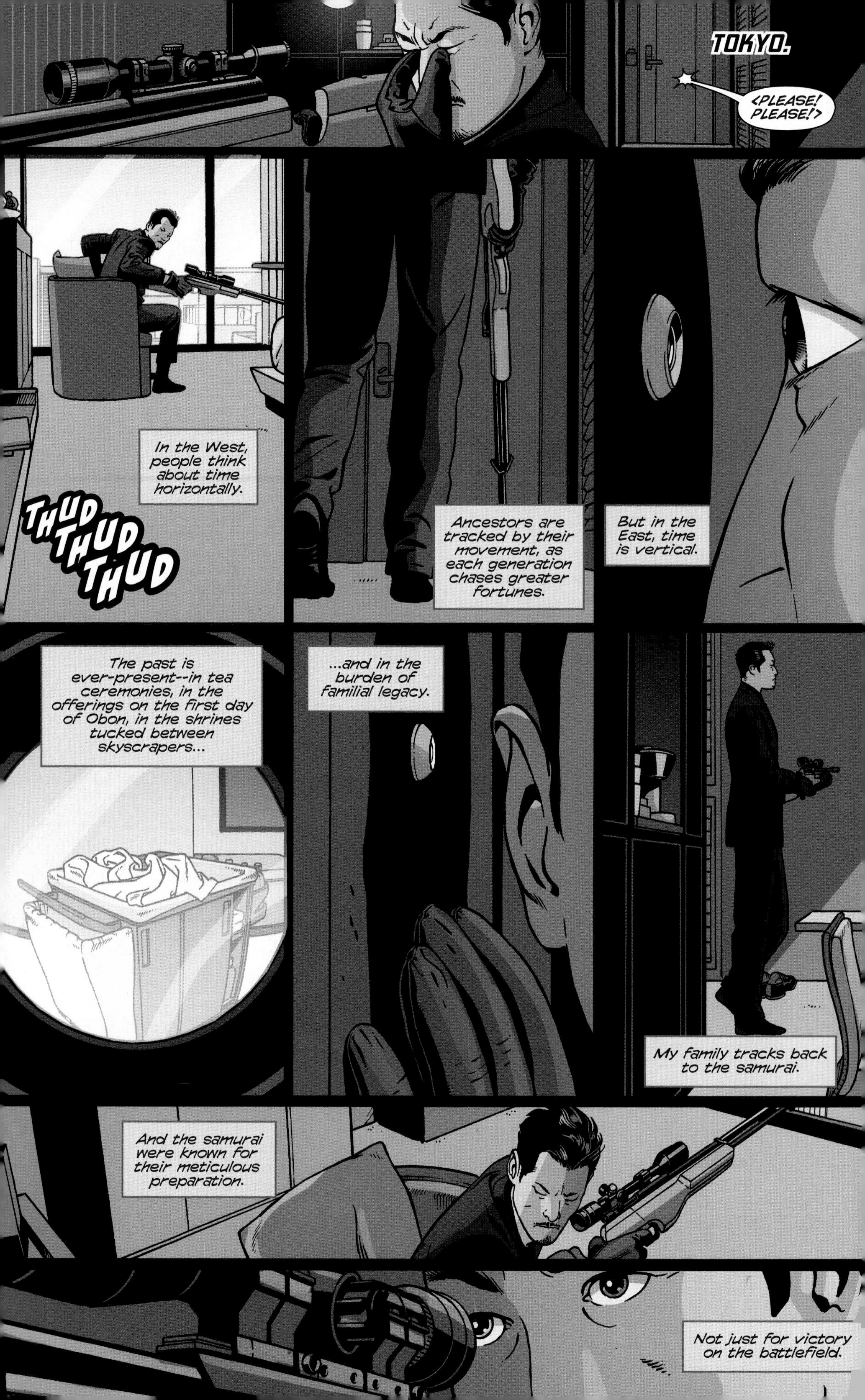
TOKYO.
<PLEASE! PLEASE!>
In the West, people think about time horizontally.
THUD THUD THUD
Ancestors are tracked by their movement, as each generation chases greater fortunes.
But in the East, time is vertical.
The past is ever-present--in tea ceremonies, in the offerings on the first day of Obon, in the shrines tucked between skyscrapers...
...and in the burden of familial legacy.
My family tracks back to the samurai.
And the samurai were known for their meticulous preparation.
Not just for victory on the battlefield.

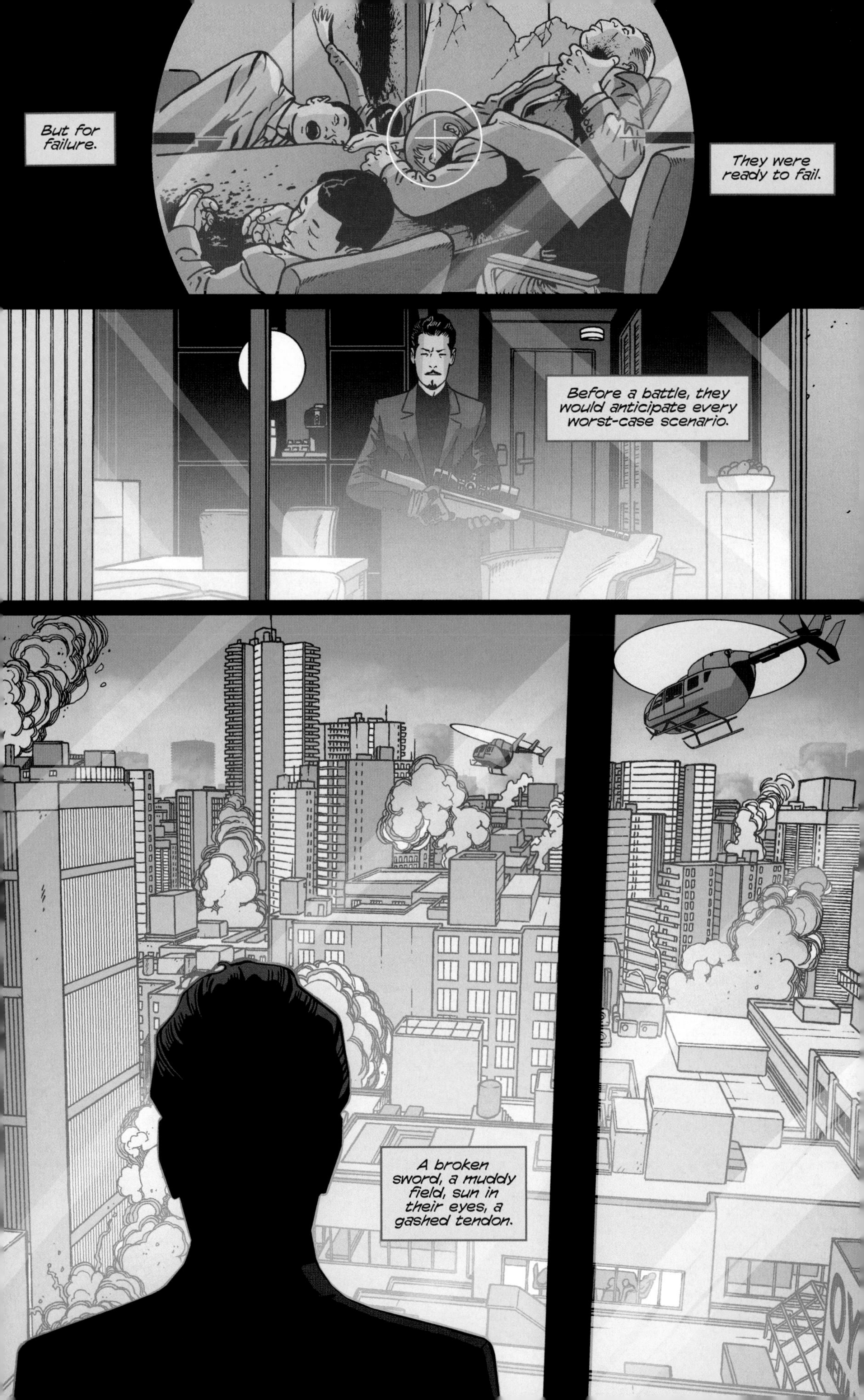
But for failure.
They were ready to fail.
Before a battle, they would anticipate every worst-case scenario.
A broken sword, a muddy field, sun in their eyes, a gashed tendon.

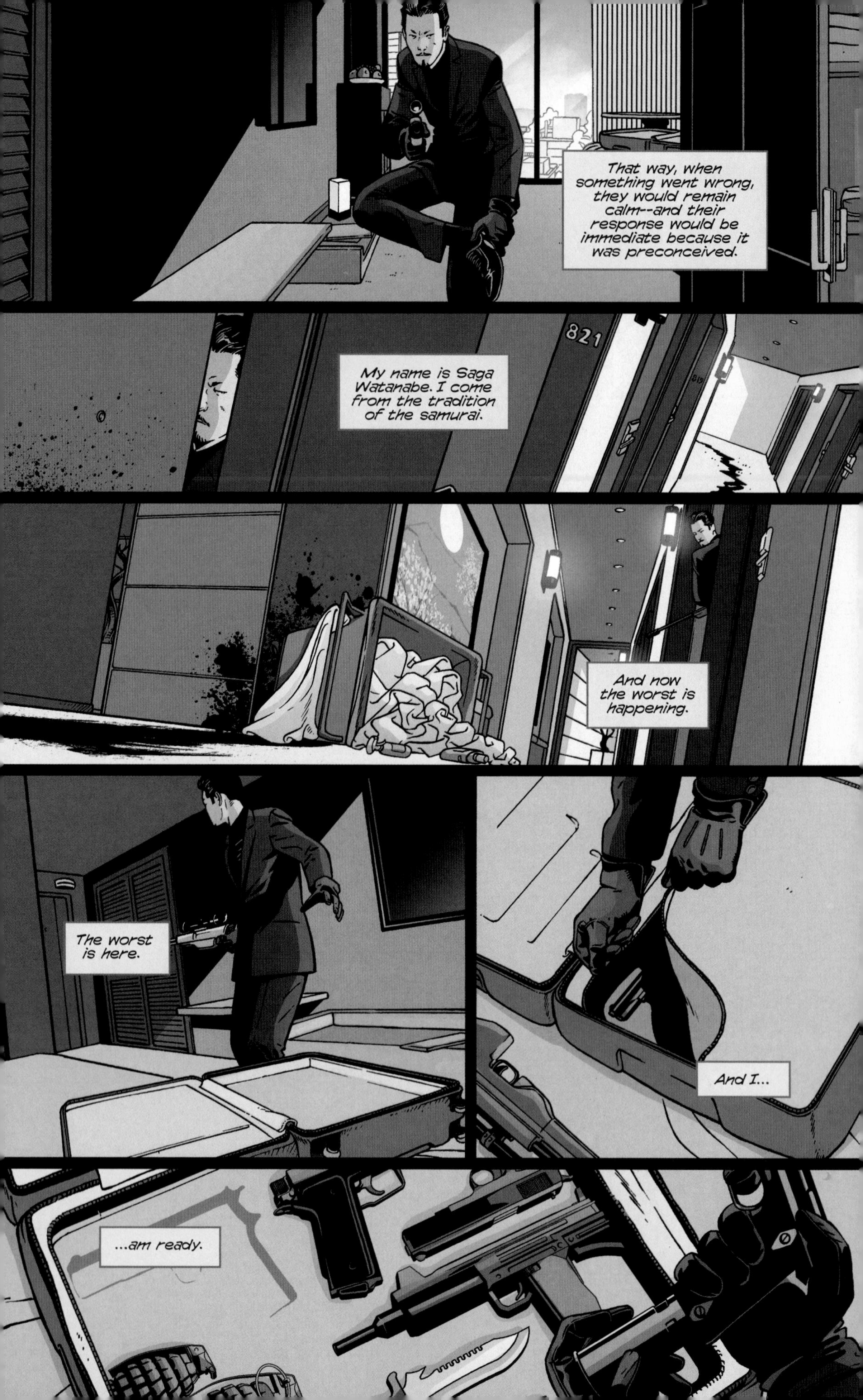
That way, when something went wrong, they would remain calm--and their response would be immediate because it was preconceived.
821
My name is Saga Watanabe. I come from the tradition of the samurai.
And now the worst is happening.
The worst is here.
And I...
...am ready.

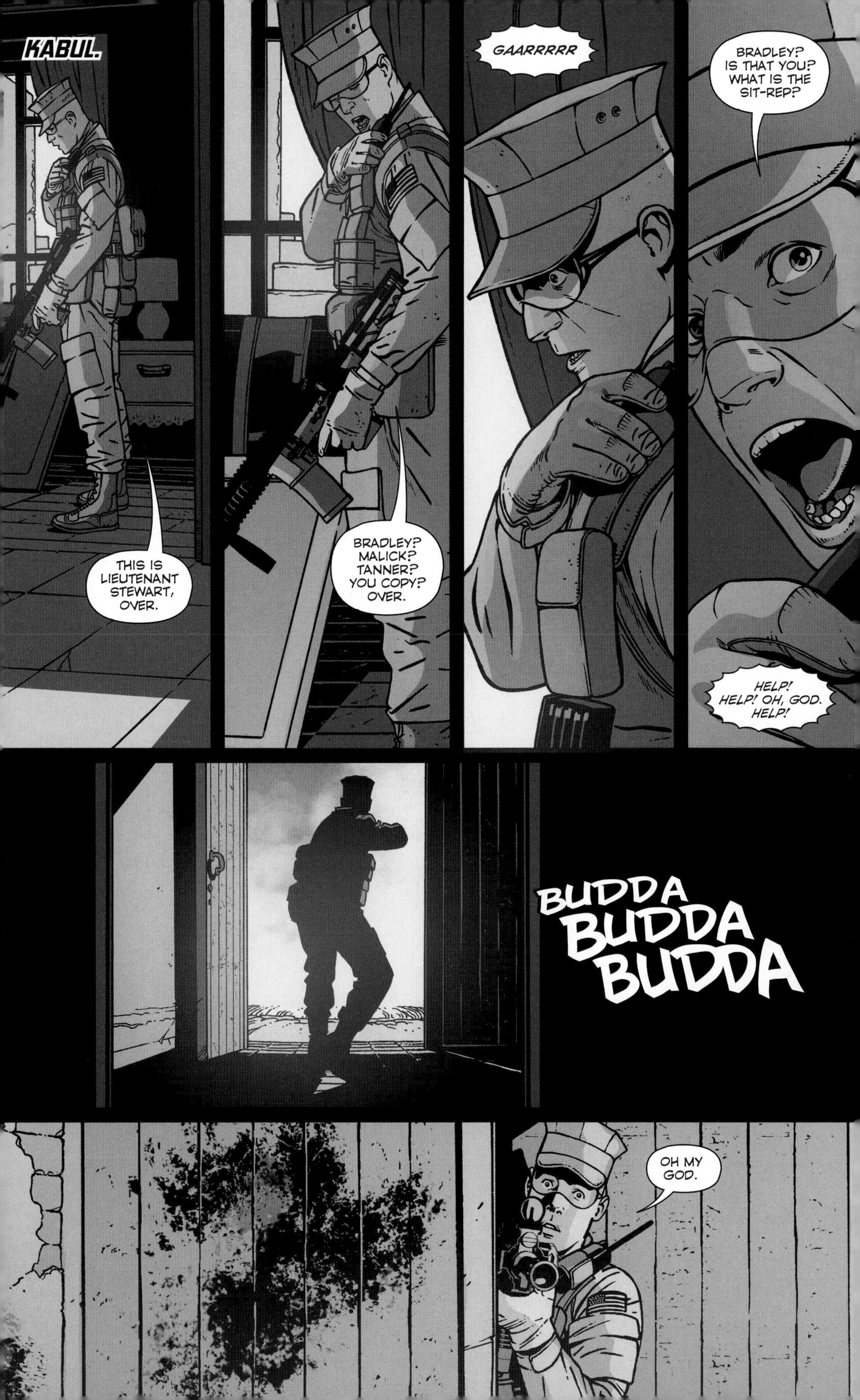
KABUL.
THIS IS LIEUTENANT STEWART, OVER.
BRADLEY? MALICK? TANNER? YOU COPY? OVER.
GAARRRRR
BRADLEY? IS THAT YOU? WHAT IS THE SIT-REP?
HELP! HELP! OH, GOD. HELP!
BUDDA BUDDA BUDDA
OH MY GOD.

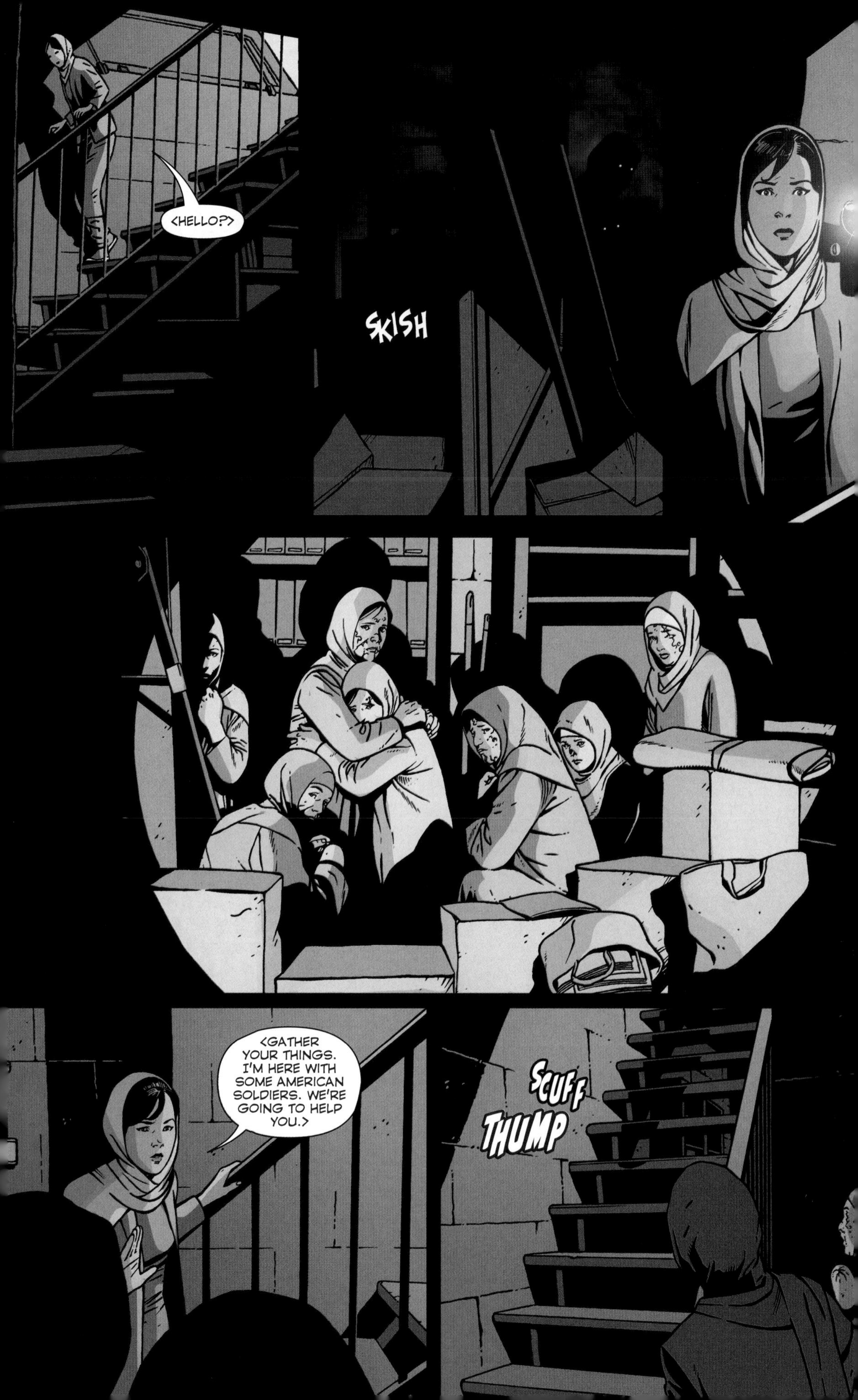
<HELLO?>
SKISH
<GATHER YOUR THINGS. I'M HERE WITH SOME AMERICAN SOLDIERS. WE'RE GOING TO HELP YOU.>
SCUFF
THUMP

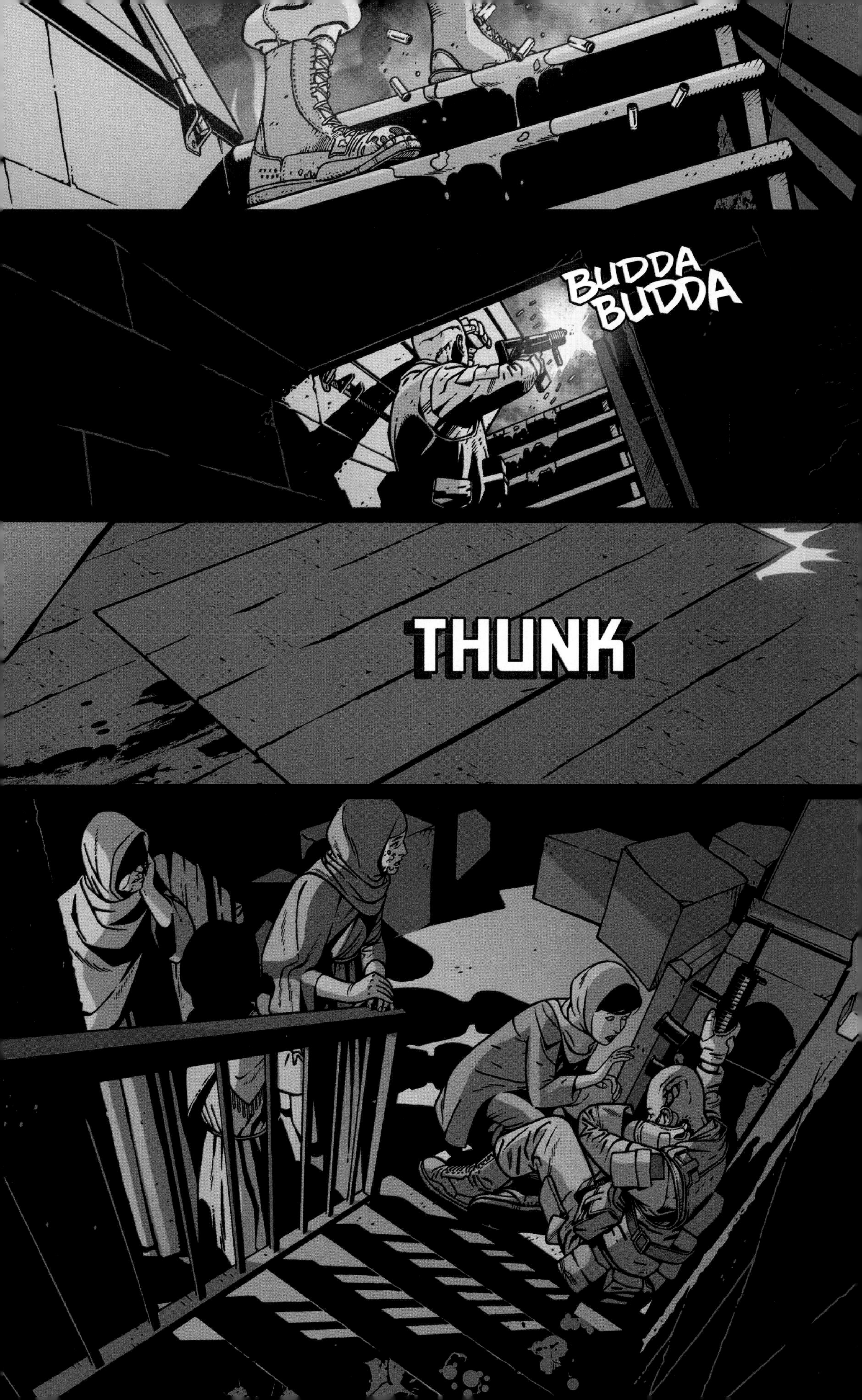
BUDDA BUDDA
THUNK

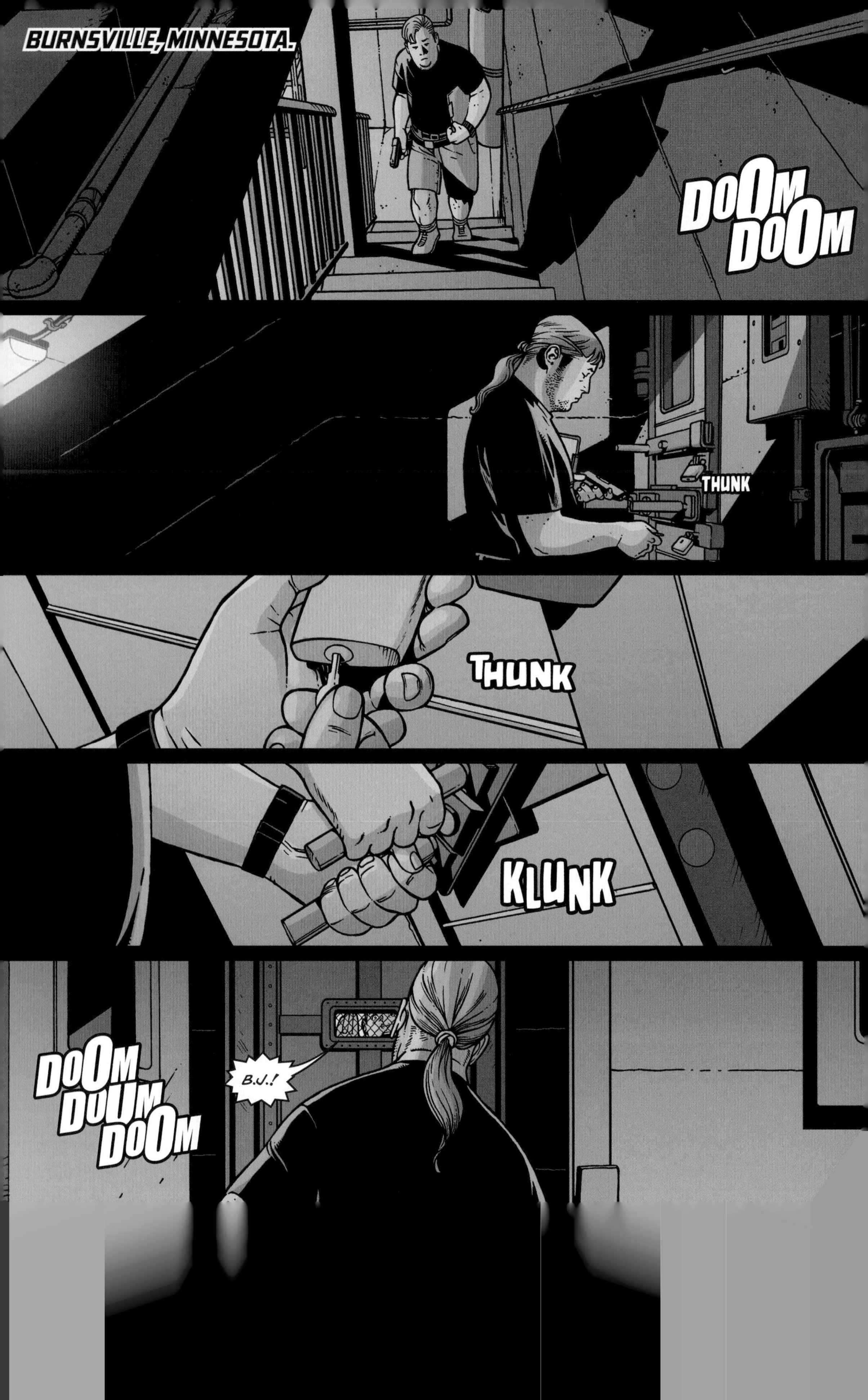
BURNSVILLE, MINNESOTA.
DOOM DOOM
THUNK
THUNK
KLUNK
DOOM DUUM DOOM
B.J.!

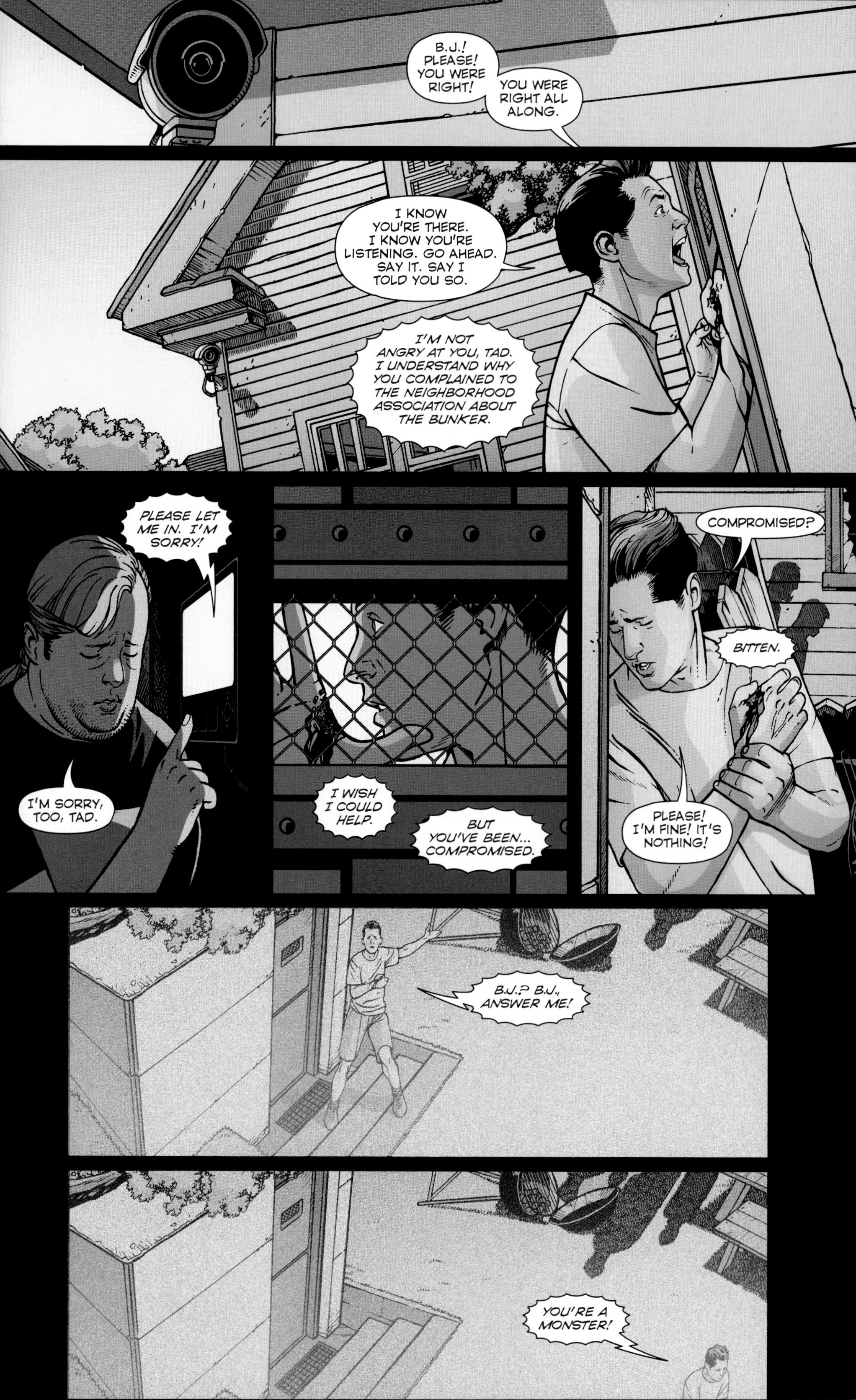
B.J.! PLEASE! YOU WERE RIGHT!
YOU WERE RIGHT ALL ALONG.
I KNOW YOU'RE THERE. I KNOW YOU'RE LISTENING. GO AHEAD. SAY IT. SAY I TOLD YOU SO.
I'M NOT ANGRY AT YOU, TAD. I UNDERSTAND WHY YOU COMPLAINED TO THE NEIGHBORHOOD ASSOCIATION ABOUT THE BUNKER.
PLEASE LET ME IN. I'M SORRY!
I'M SORRY, TOO, TAD.
I WISH I COULD HELP.
BUT YOU'VE BEEN... COMPROMISED.
COMPROMISED?
BITTEN.
PLEASE! I'M FINE! IT'S NOTHING!
B.J.? B.J., ANSWER ME!
YOU'RE A MONSTER!

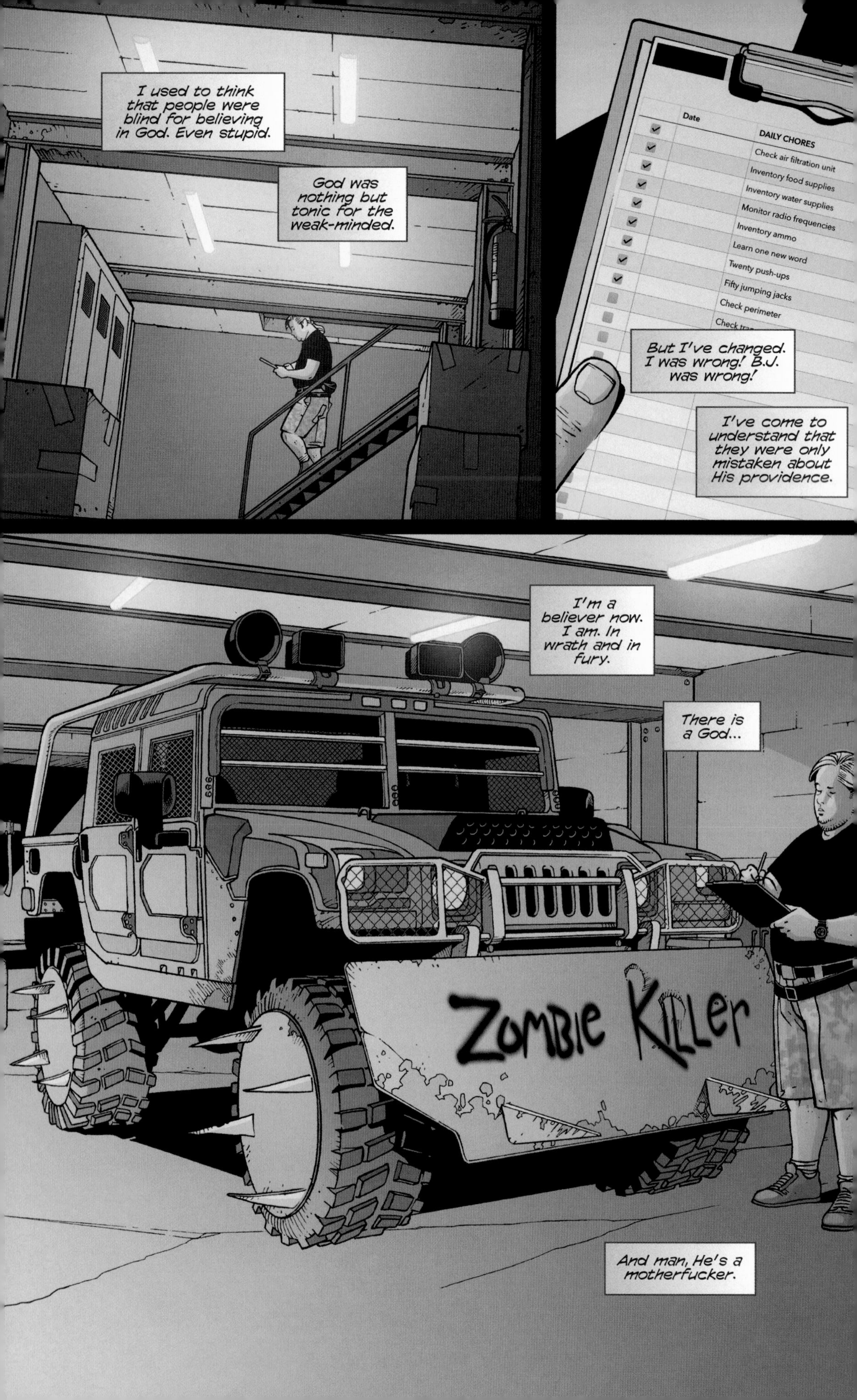
I used to think that people were blind for believing in God. Even stupid.
God was nothing but tonic for the weak-minded.
Date
DAILY CHORES
Check air filtration unit
Inventory food supplies
Inventory water supplies
Monitor radio frequencies
Inventory ammo
Learn one new word
Twenty push-ups
Fifty jumping jacks
Check perimeter
But I've changed. I was wrong! B.J. was wrong!
I've come to understand that they were only mistaken about His providence.
I'm a believer now. I am. In wrath and in fury.
There is a God...
ZOMBIE KILLER
And man, He's a motherfucker.

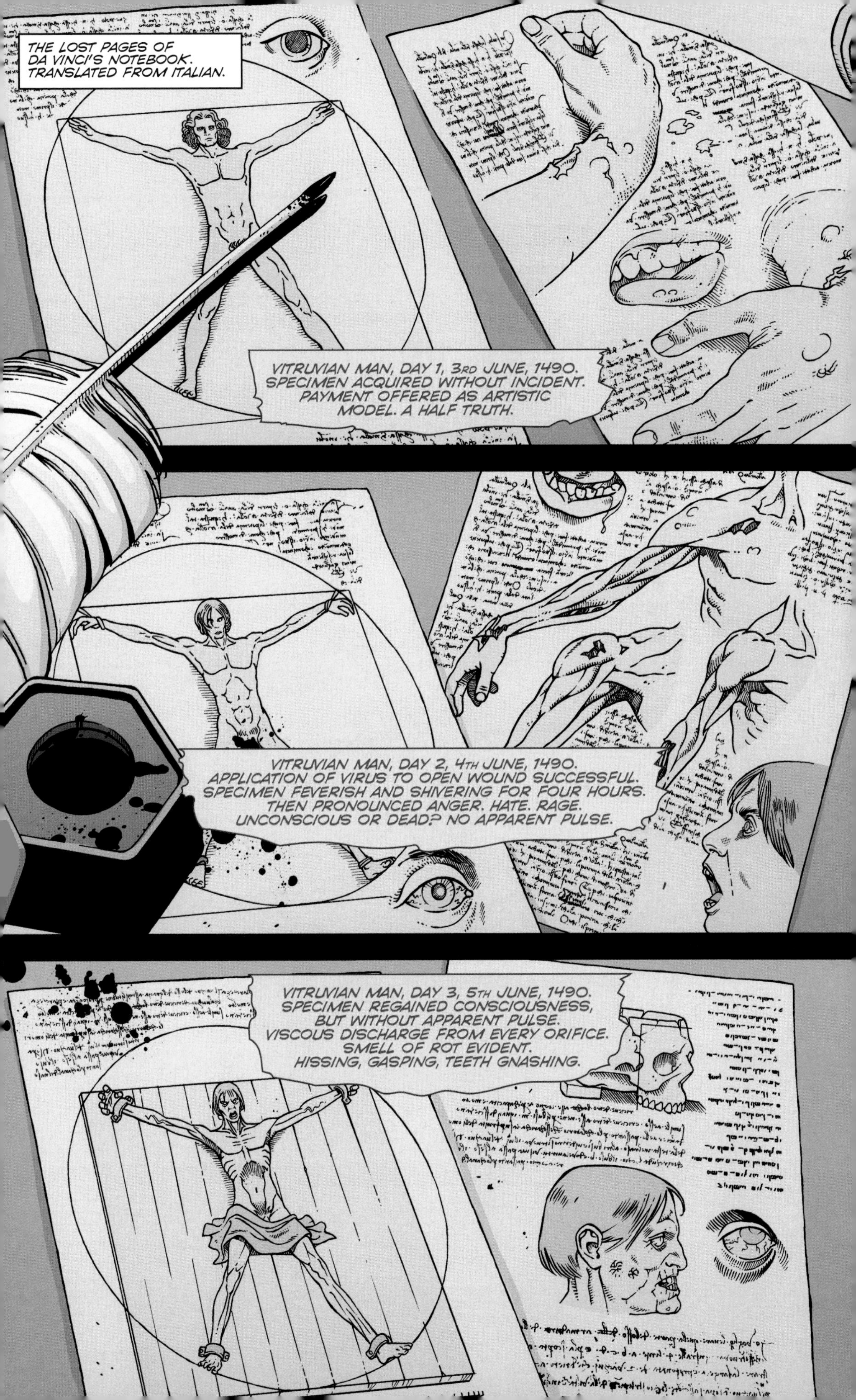
THE LOST PAGES OF DA VINCI'S NOTEBOOK. TRANSLATED FROM ITALIAN.
VITRUVIAN MAN, DAY 1, 3RD JUNE, 1490. SPECIMEN ACQUIRED WITHOUT INCIDENT. PAYMENT OFFERED AS ARTISTIC MODEL. A HALF TRUTH.
VITRUVIAN MAN, DAY 2, 4TH JUNE, 1490. APPLICATION OF VIRUS TO OPEN WOUND SUCCESSFUL. SPECIMEN FEVERISH AND SHIVERING FOR FOUR HOURS. THEN PRONOUNCED ANGER. HATE. RAGE. UNCONSCIOUS OR DEAD? NO APPARENT PULSE.
VITRUVIAN MAN, DAY 3, 5TH JUNE, 1490. SPECIMEN REGAINED CONSCIOUSNESS, BUT WITHOUT APPARENT PULSE. VISCOUS DISCHARGE FROM EVERY ORIFICE. SMELL OF ROT EVIDENT. HISSING, GASPING, TEETH GNASHING.

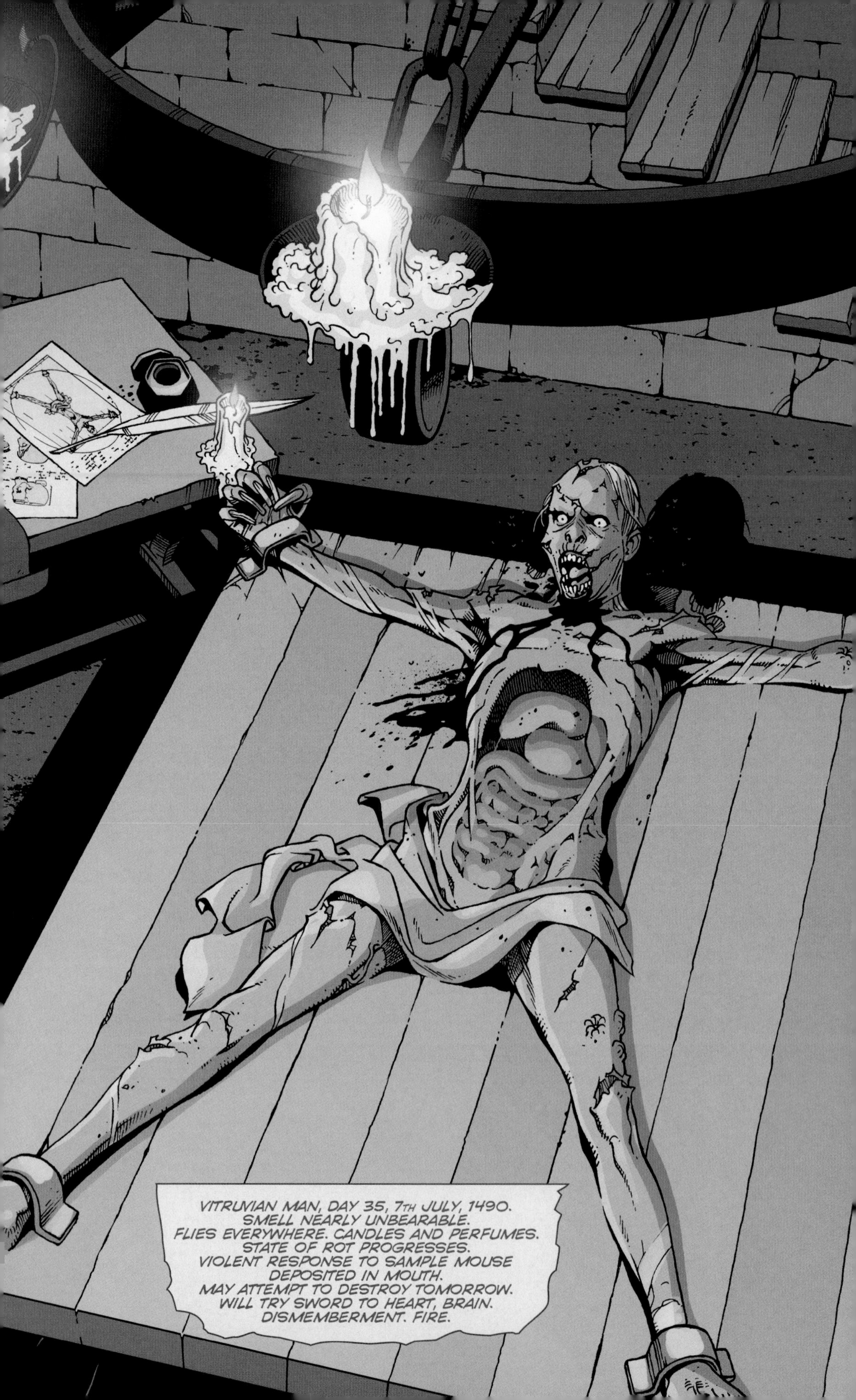
VITRUVIAN MAN, DAY 35, 7TH JULY, 1490. SMELL NEARLY UNBEARABLE. FLIES EVERYWHERE. CANDLES AND PERFUMES. STATE OF ROT PROGRESSES. VIOLENT RESPONSE TO SAMPLE MOUSE DEPOSITED IN MOUTH. MAY ATTEMPT TO DESTROY TOMORROW. WILL TRY SWORD TO HEART, BRAIN. DISMEMBERMENT. FIRE.

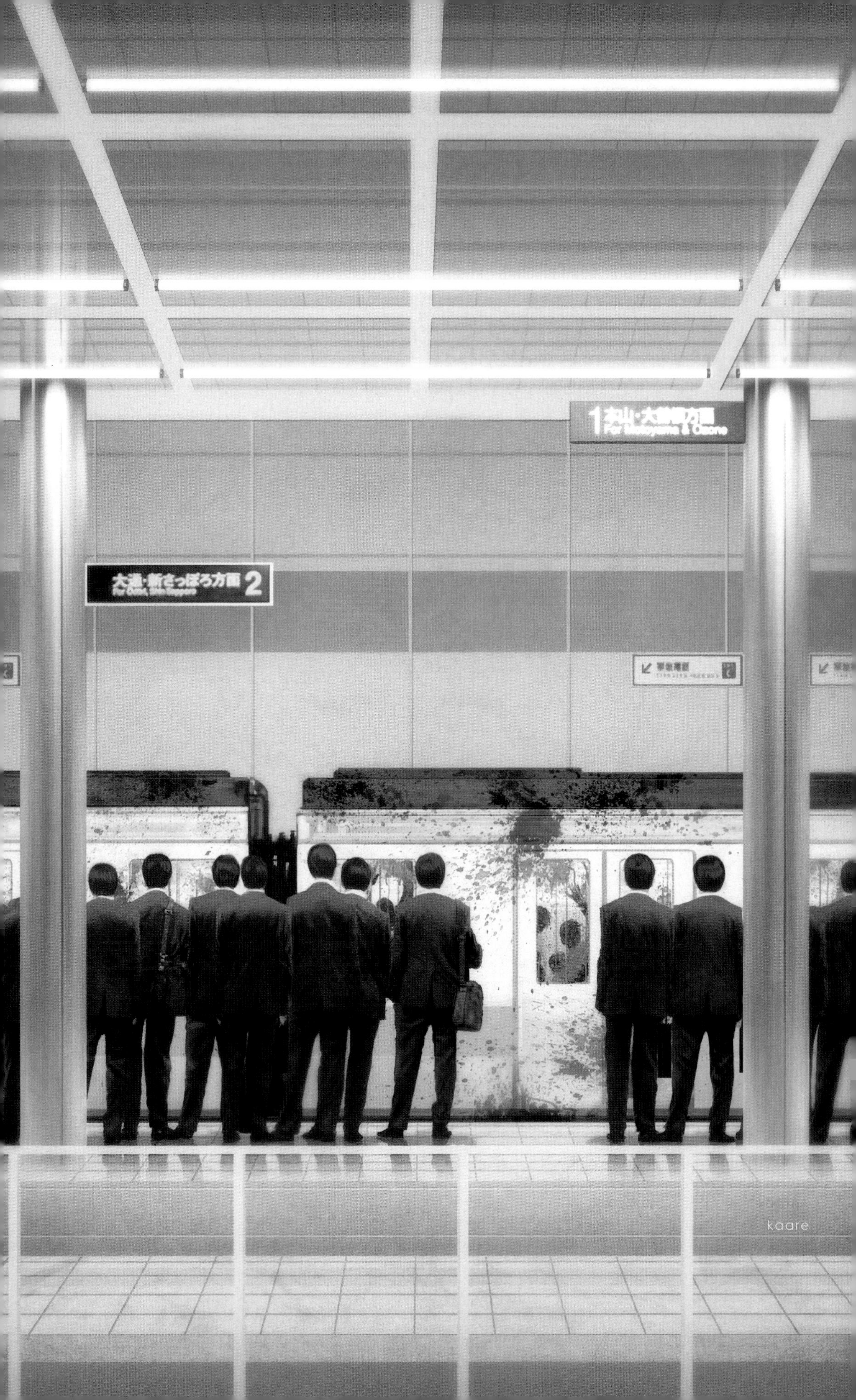
大通・新さっぽろ方面 2
kaare

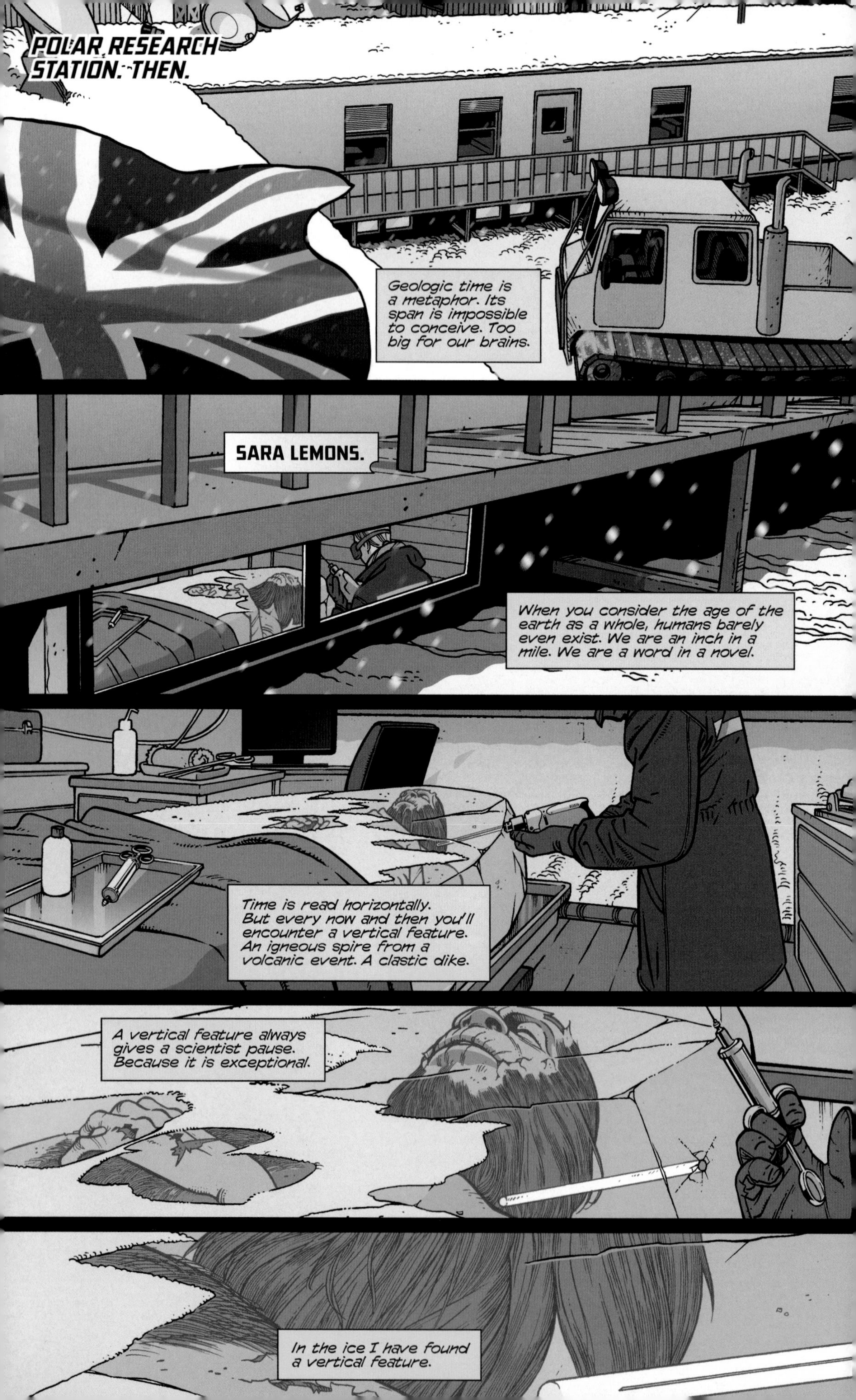
POLAR RESEARCH STATION. THEN.
Geologic time is a metaphor. Its span is impossible to conceive. Too big for our brains.
SARA LEMONS.
When you consider the age of the earth as a whole, humans barely even exist. We are an inch in a mile. We are a word in a novel.
Time is read horizontally. But every now and then you'll encounter a vertical feature. An igneous spire from a volcanic event. A clastic dike.
A vertical feature always gives a scientist pause. Because it is exceptional.
In the ice I have found a vertical feature.

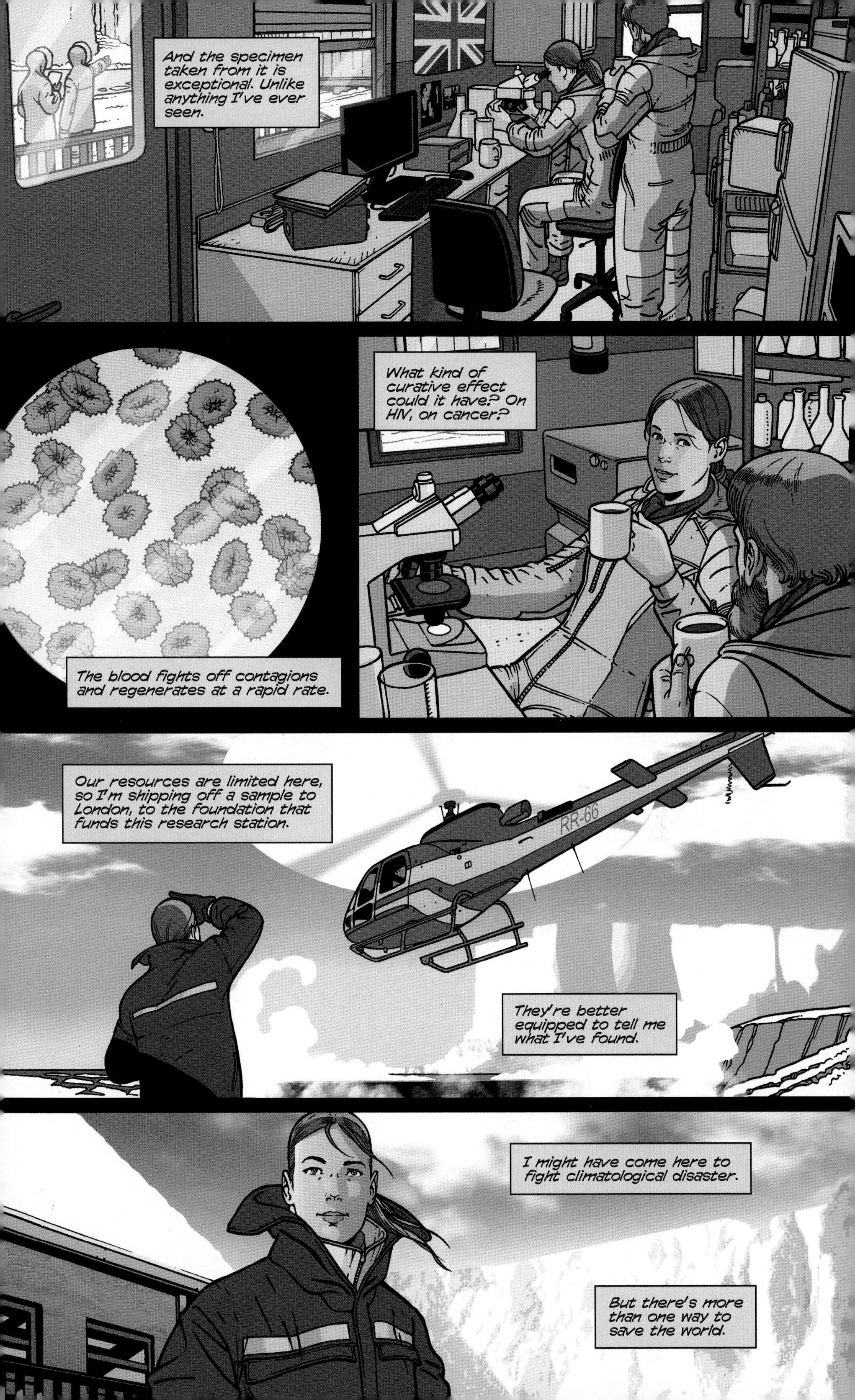
And the specimen taken from it is exceptional. Unlike anything I've ever seen.
The blood fights off contagions and regenerates at a rapid rate.
What kind of curative effect could it have? On HIV, on cancer?
Our resources are limited here, so I'm shipping off a sample to London, to the foundation that funds this research station.
RR-66
They're better equipped to tell me what I've found.
I might have come here to fight climatological disaster.
But there's more than one way to save the world.

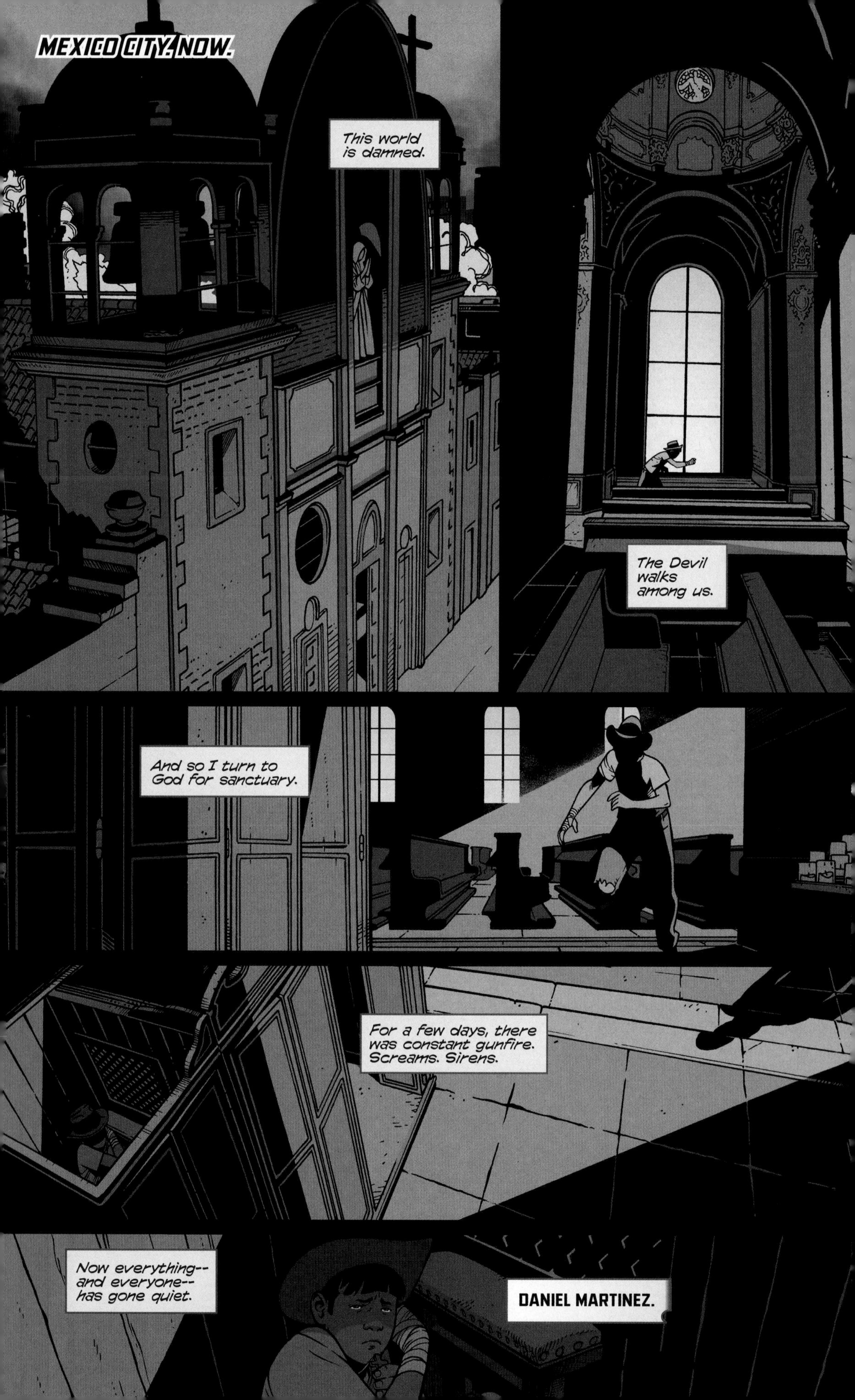
MEXICO CITY, NOW.
This world is damned.
The Devil walks among us.
And so I turn to God for sanctuary.
For a few days, there was constant gunfire. Screams. Sirens.
Now everything--and everyone--has gone quiet.
DANIEL MARTINEZ.

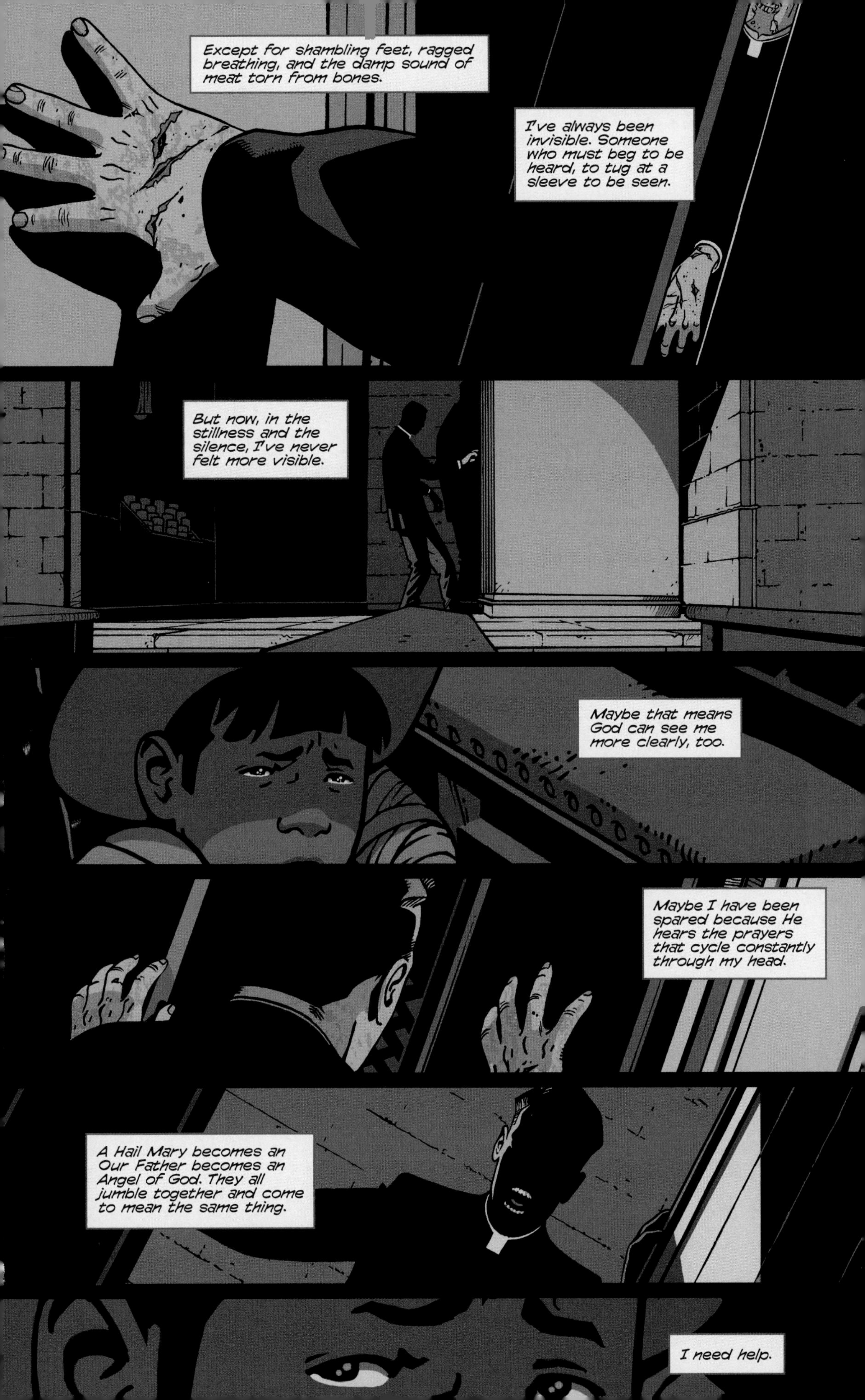
Except for shambling feet, ragged breathing, and the damp sound of meat torn from bones.
I've always been invisible. Someone who must beg to be heard, to tug at a sleeve to be seen.
But now, in the stillness and the silence, I've never felt more visible.
Maybe that means God can see me more clearly, too.
Maybe I have been spared because He hears the prayers that cycle constantly through my head.
A Hail Mary becomes an Our Father becomes an Angel of God. They all jumble together and come to mean the same thing.
I need help.

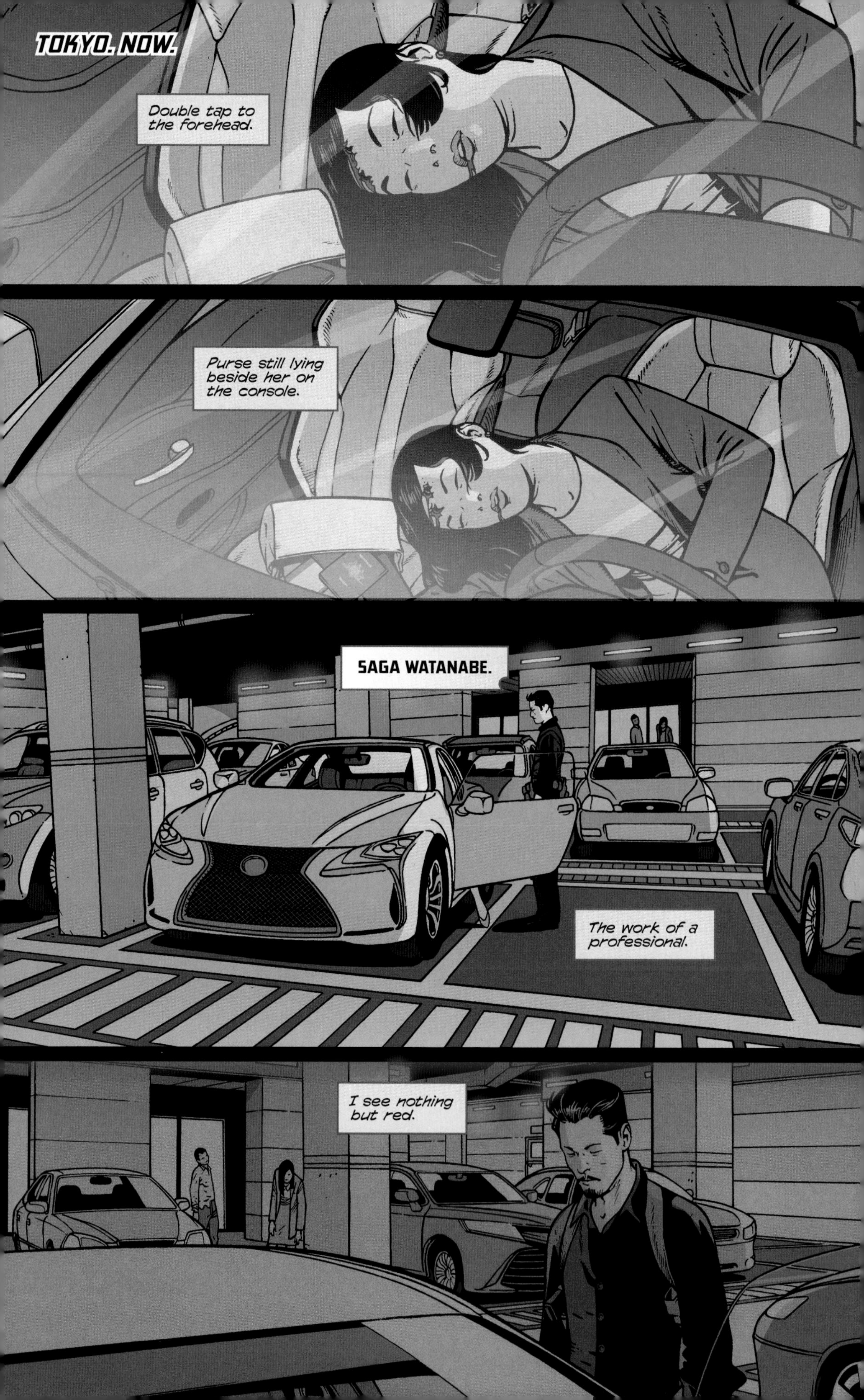
TOKYO. NOW.
Double tap to the forehead.
Purse still lying beside her on the console.
SAGA WATANABE.
The work of a professional.
I see nothing but red.

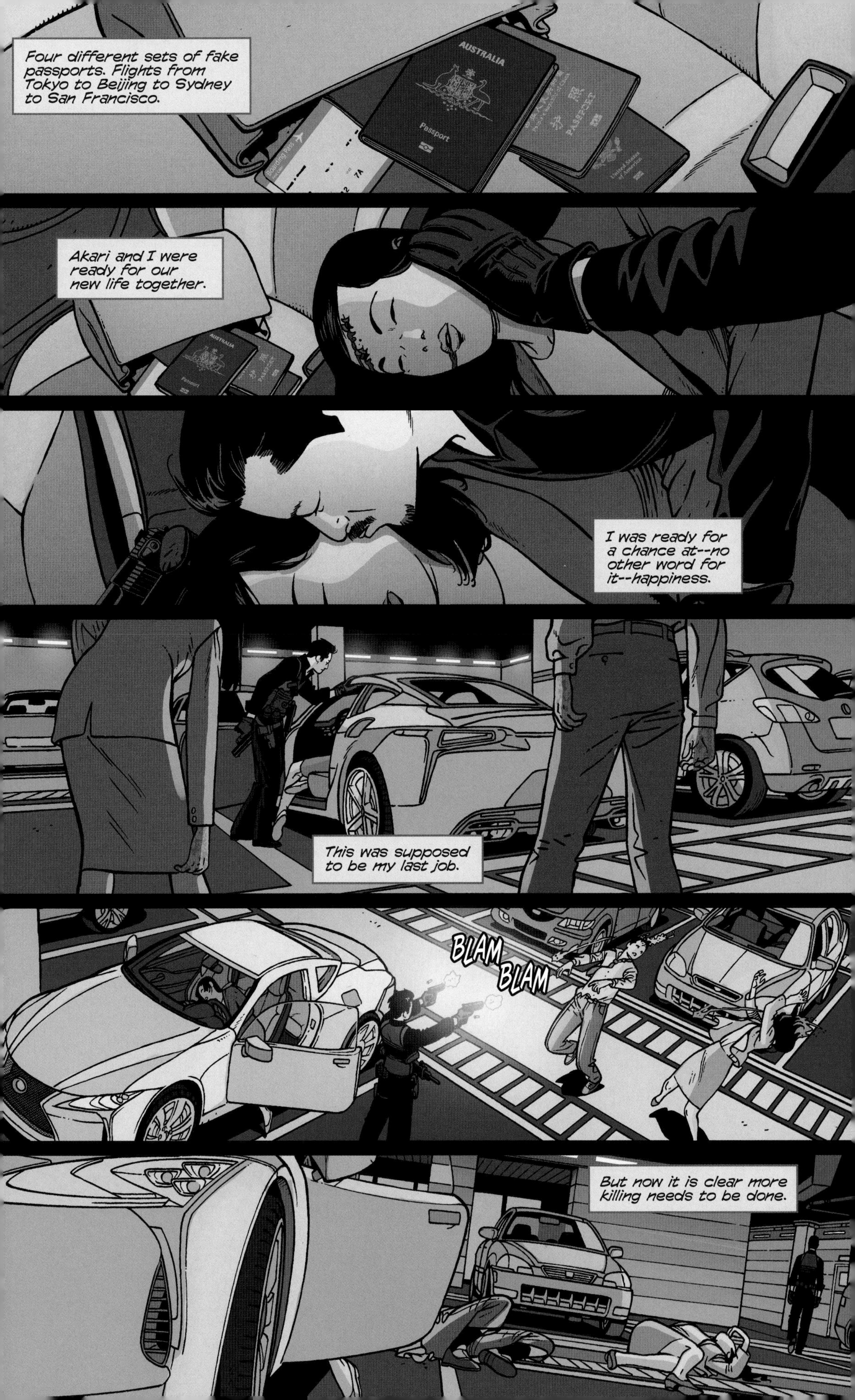
Four different sets of fake passports. Flights from Tokyo to Beijing to Sydney to San Francisco.
AUSTRALIA
Passport
PASSPORT
Boarding Pass
7A
Akari and I were ready for our new life together.
AUSTRALIA
Passport
I was ready for a chance at--no other word for it--happiness.
This was supposed to be my last job.
BLAM
BLAM
But now it is clear more killing needs to be done.

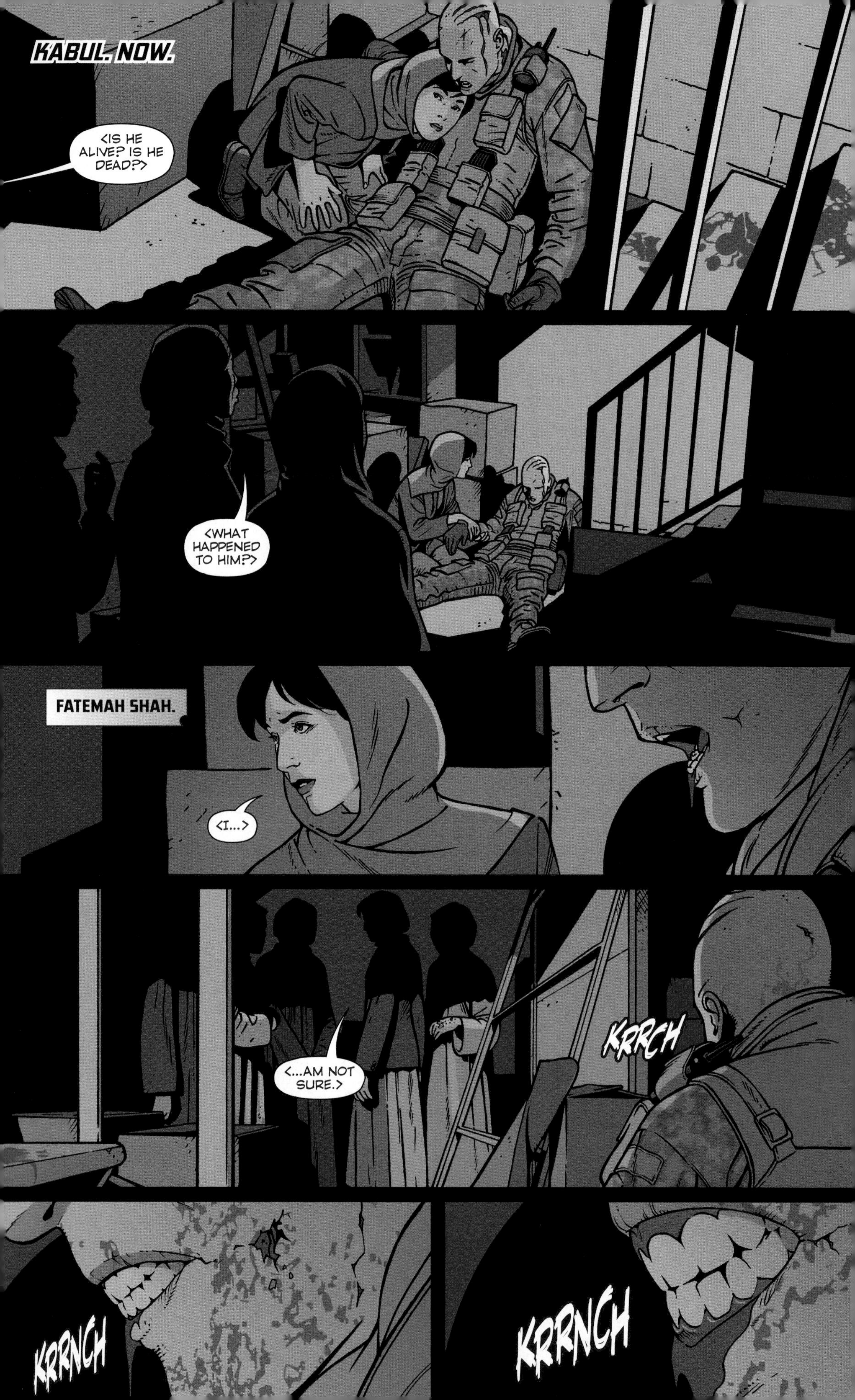
KABUL. NOW.
<IS HE ALIVE? IS HE DEAD?>
<WHAT HAPPENED TO HIM?>
FATEMAH SHAH.
<I...>
<...AM NOT SURE.>
KRRCH
KRRNCH
KRRNCH

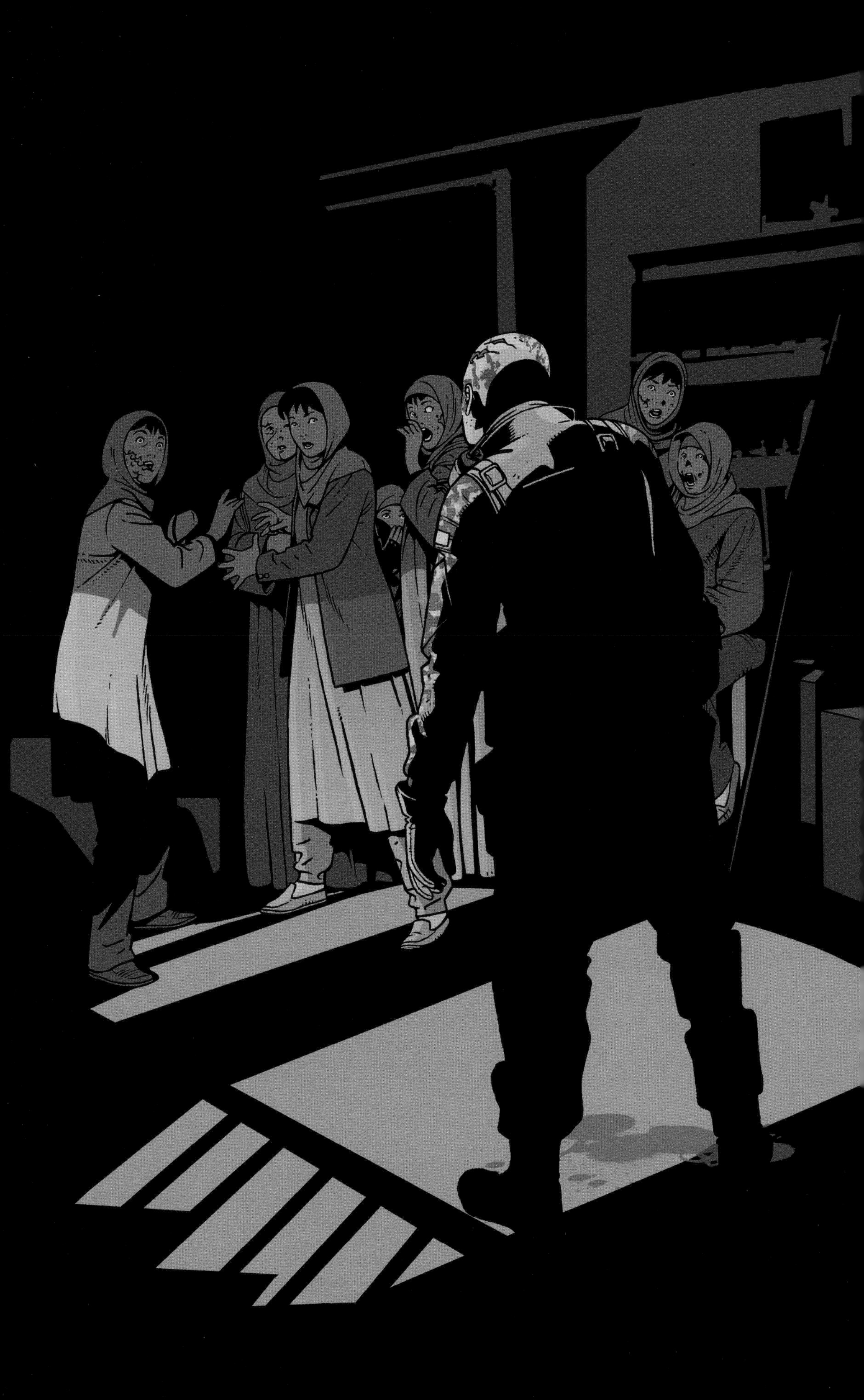

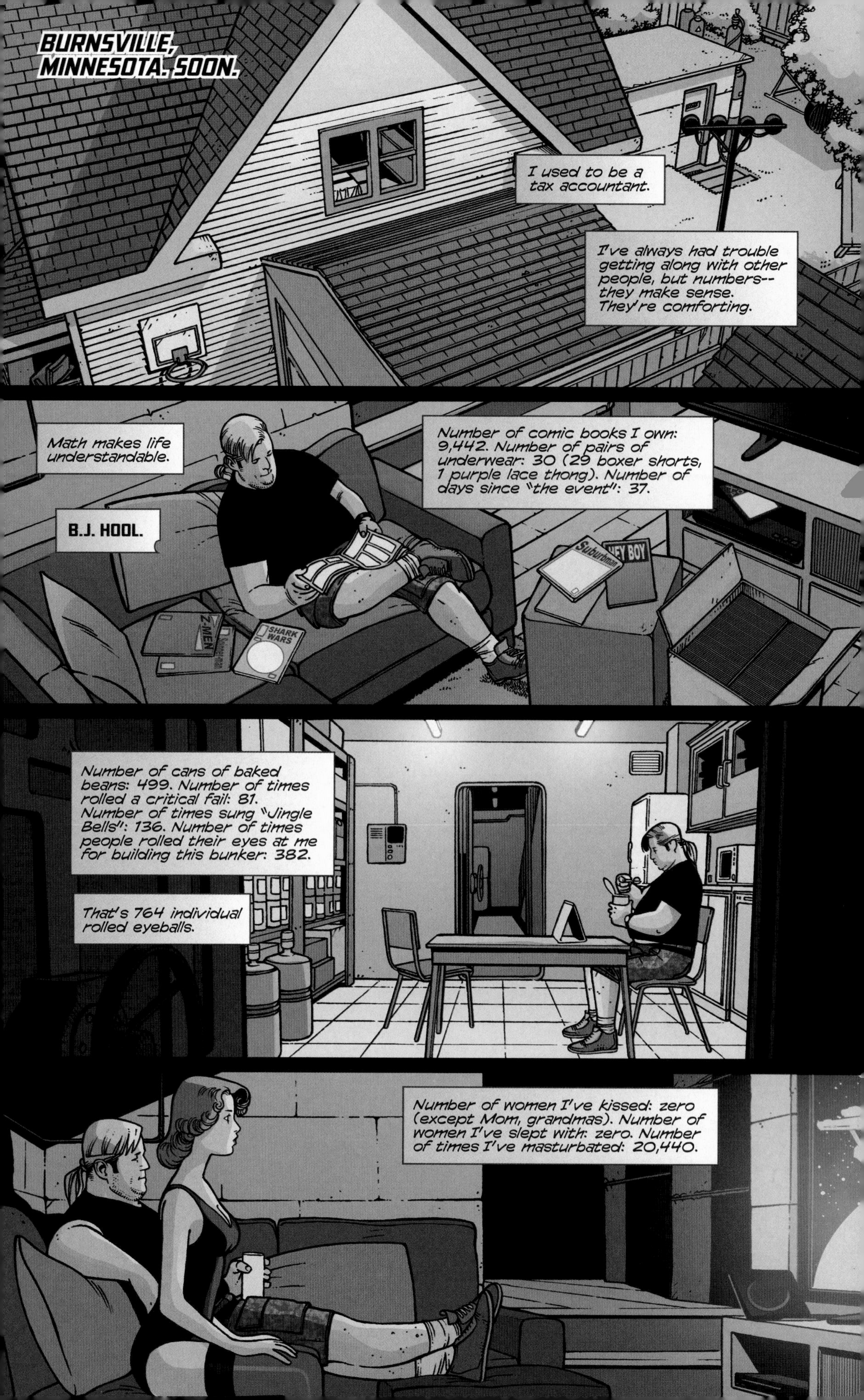

BURNSVILLE, MINNESOTA. SOON.
I used to be a tax accountant.
I've always had trouble getting along with other people, but numbers-- they make sense. They're comforting.
Math makes life understandable.
B.J. HOOL.
Number of comic books I own: 9,442. Number of pairs of underwear: 30 (29 boxer shorts, 1 purple lace thong). Number of days since "the event": 37.
Z-MEN
SHARK WARS
Suburbman
HEY BOY
Number of cans of baked beans: 499. Number of times rolled a critical fail: 81. Number of times sung "Jingle Bells": 136. Number of times people rolled their eyes at me for building this bunker: 382.
That's 764 individual rolled eyeballs.
Number of women I've kissed: zero (except Mom, grandmas). Number of women I've slept with: zero. Number of times I've masturbated: 20,440.

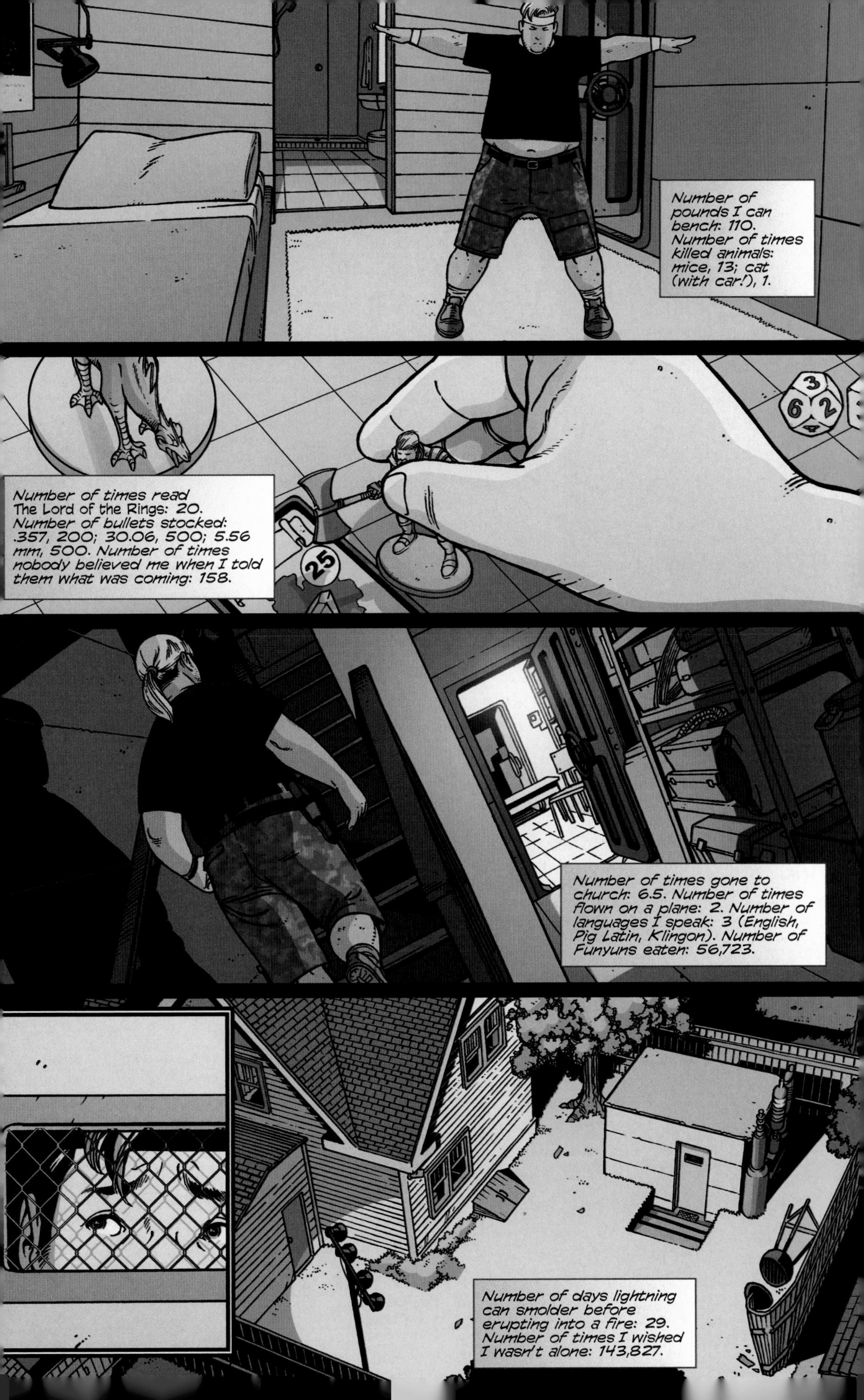
Number of pounds I can bench: 110. Number of times killed animals: mice, 13; cat (with car!), 1.
Number of times read The Lord of the Rings: 20. Number of bullets stocked: .357, 200; 30.06, 500; 5.56 mm, 500. Number of times nobody believed me when I told them what was coming: 158.
25
Number of times gone to church: 6.5. Number of times flown on a plane: 2. Number of languages I speak: 3 (English, Pig Latin, Klingon). Number of Funyuns eaten: 56,723.
Number of days lightning can smolder before erupting into a fire: 29. Number of times I wished I wasn't alone: 143,827.

MEXICO CITY.

Once I prayed for proof that God was listening, and a butterfly--with wings like stained glass--landed on my knee.

KRINSH

Once I prayed for food, and the next morning I found a perfect pink concha on the sidewalk.

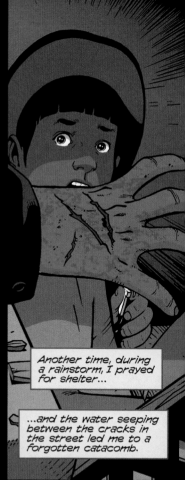

Another time, during a rainstorm, I prayed for shelter...

...and the water seeping between the cracks in the street led me to a forgotten catacomb.

God is listening, but sometimes He answers in curious ways.

BLAM

Such as now...

SCREE

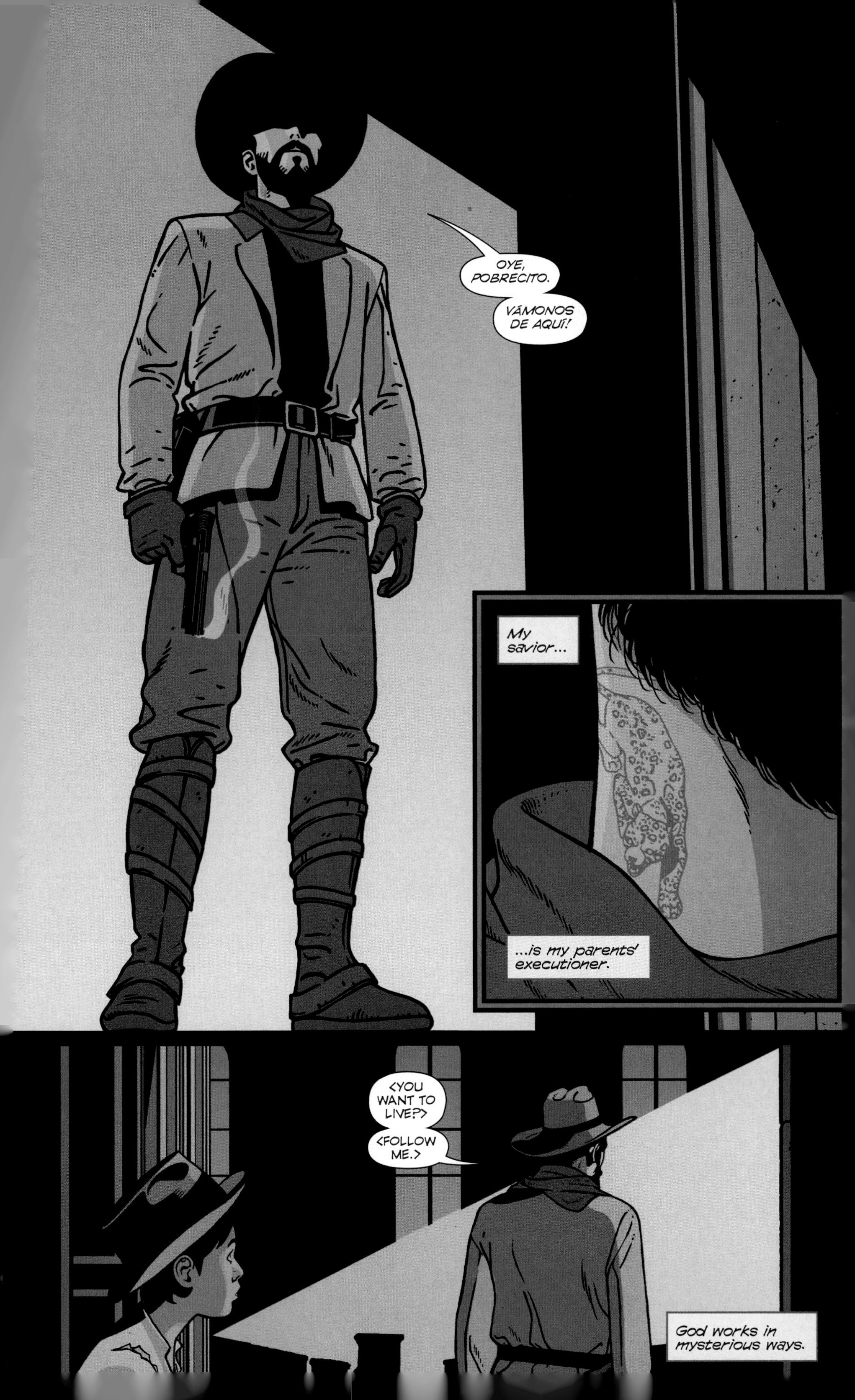
OYE, POBRECITO.
VÁMONOS DE AQUÍ!
My savior...
...is my parents' executioner.
<YOU WANT TO LIVE?>
<FOLLOW ME.>
God works in mysterious ways.

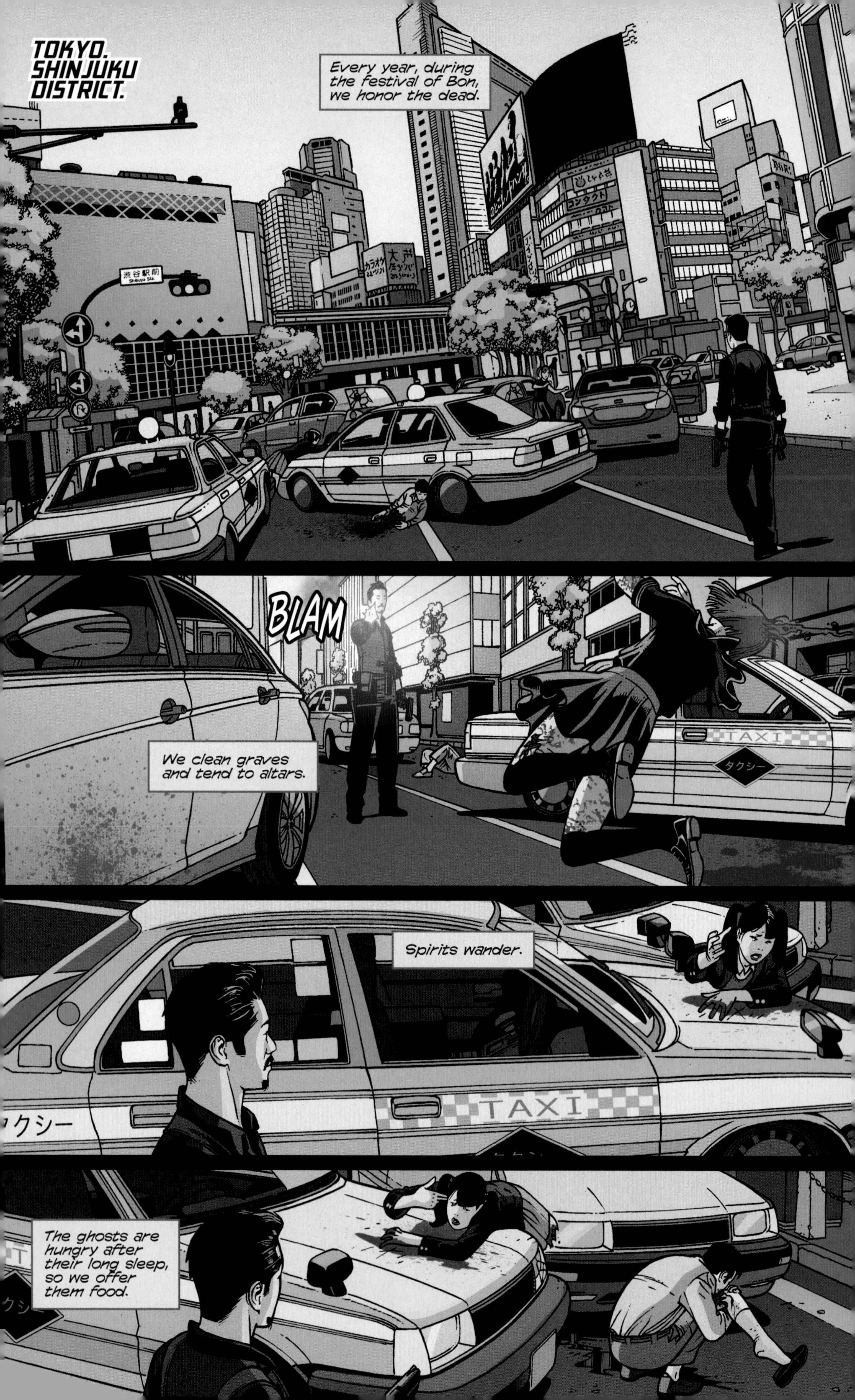
TOKYO. SHINJUKU DISTRICT.
Every year, during the festival of Bon, we honor the dead.
渋谷駅前
BLAM
We clean graves and tend to altars.
TAXI
タクシー
Spirits wander.
TAXI
クシー
The ghosts are hungry after their long sleep, so we offer them food.

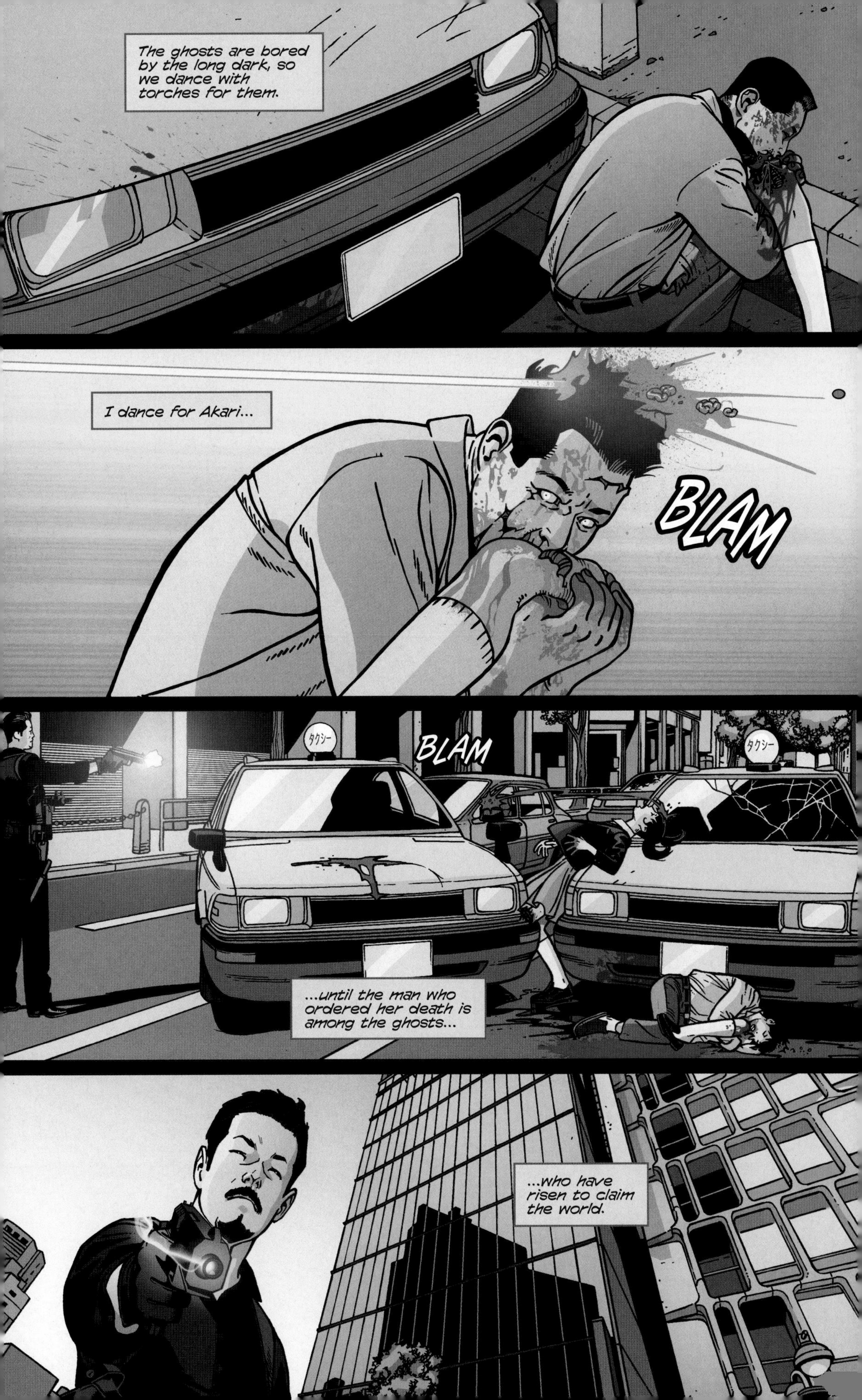
The ghosts are bored by the long dark, so we dance with torches for them.
I dance for Akari...
BLAM
BLAM
タクシー
タクシー
...until the man who ordered her death is among the ghosts...
...who have risen to claim the world.

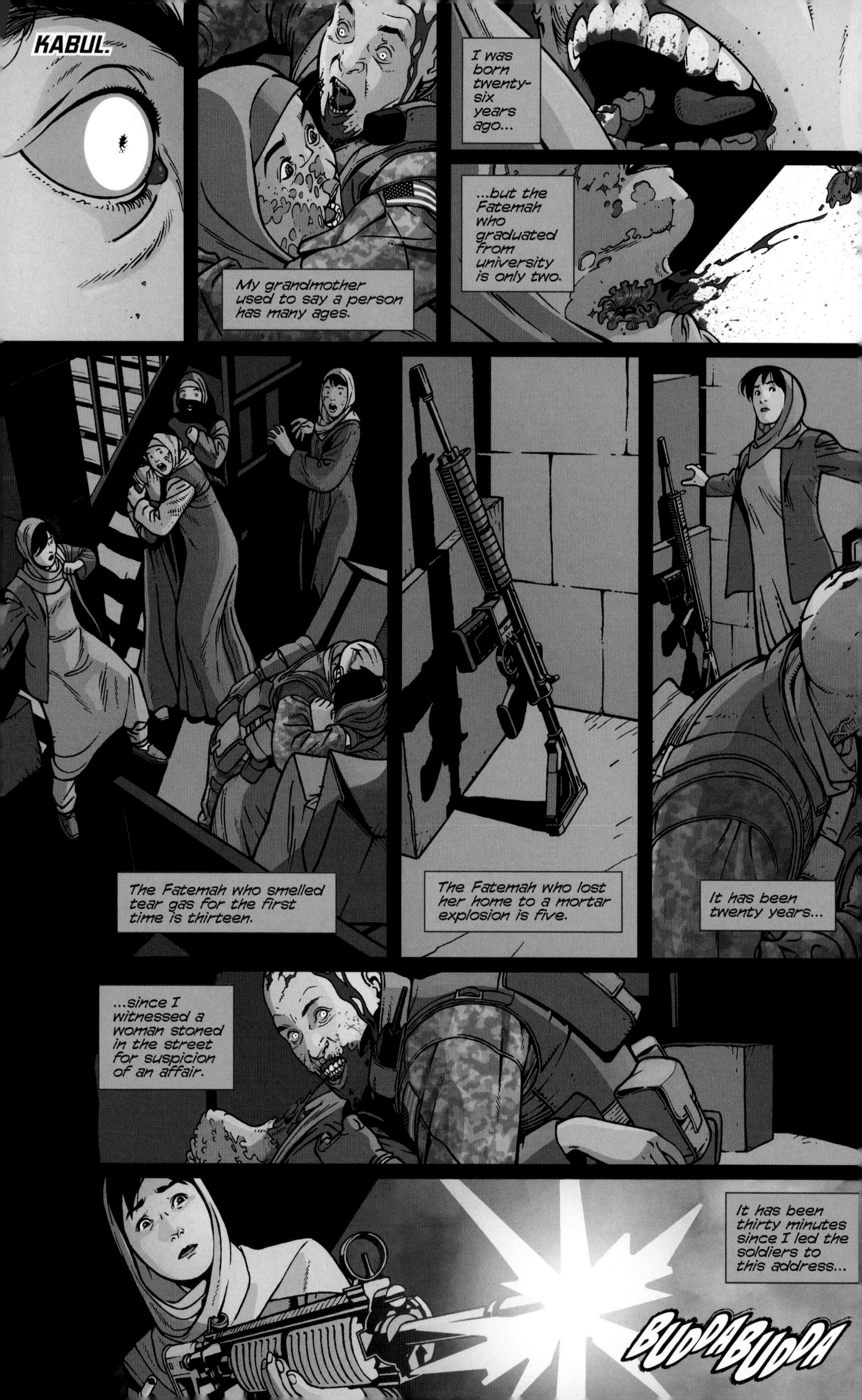
KABUL.
My grandmother used to say a person has many ages.
I was born twenty-six years ago...
...but the Fatemah who graduated from university is only two.
The Fatemah who smelled tear gas for the first time is thirteen.
The Fatemah who lost her home to a mortar explosion is five.
It has been twenty years...
...since I witnessed a woman stoned in the street for suspicion of an affair.
It has been thirty minutes since I led the soldiers to this address...
BUDDABUDDA

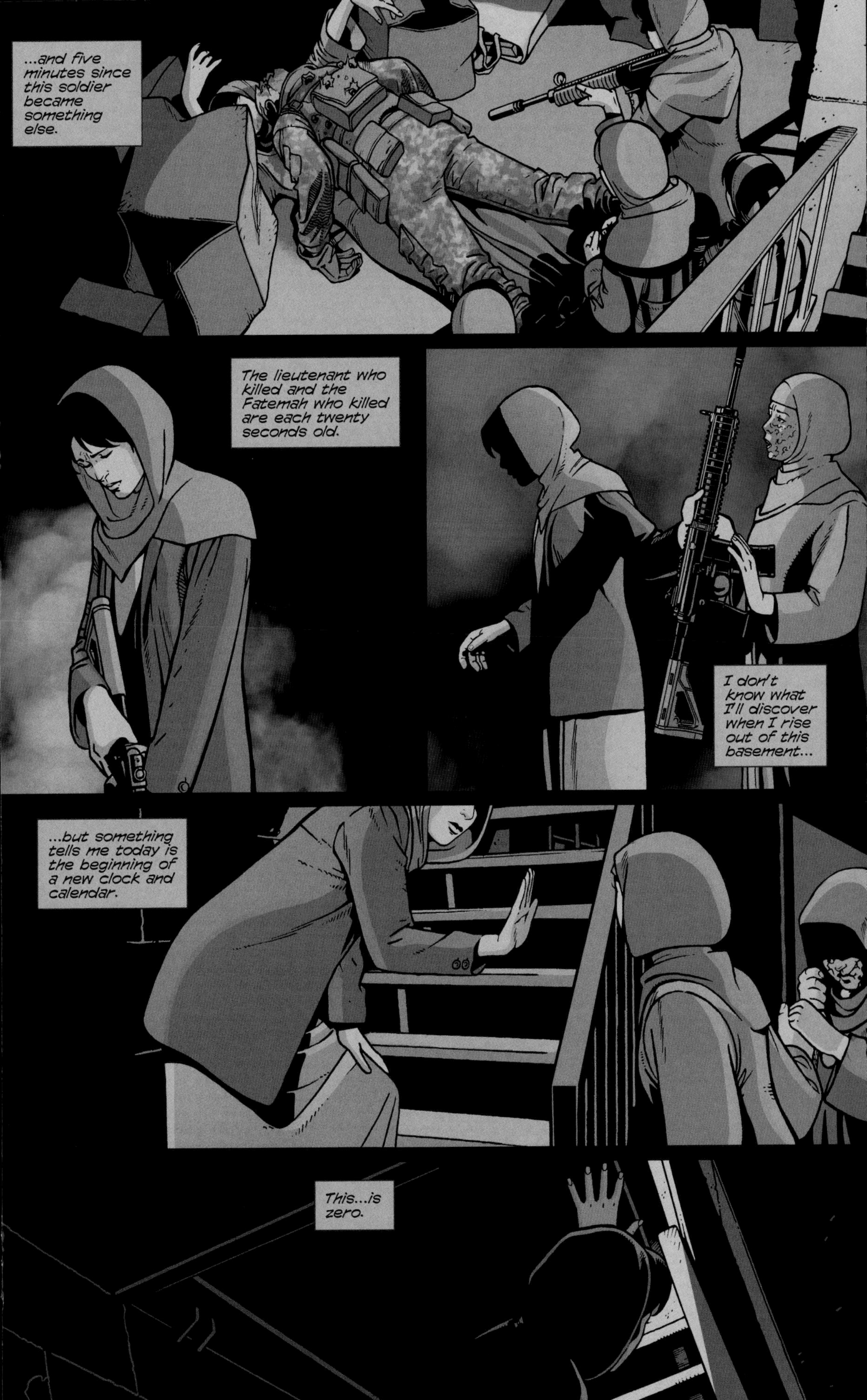
...and five minutes since this soldier became something else.
The lieutenant who killed and the Fatemah who killed are each twenty seconds old.
I don't know what I'll discover when I rise out of this basement...
...but something tells me today is the beginning of a new clock and calendar.
This...is zero.

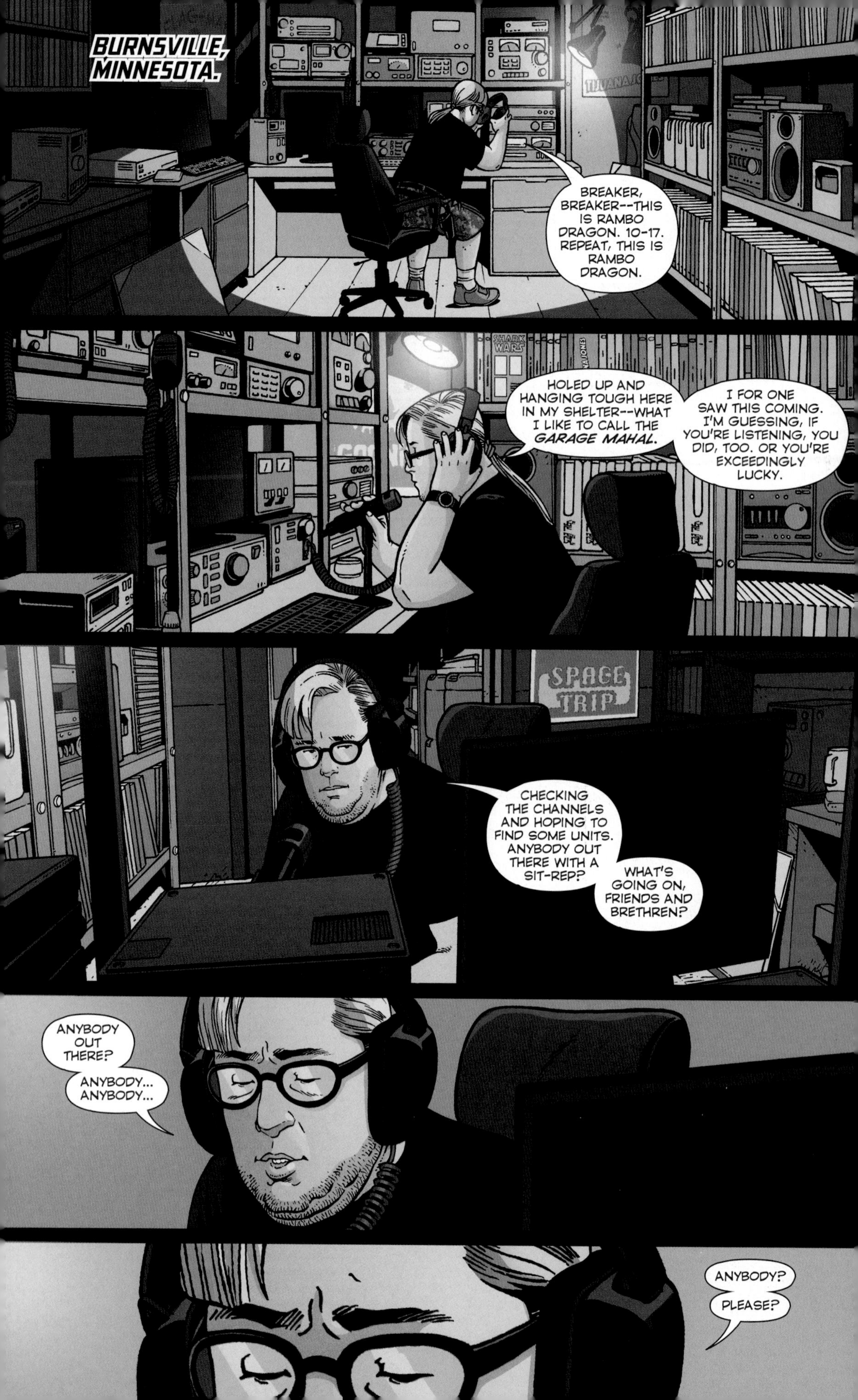
BURNSVILLE, MINNESOTA.
BREAKER, BREAKER--THIS IS RAMBO DRAGON. 10-17. REPEAT, THIS IS RAMBO DRAGON.
SHARK WARS
HOLED UP AND HANGING TOUGH HERE IN MY SHELTER--WHAT I LIKE TO CALL THE *GARAGE MAHAL*.
I FOR ONE SAW THIS COMING. I'M GUESSING, IF YOU'RE LISTENING, YOU DID, TOO. OR YOU'RE EXCEEDINGLY LUCKY.
SPACE TRIP
CHECKING THE CHANNELS AND HOPING TO FIND SOME UNITS. ANYBODY OUT THERE WITH A SIT-REP?
WHAT'S GOING ON, FRIENDS AND BRETHREN?
ANYBODY OUT THERE?
ANYBODY... ANYBODY...
ANYBODY?
PLEASE?

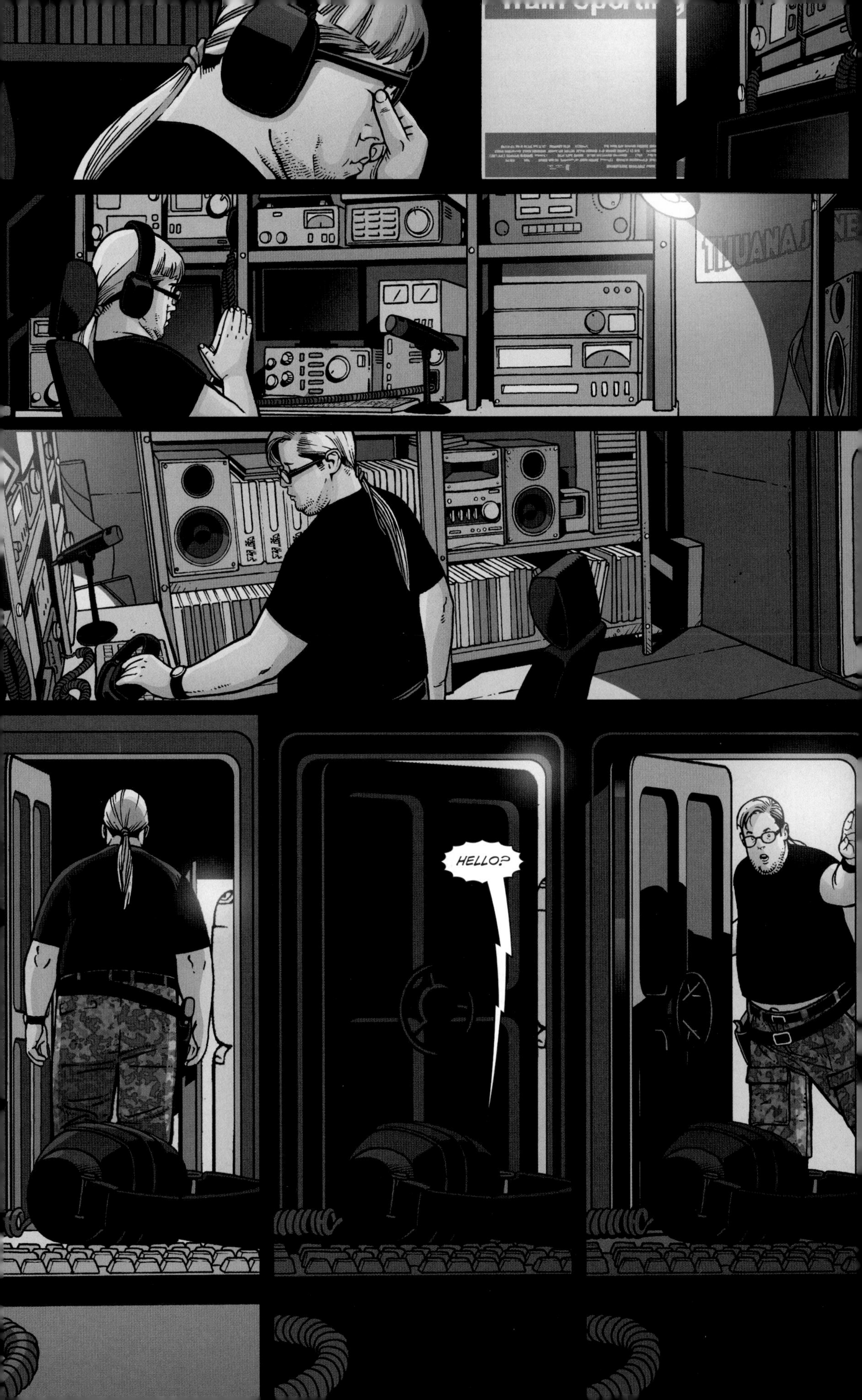
HELLO?

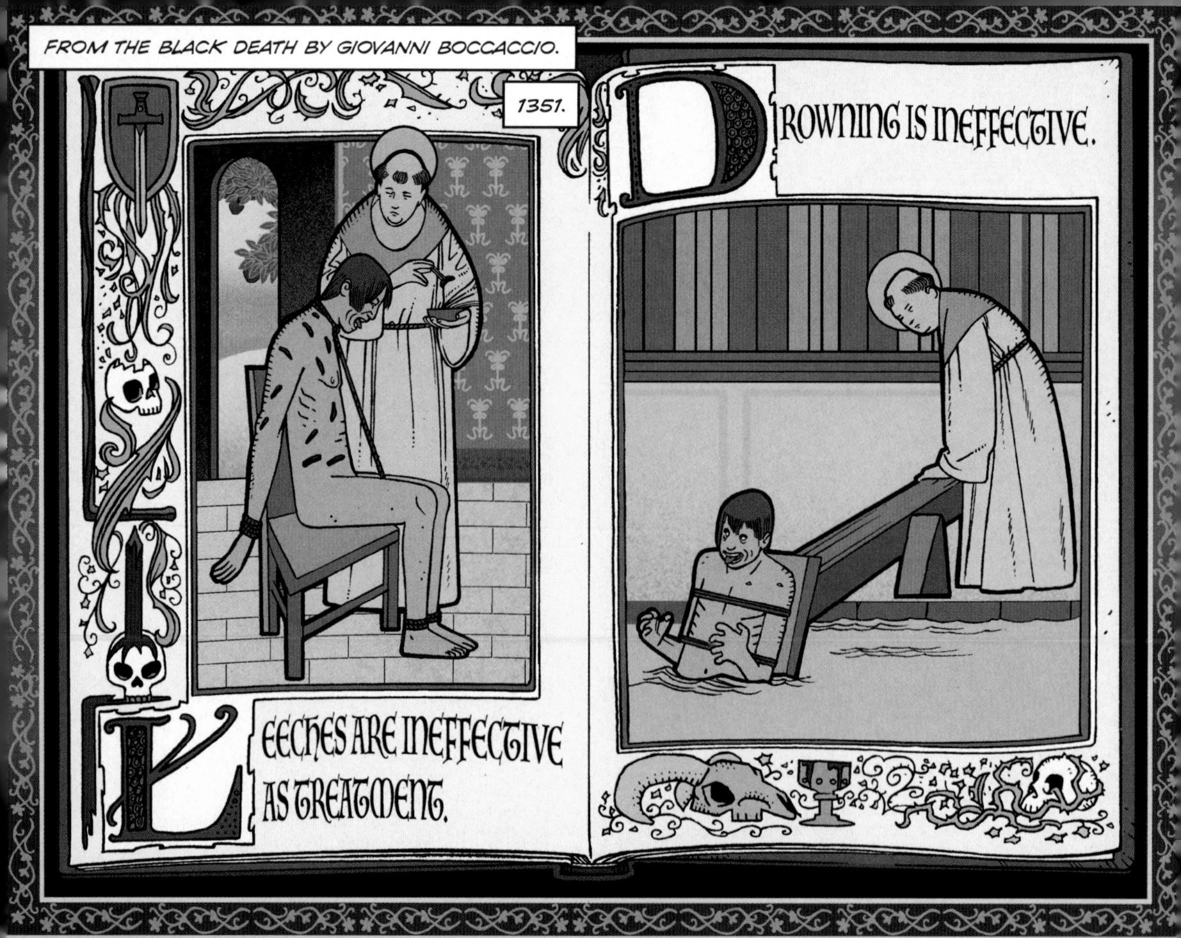
FROM THE BLACK DEATH BY GIOVANNI BOCCACCIO.
1351.
LEECHES ARE INEFFECTIVE AS TREATMENT.
DROWNING IS INEFFECTIVE.

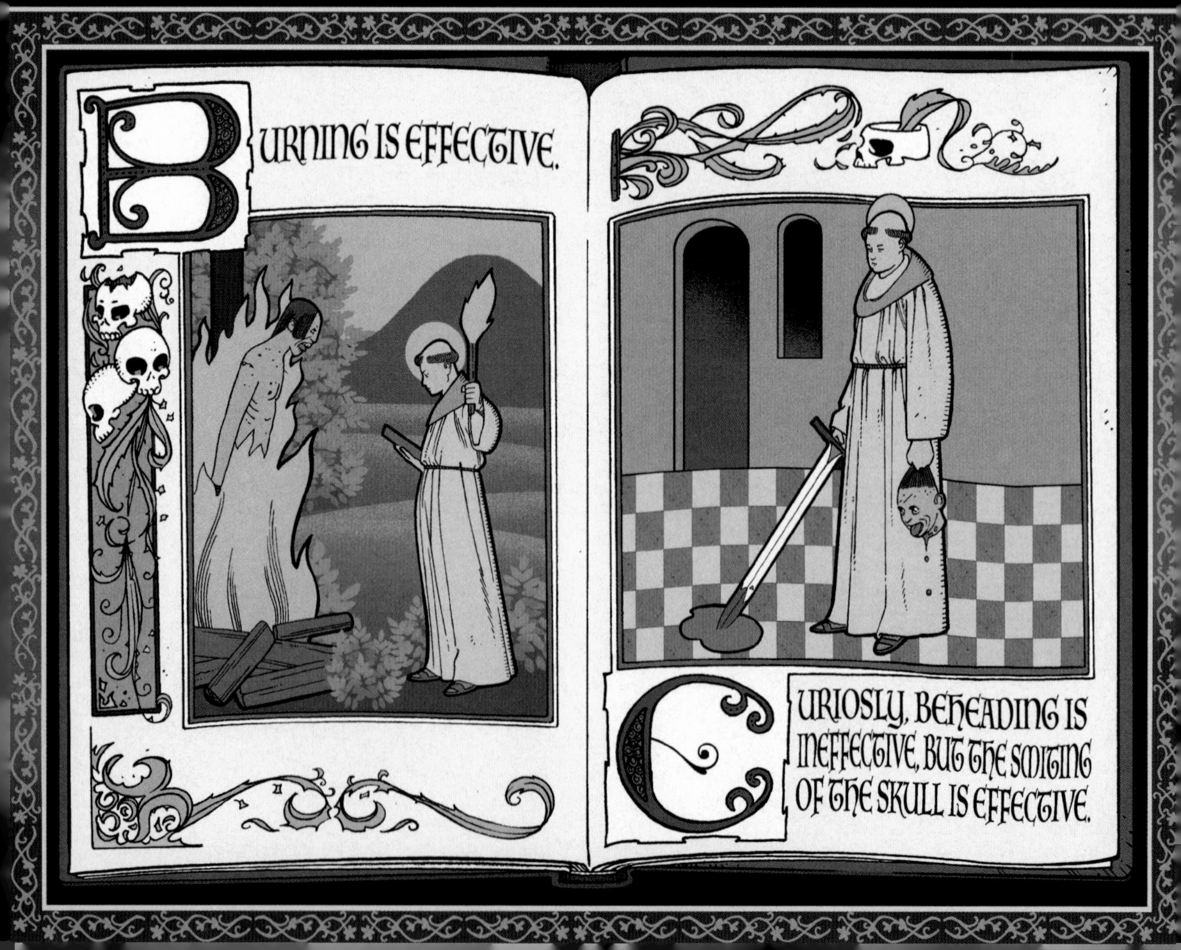
BURNING IS EFFECTIVE.
CURIOSLY, BEHEADING IS INEFFECTIVE, BUT THE SMITING OF THE SKULL IS EFFECTIVE.

THEY CALLED IT THE PEASANT'S CURSE, BUT THEN IT CAME FOR ALL.

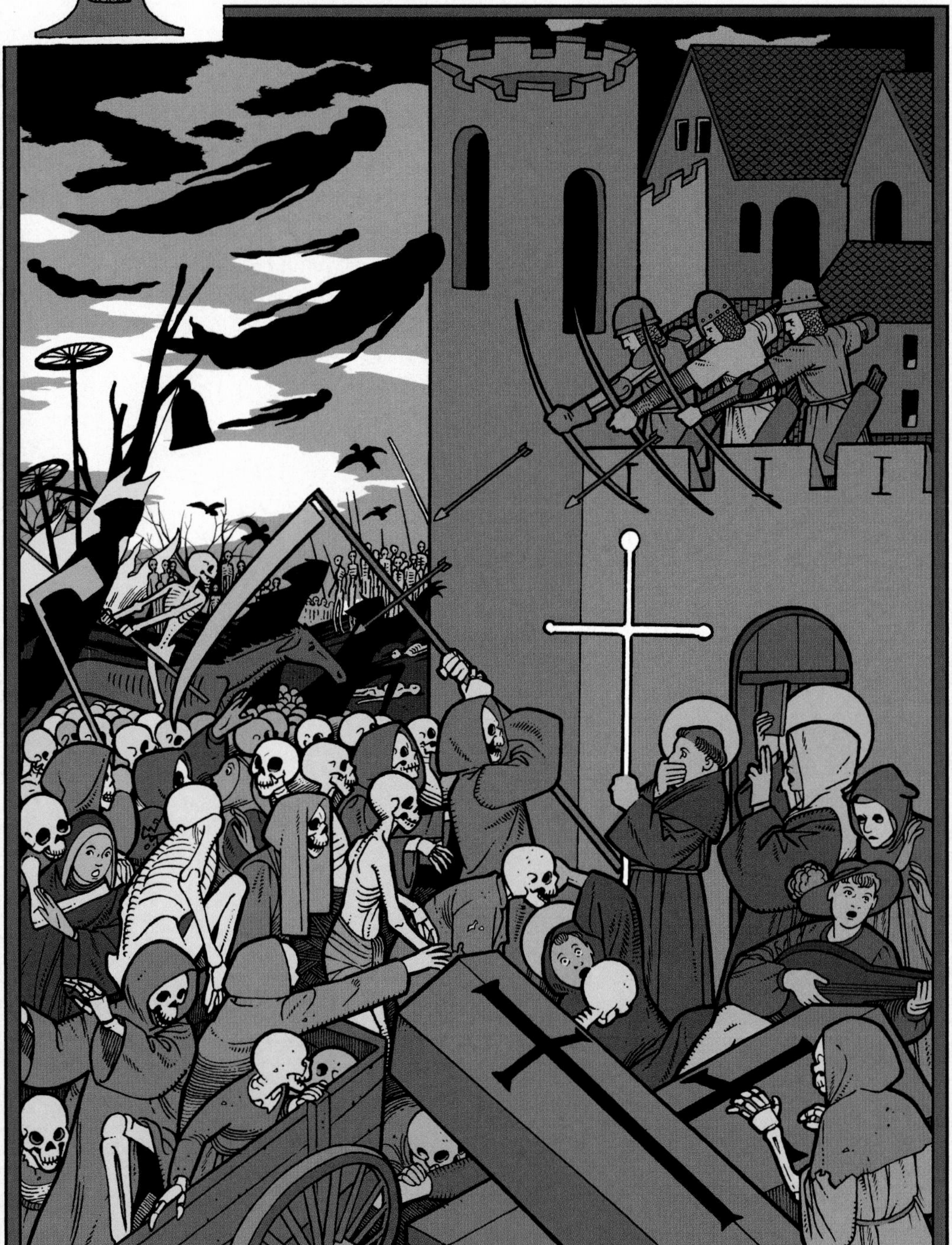

A BLACK DEATH.

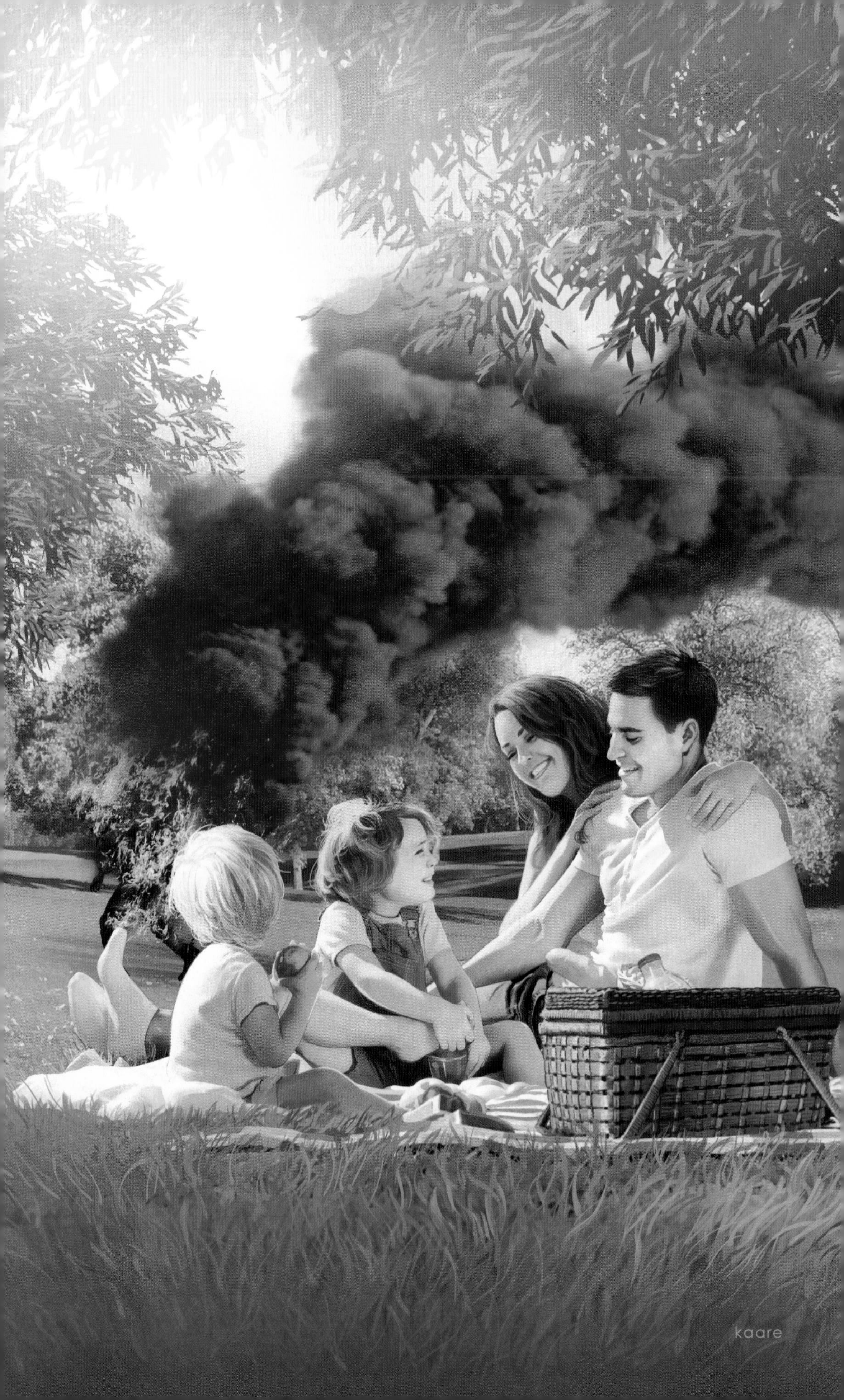
kaare

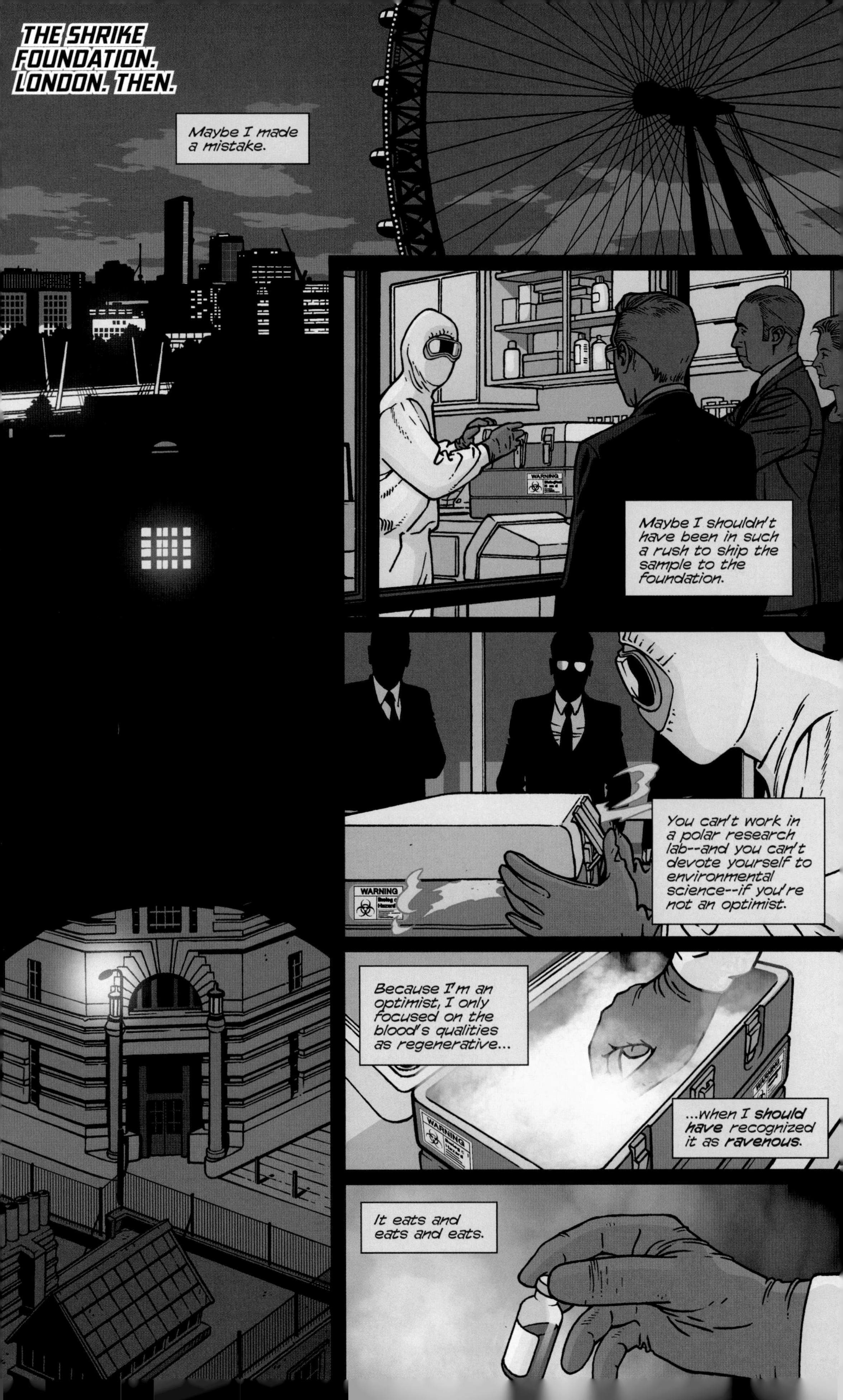
THE SHRIKE FOUNDATION. LONDON. THEN.
Maybe I made a mistake.
Maybe I shouldn't have been in such a rush to ship the sample to the foundation.
You can't work in a polar research lab--and you can't devote yourself to environmental science--if you're not an optimist.
WARNING
Because I'm an optimist, I only focused on the blood's qualities as regenerative...
...when I should have recognized it as ravenous.
It eats and eats and eats.

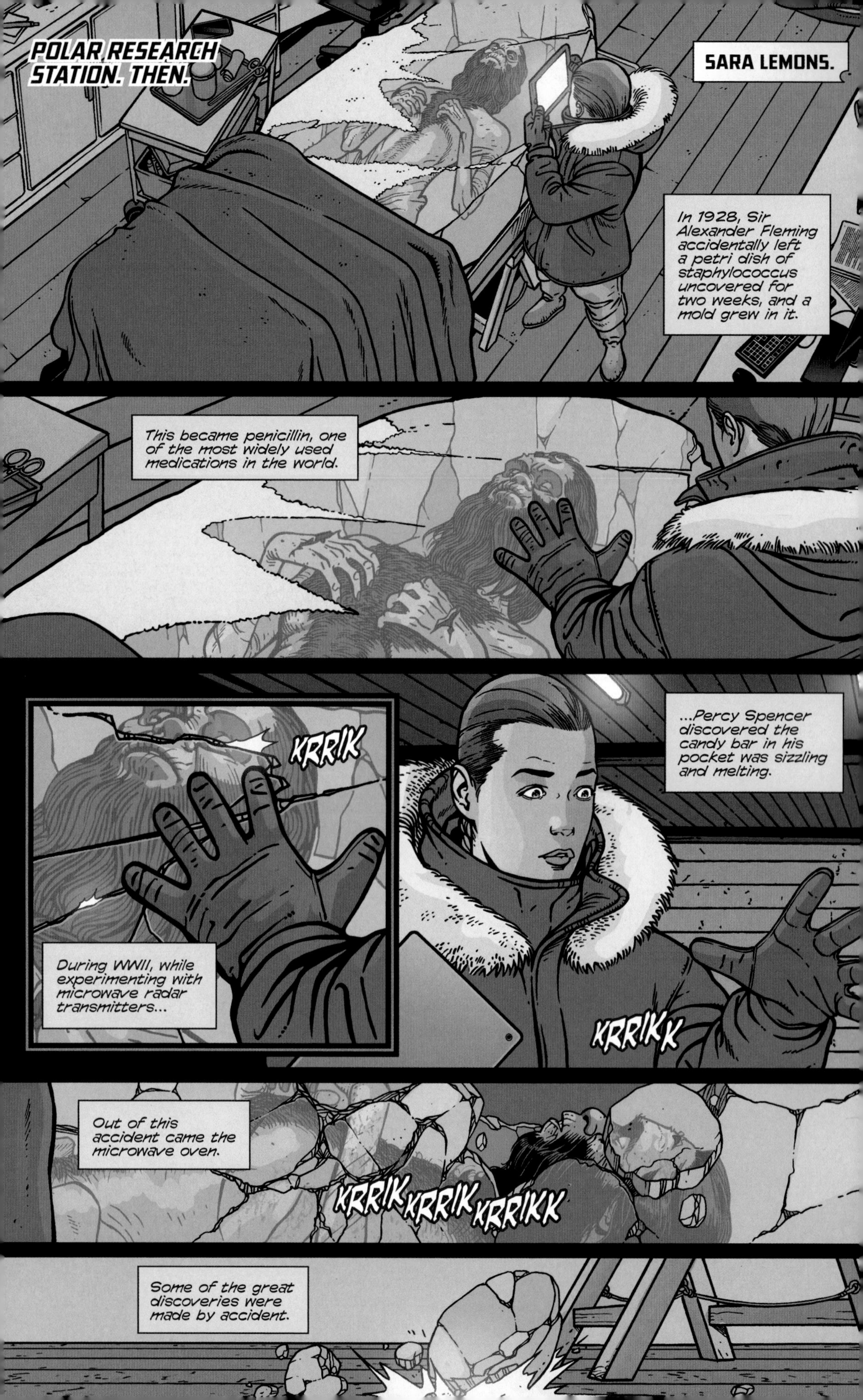

POLAR RESEARCH STATION. THEN.
SARA LEMONS.
In 1928, Sir Alexander Fleming accidentally left a petri dish of staphylococcus uncovered for two weeks, and a mold grew in it.
This became penicillin, one of the most widely used medications in the world.
KRRIK
During WWII, while experimenting with microwave radar transmitters...
...Percy Spencer discovered the candy bar in his pocket was sizzling and melting.
KRRIKK
Out of this accident came the microwave oven.
KRRIK KRRIK KRRIKK
Some of the great discoveries were made by accident.

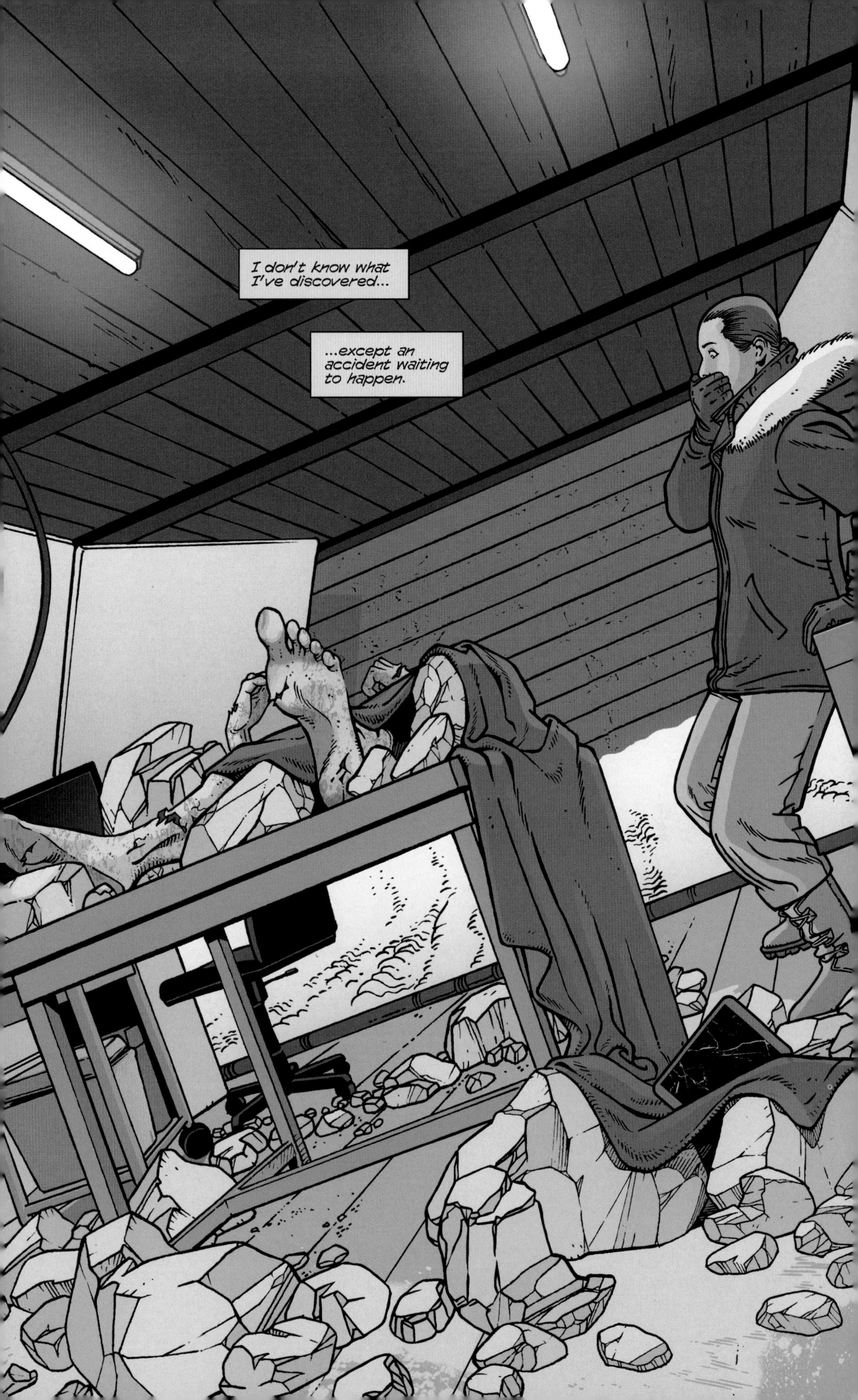
I don't know what I've discovered...
...except an accident waiting to happen.

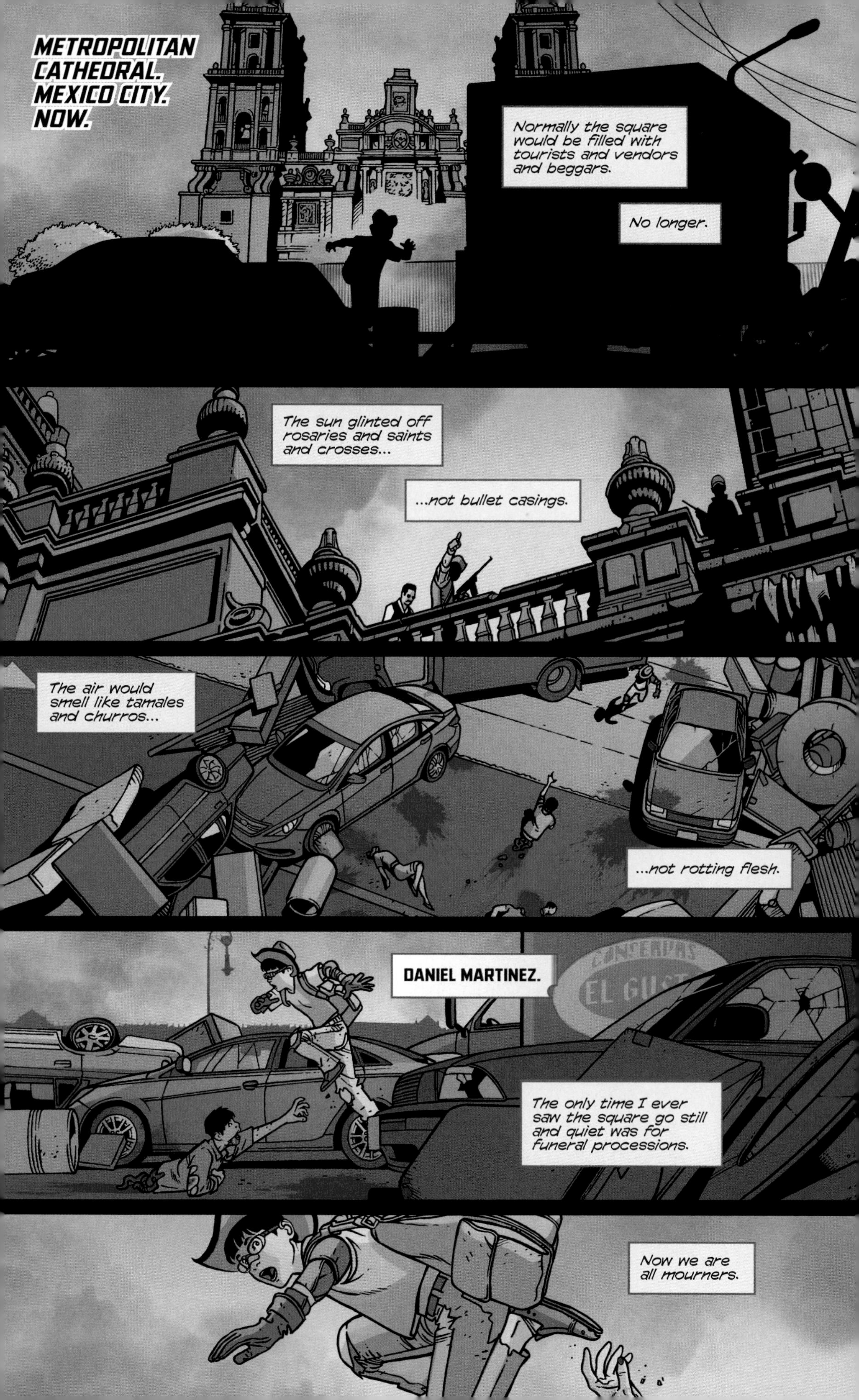
METROPOLITAN CATHEDRAL. MEXICO CITY. NOW.
Normally the square would be filled with tourists and vendors and beggars.
No longer.
The sun glinted off rosaries and saints and crosses...
...not bullet casings.
The air would smell like tamales and churros...
...not rotting flesh.
DANIEL MARTINEZ.
The only time I ever saw the square go still and quiet was for funeral processions.
Now we are all mourners.

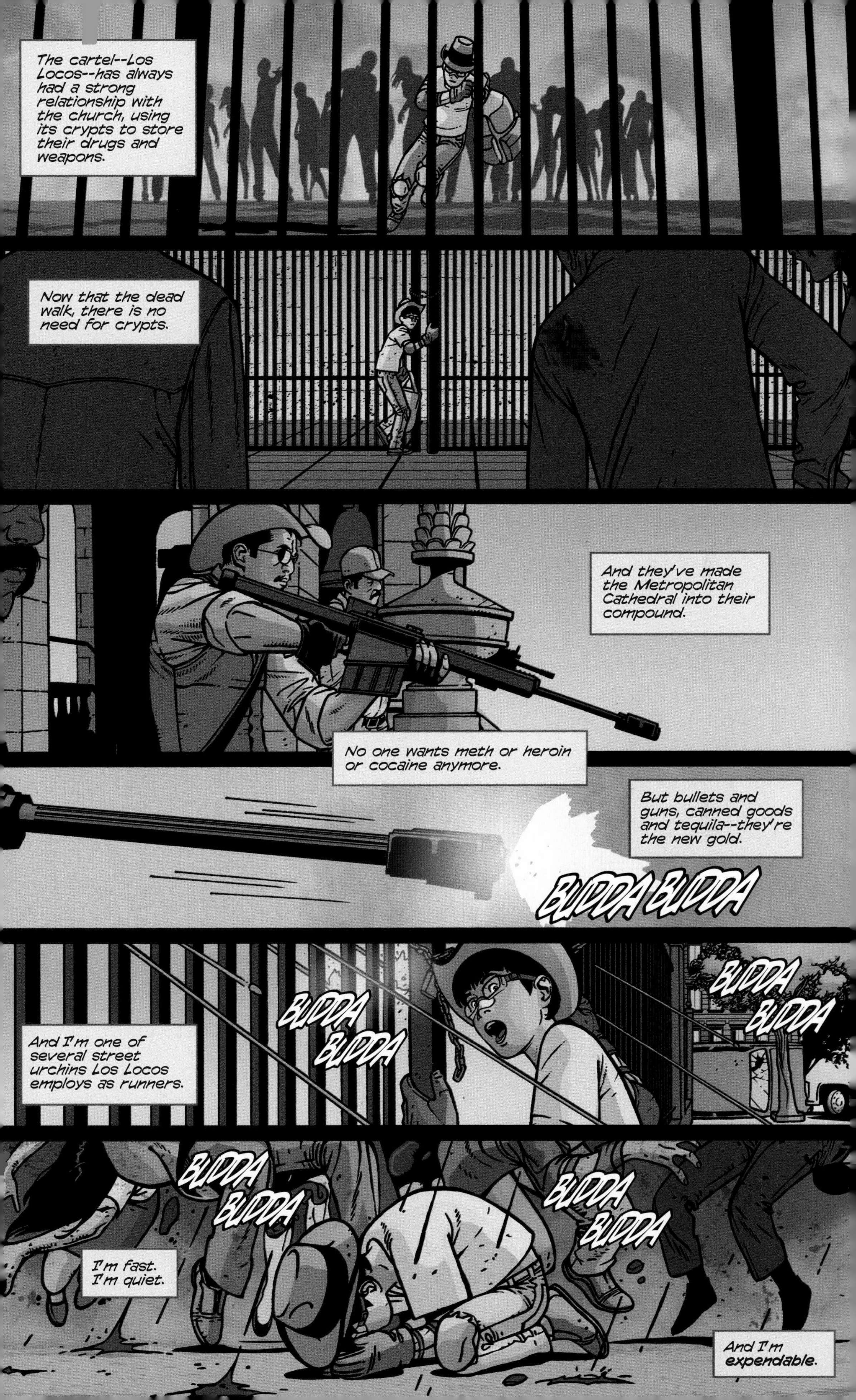
The cartel--Los Locos--has always had a strong relationship with the church, using its crypts to store their drugs and weapons.
Now that the dead walk, there is no need for crypts.
And they've made the Metropolitan Cathedral into their compound.
No one wants meth or heroin or cocaine anymore.
But bullets and guns, canned goods and tequila--they're the new gold.
BUDDA BUDDA
And I'm one of several street urchins Los Locos employs as runners.
BUDDA BUDDA
BUDDA BUDDA
BUDDA BUDDA
BUDDA BUDDA
I'm fast. I'm quiet.
And I'm expendable.

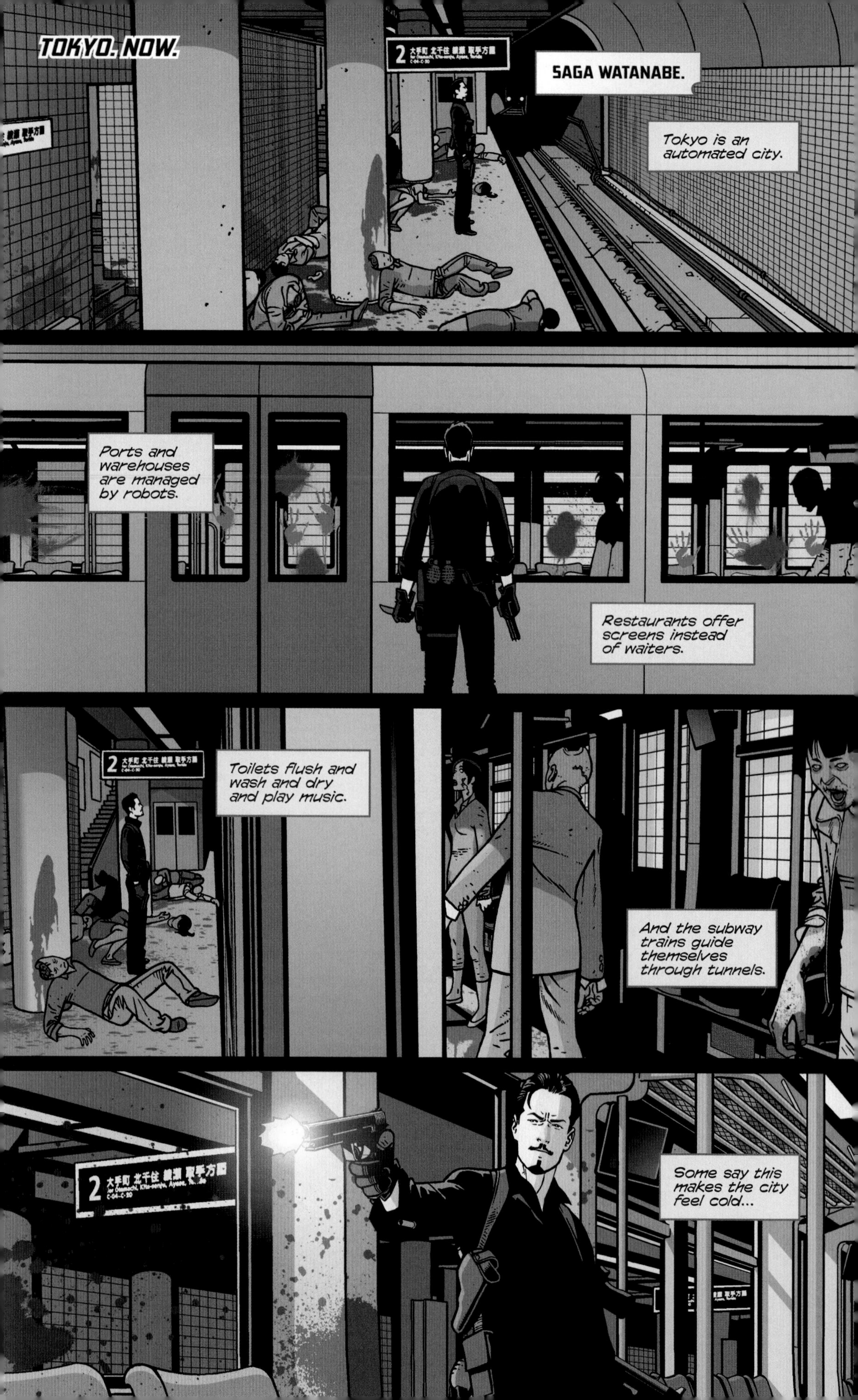
TOKYO. NOW.
SAGA WATANABE.
Tokyo is an automated city.
Ports and warehouses are managed by robots.
Restaurants offer screens instead of waiters.
Toilets flush and wash and dry and play music.
And the subway trains guide themselves through tunnels.
Some say this makes the city feel cold...

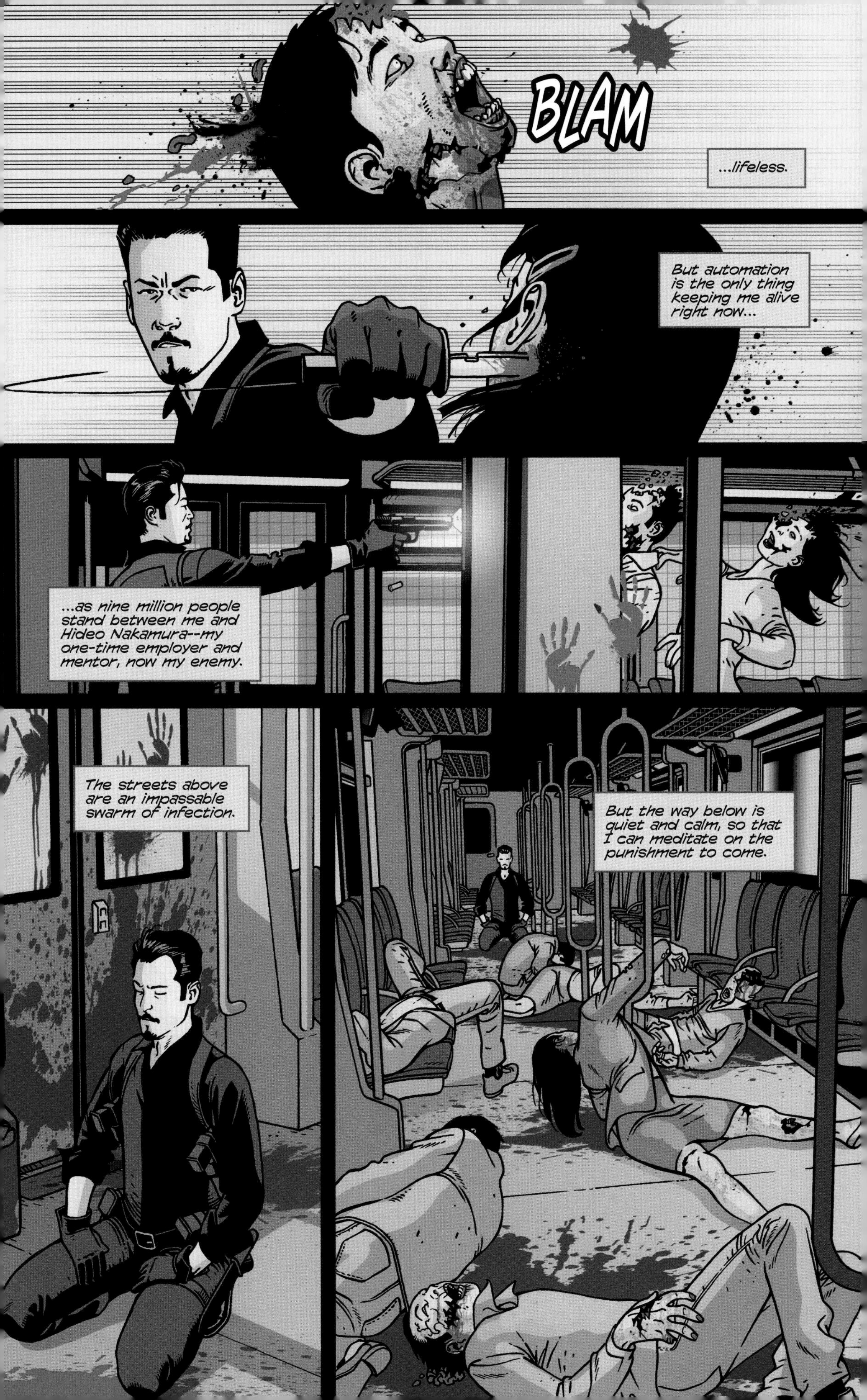
BLAM
...lifeless.
But automation is the only thing keeping me alive right now...
...as nine million people stand between me and Hideo Nakamura--my one-time employer and mentor, now my enemy.
The streets above are an impassable swarm of infection.
But the way below is quiet and calm, so that I can meditate on the punishment to come.

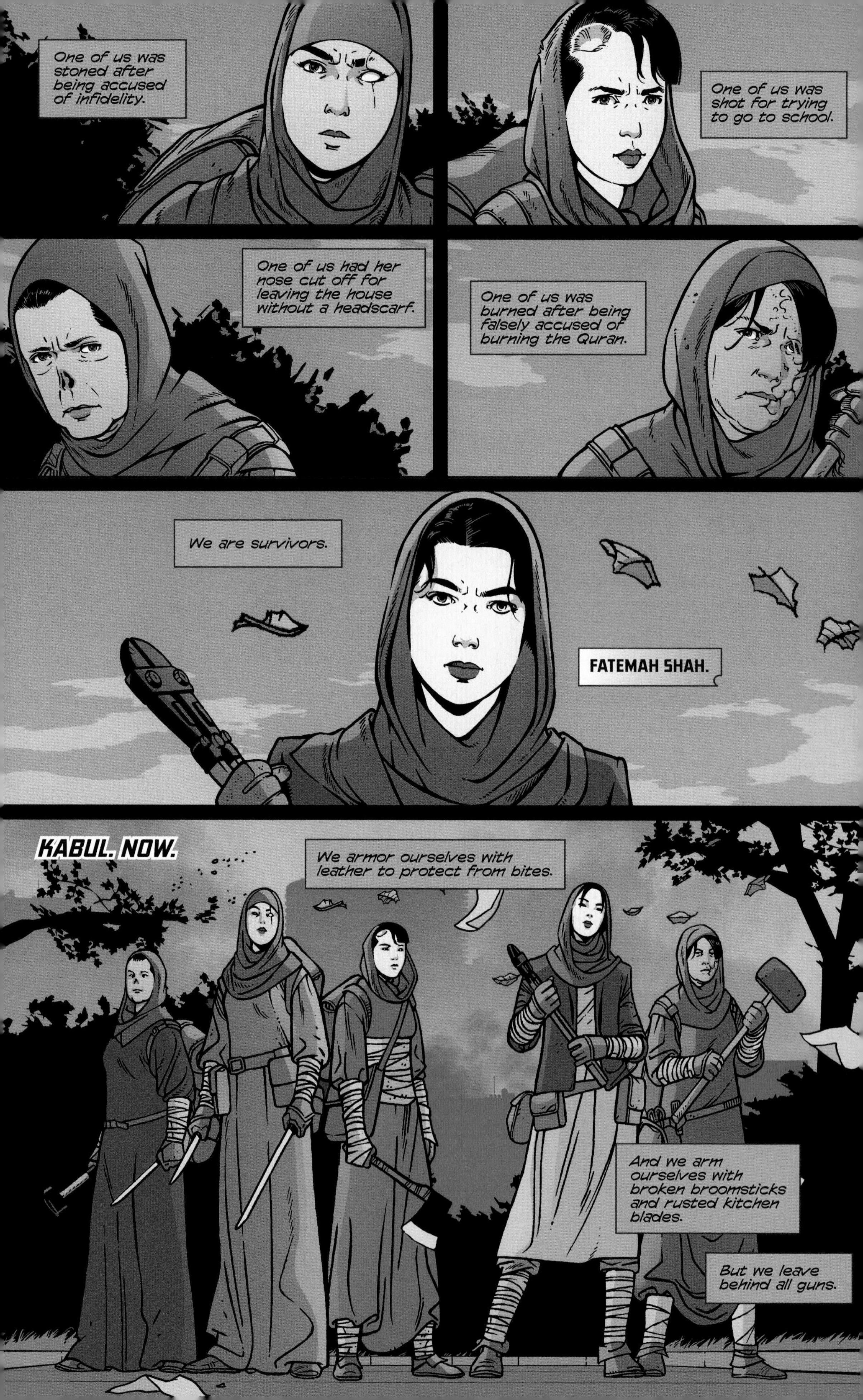
One of us was stoned after being accused of infidelity.
One of us was shot for trying to go to school.
One of us had her nose cut off for leaving the house without a headscarf.
One of us was burned after being falsely accused of burning the Quran.
We are survivors.
FATEMAH SHAH.
KABUL. NOW.
We armor ourselves with leather to protect from bites.
And we arm ourselves with broken broomsticks and rusted kitchen blades.
But we leave behind all guns.

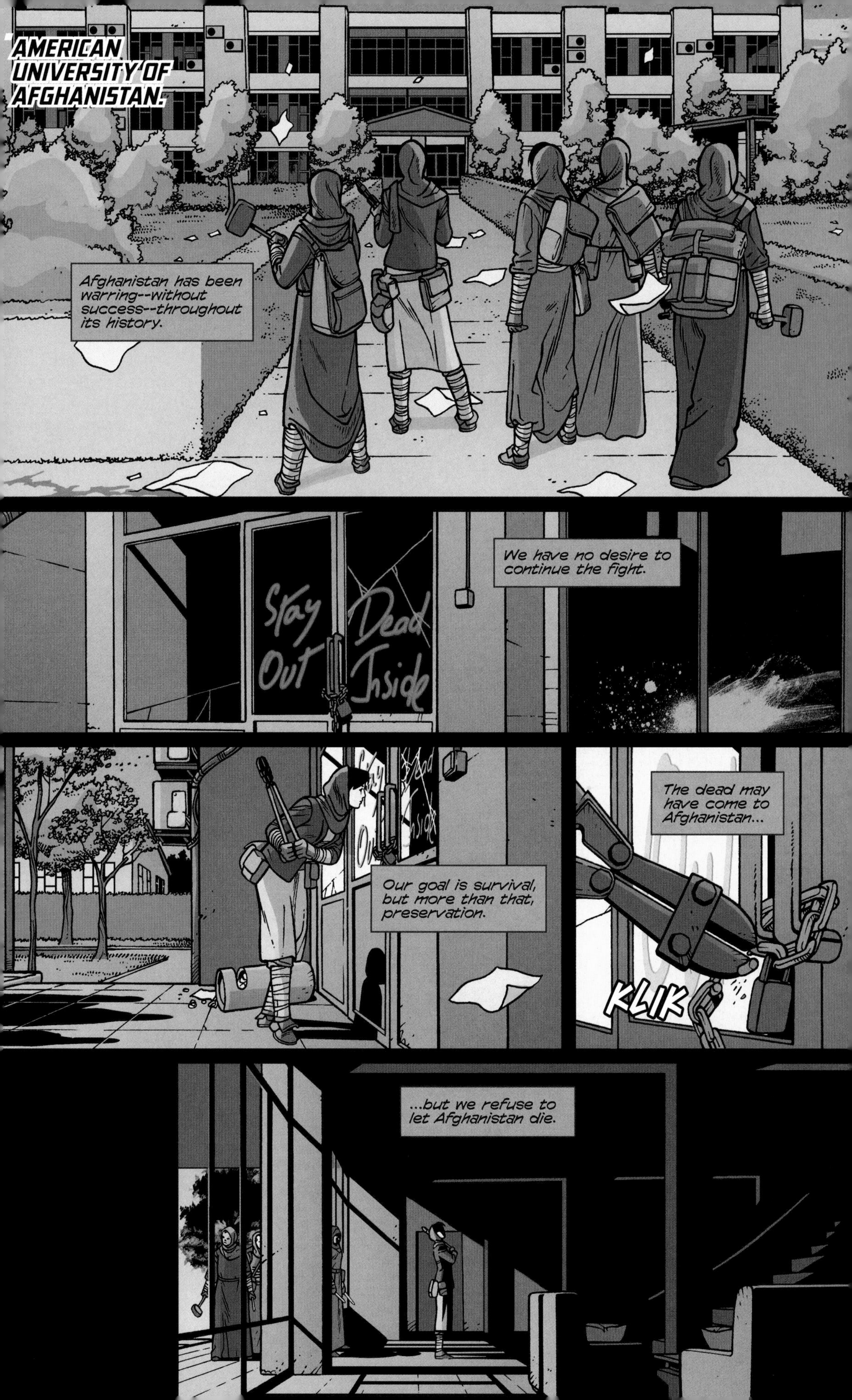
AMERICAN UNIVERSITY OF AFGHANISTAN.
Afghanistan has been warring--without success--throughout its history.
We have no desire to continue the fight.
Stay Out
Dead Inside
Our goal is survival, but more than that, preservation.
The dead may have come to Afghanistan...
KLIK
...but we refuse to let Afghanistan die.

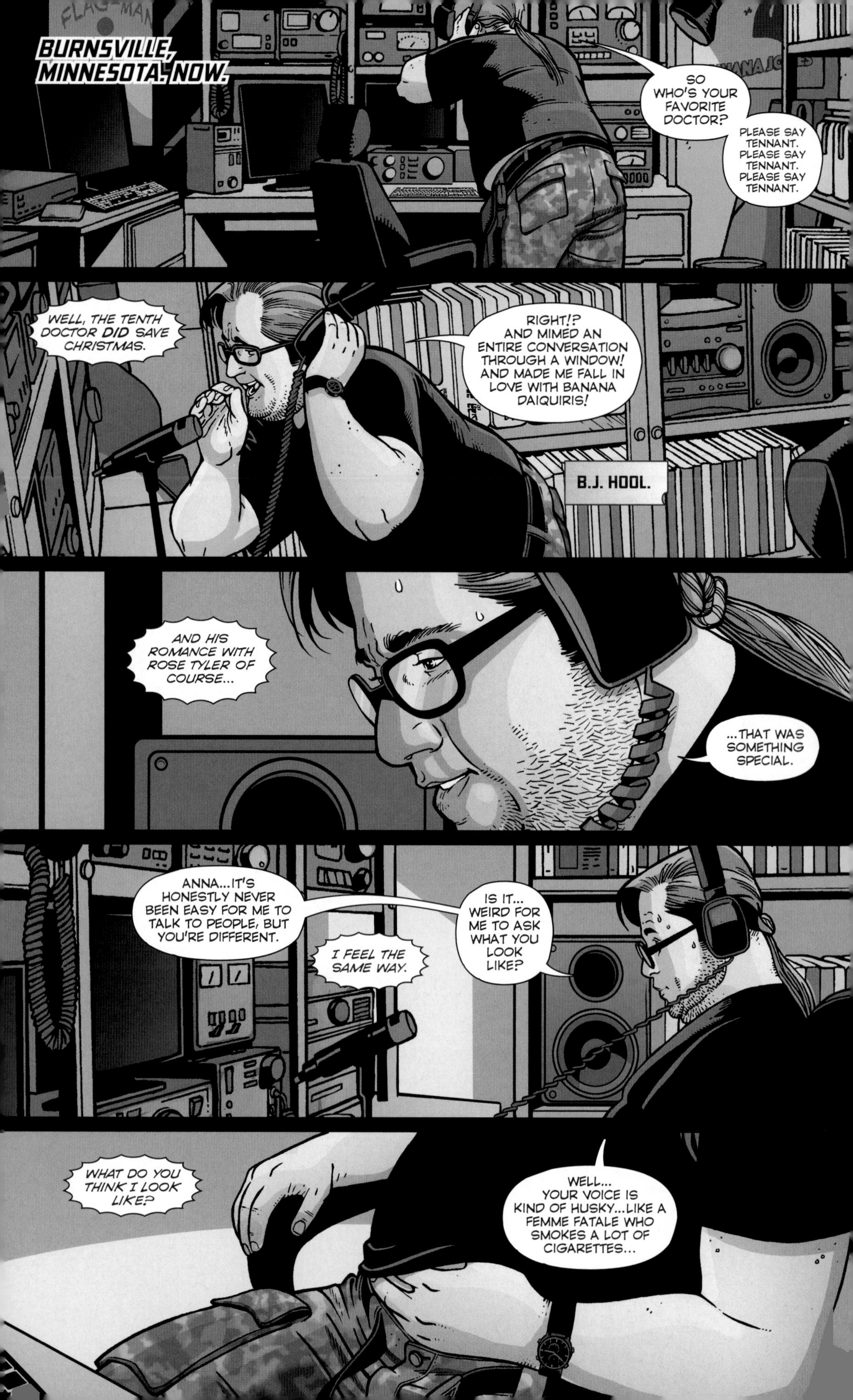
BURNSVILLE, MINNESOTA. NOW.
SO WHO'S YOUR FAVORITE DOCTOR?
PLEASE SAY TENNANT. PLEASE SAY TENNANT. PLEASE SAY TENNANT.
WELL, THE TENTH DOCTOR DID SAVE CHRISTMAS.
RIGHT!? AND MIMED AN ENTIRE CONVERSATION THROUGH A WINDOW! AND MADE ME FALL IN LOVE WITH BANANA DAIQUIRIS!
B.J. HOOL.
AND HIS ROMANCE WITH ROSE TYLER OF COURSE...
...THAT WAS SOMETHING SPECIAL.
ANNA...IT'S HONESTLY NEVER BEEN EASY FOR ME TO TALK TO PEOPLE, BUT YOU'RE DIFFERENT.
I FEEL THE SAME WAY.
IS IT... WEIRD FOR ME TO ASK WHAT YOU LOOK LIKE?
WHAT DO YOU THINK I LOOK LIKE?
WELL... YOUR VOICE IS KIND OF HUSKY...LIKE A FEMME FATALE WHO SMOKES A LOT OF CIGARETTES...

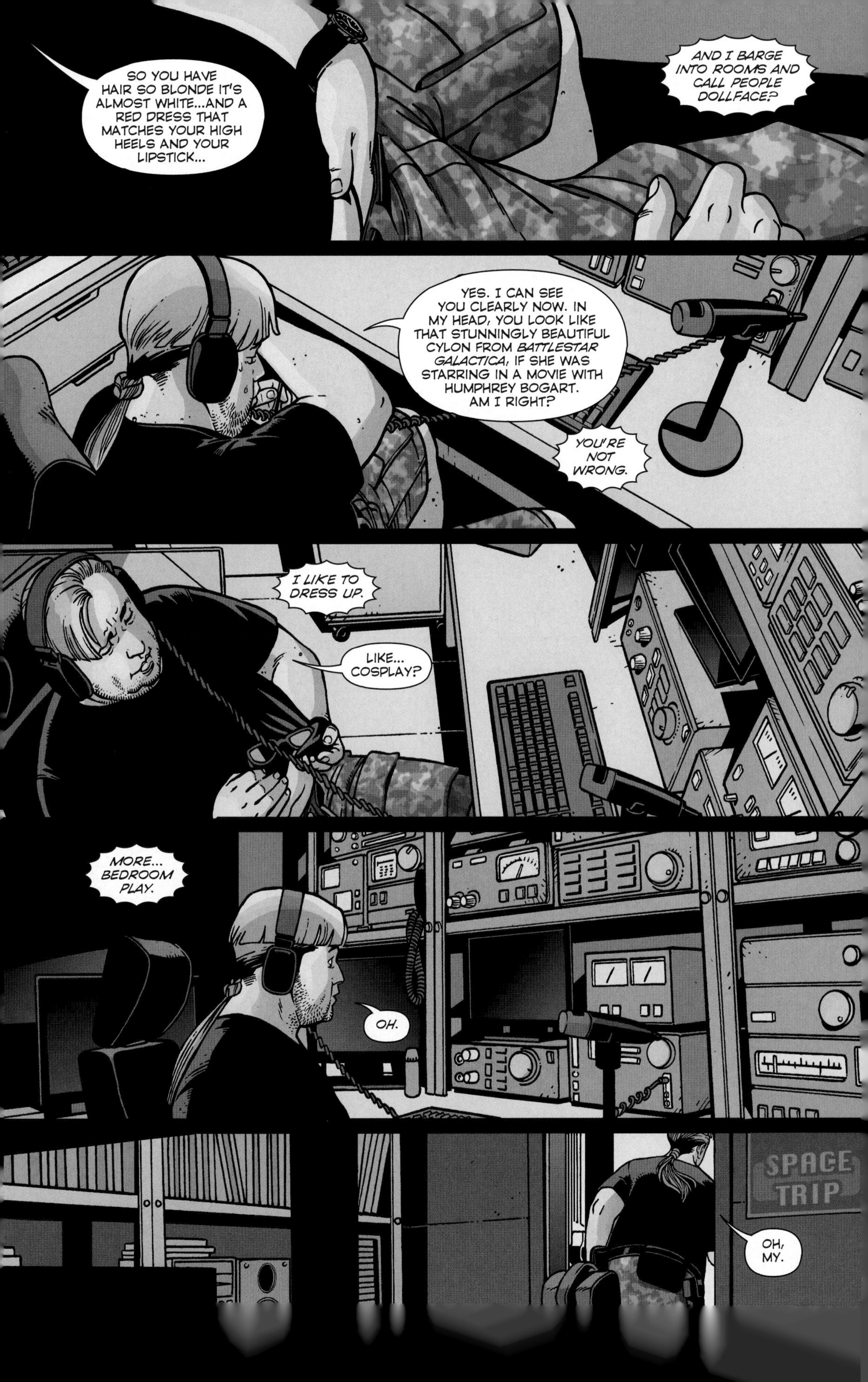
SO YOU HAVE HAIR SO BLONDE IT'S ALMOST WHITE...AND A RED DRESS THAT MATCHES YOUR HIGH HEELS AND YOUR LIPSTICK...
AND I BARGE INTO ROOMS AND CALL PEOPLE DOLLFACE?
YES. I CAN SEE YOU CLEARLY NOW. IN MY HEAD, YOU LOOK LIKE THAT STUNNINGLY BEAUTIFUL CYLON FROM *BATTLESTAR GALACTICA,* IF SHE WAS STARRING IN A MOVIE WITH HUMPHREY BOGART. AM I RIGHT?
YOU'RE NOT WRONG.
I LIKE TO DRESS UP.
LIKE... COSPLAY?
MORE... BEDROOM PLAY.
OH.
SPACE TRIP
OH, MY.

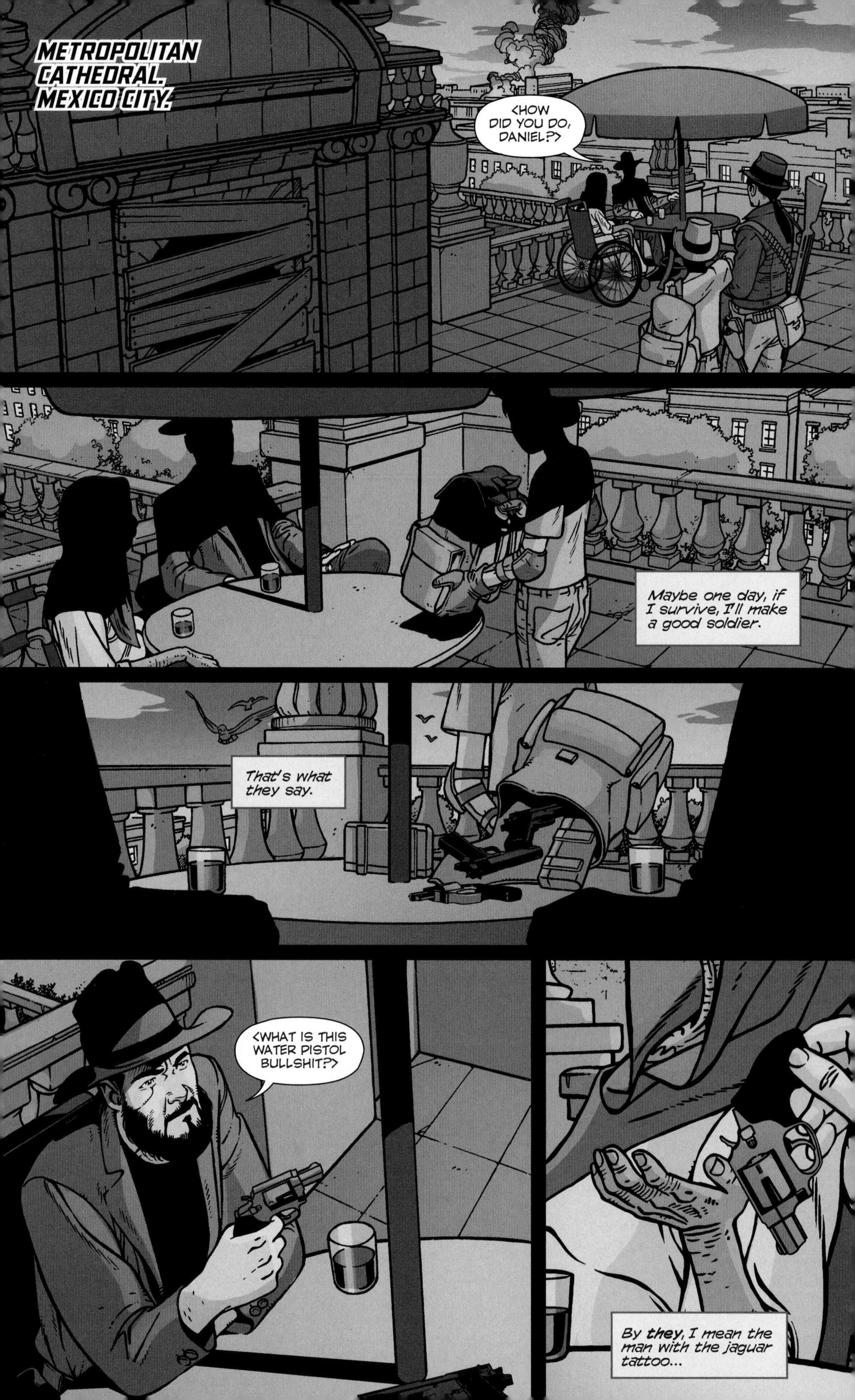
METROPOLITAN CATHEDRAL, MEXICO CITY.
<HOW DID YOU DO, DANIEL?>
Maybe one day, if I survive, I'll make a good soldier.
That's what they say.
<WHAT IS THIS WATER PISTOL BULLSHIT?>
By they, I mean the man with the jaguar tattoo...

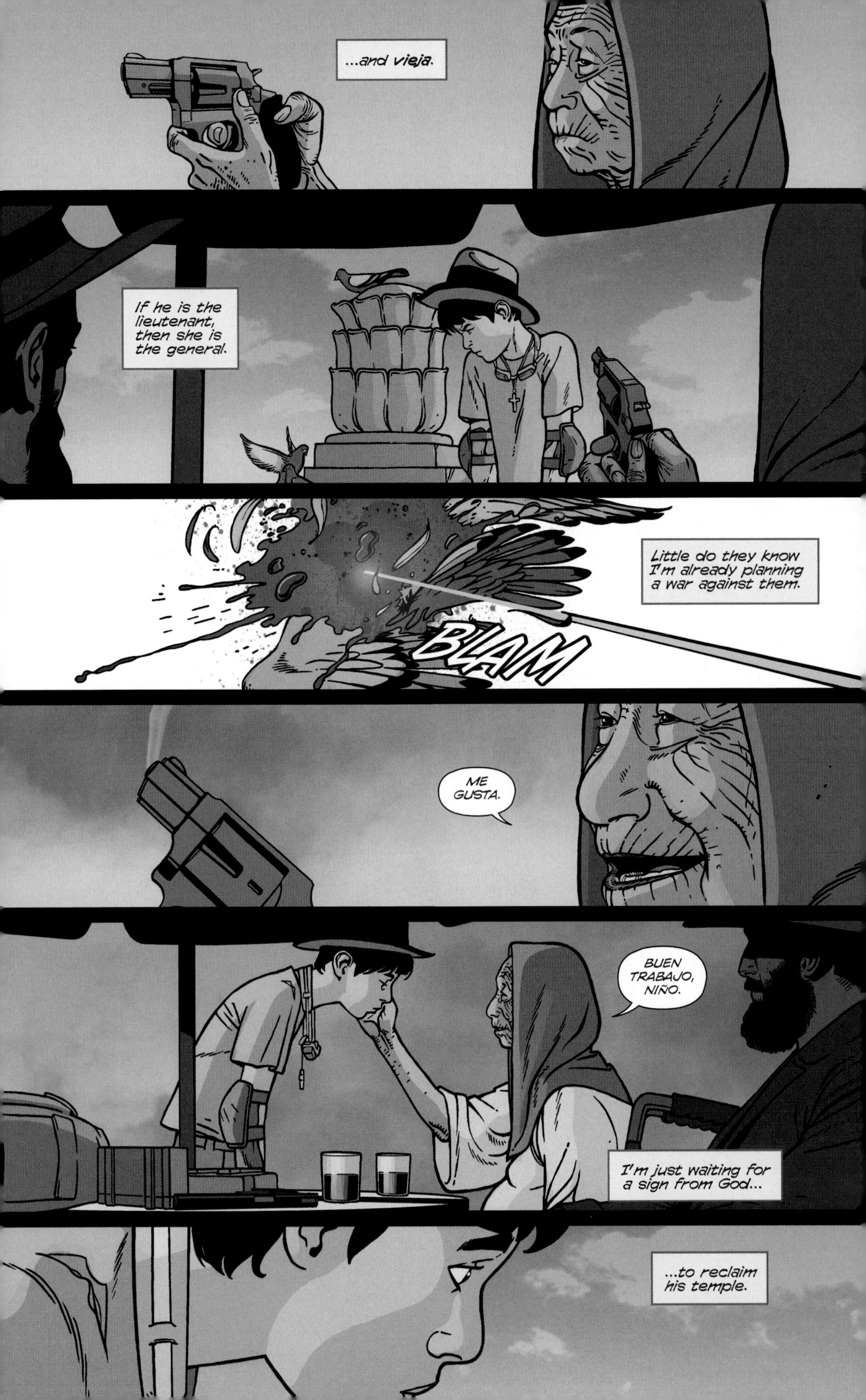
...and vieja.
If he is the lieutenant, then she is the general.
Little do they know I'm already planning a war against them.
BLAM
ME GUSTA.
BUEN TRABAJO, NIÑO.
I'm just waiting for a sign from God...
...to reclaim his temple.

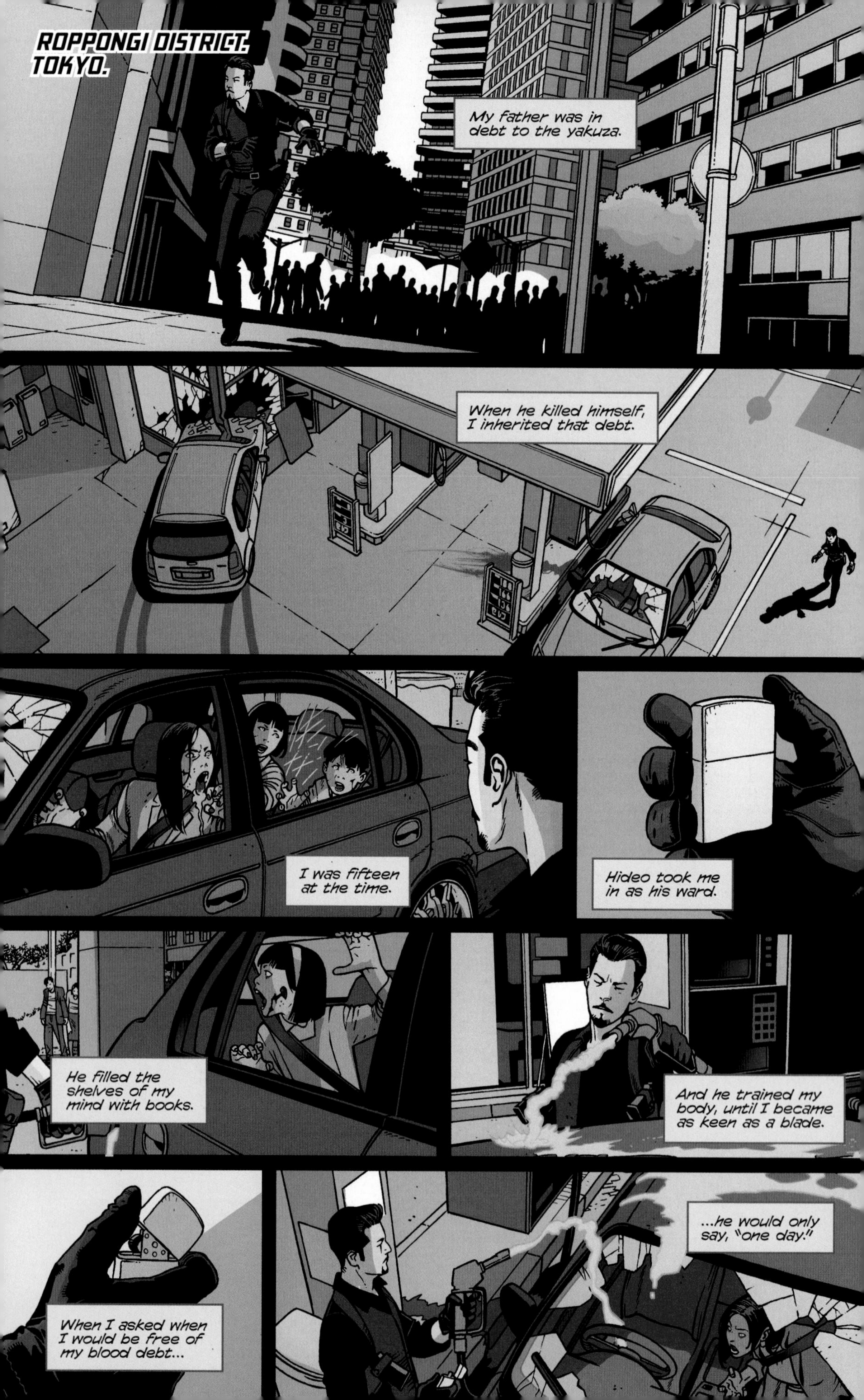
ROPPONGI DISTRICT.
TOKYO.
My father was in debt to the yakuza.
When he killed himself, I inherited that debt.
I was fifteen at the time.
Hideo took me in as his ward.
He filled the shelves of my mind with books.
And he trained my body, until I became as keen as a blade.
When I asked when I would be free of my blood debt...
...he would only say, "one day."

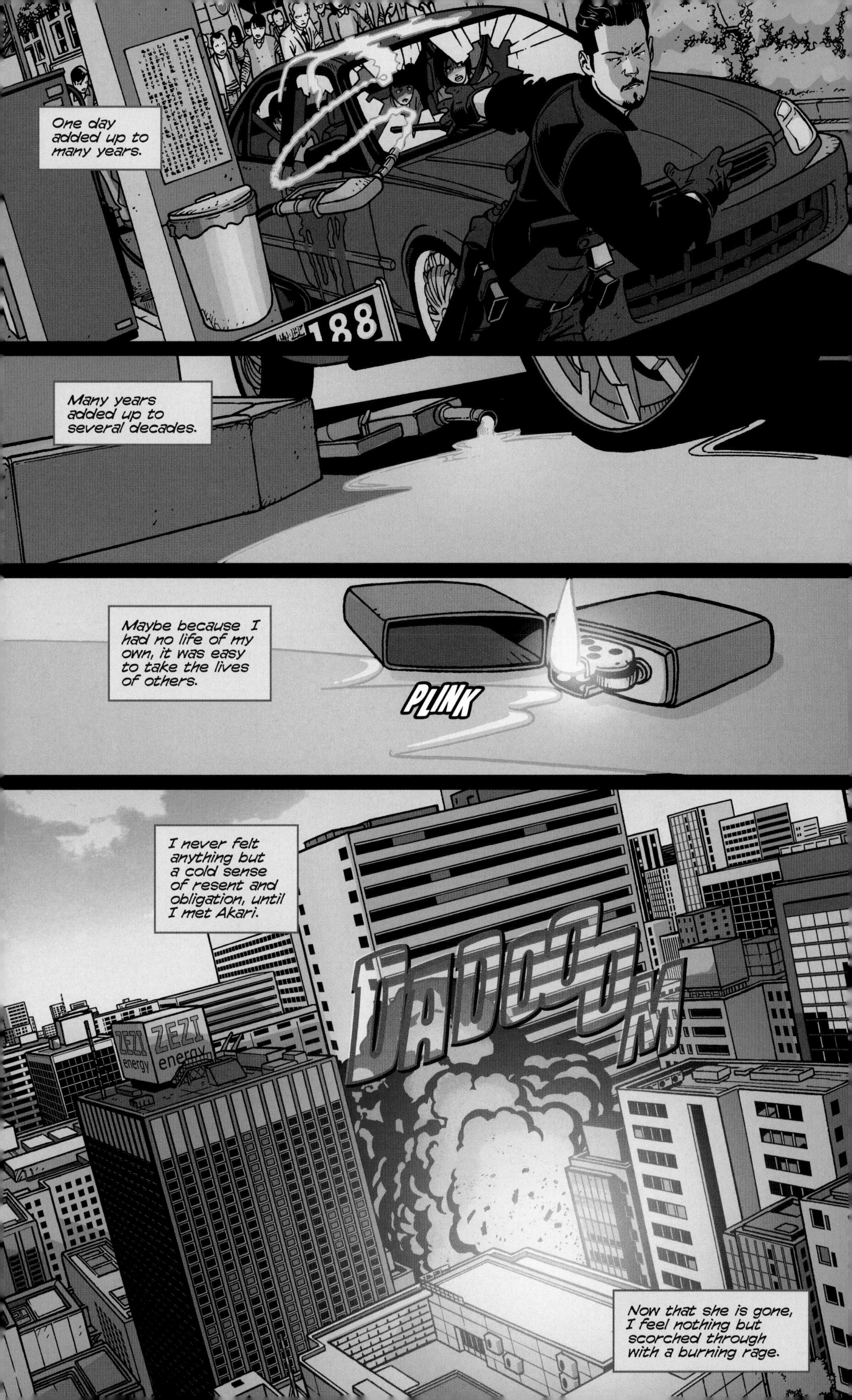
One day added up to many years.
Many years added up to several decades.
Maybe because I had no life of my own, it was easy to take the lives of others.
PLINK
I never felt anything but a cold sense of resent and obligation, until I met Akari.
ZEZI energy
Now that she is gone, I feel nothing but scorched through with a burning rage.

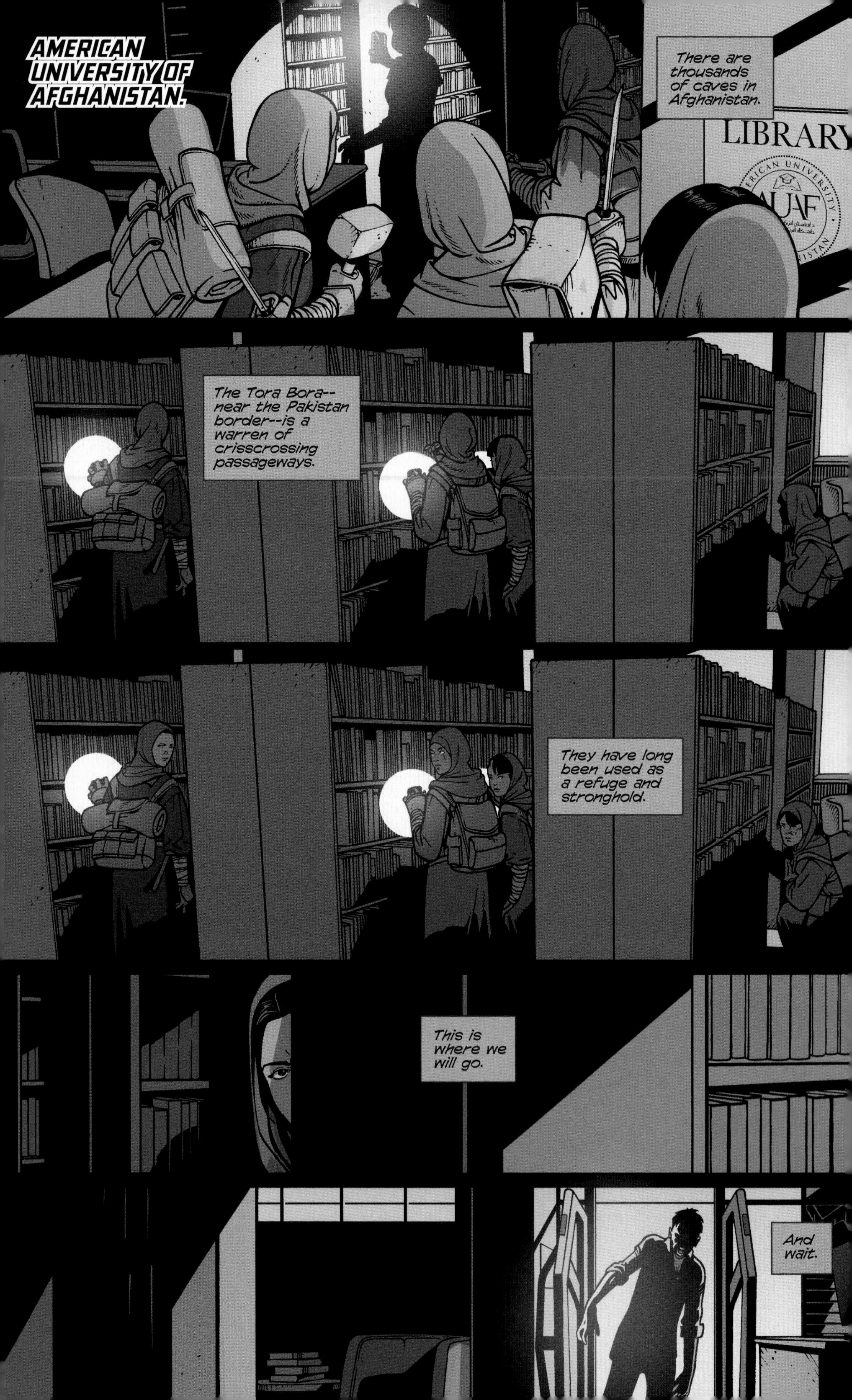
AMERICAN UNIVERSITY OF AFGHANISTAN.
There are thousands of caves in Afghanistan.
LIBRARY
AMERICAN UNIVERSITY
AUAF
AFGHANISTAN
The Tora Bora--near the Pakistan border--is a warren of crisscrossing passageways.
They have long been used as a refuge and stronghold.
This is where we will go.
And wait.

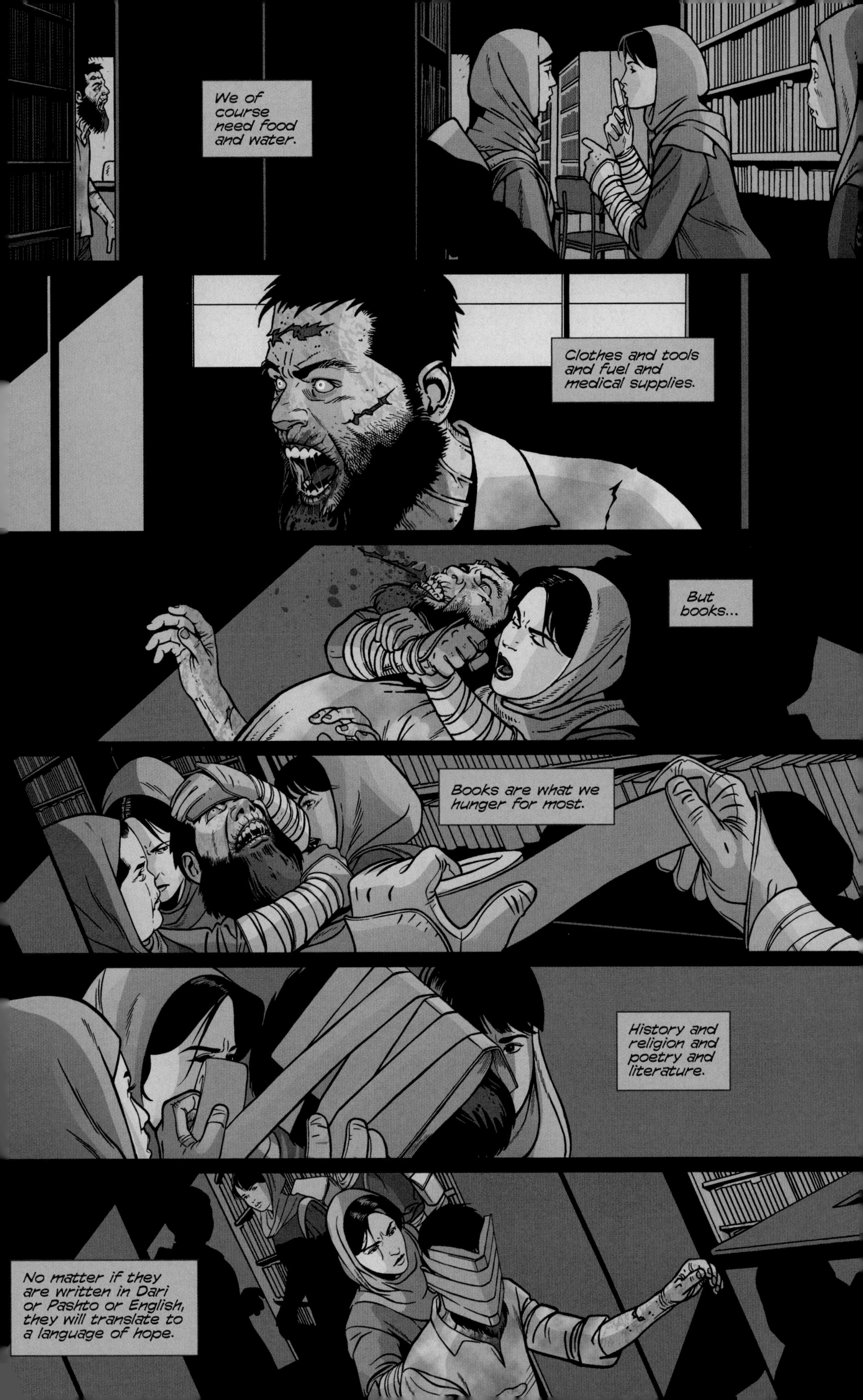
We of course need food and water.
Clothes and tools and fuel and medical supplies.
But books...
Books are what we hunger for most.
History and religion and poetry and literature.
No matter if they are written in Dari or Pashto or English, they will translate to a language of hope.

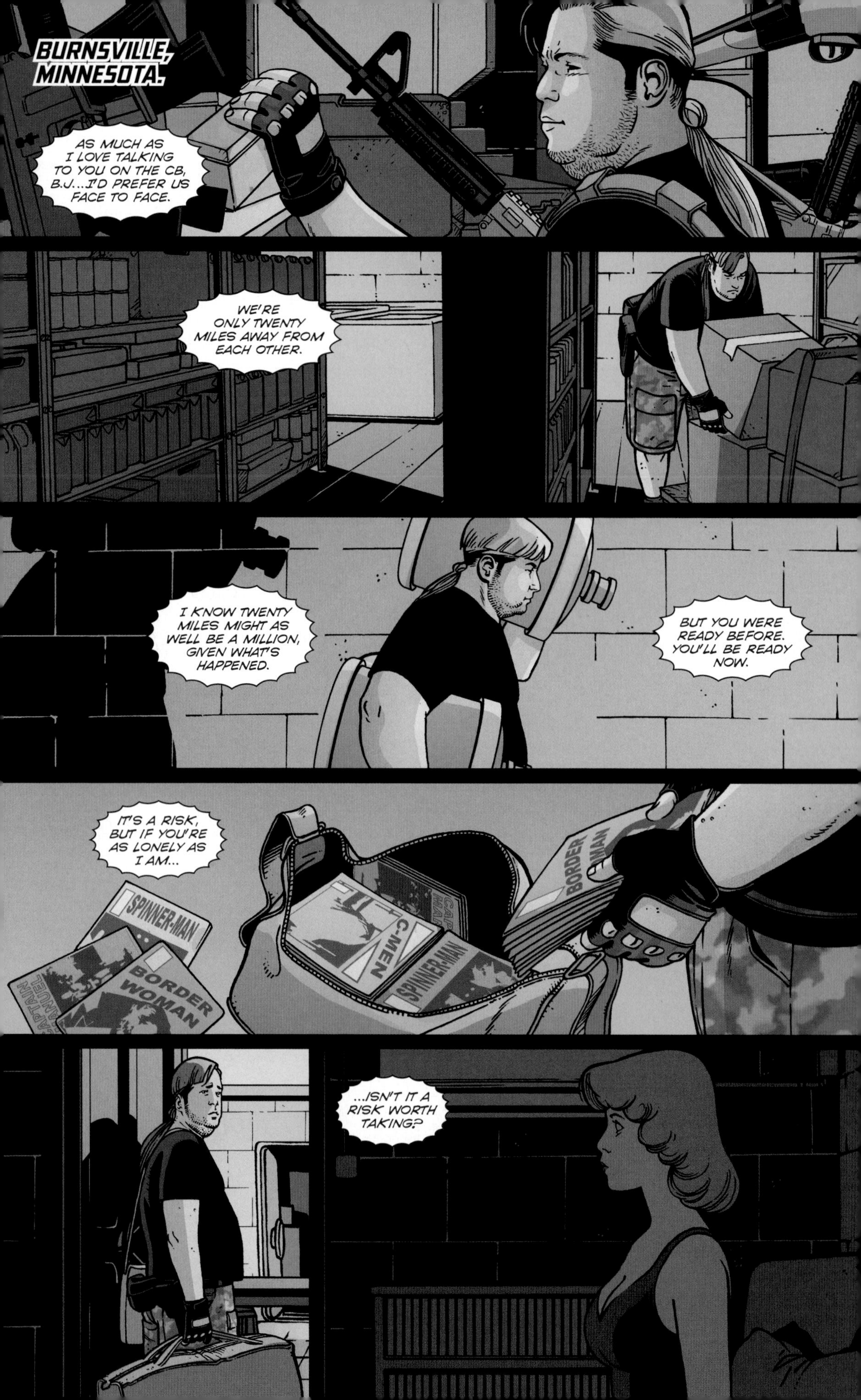
BURNSVILLE, MINNESOTA.
AS MUCH AS I LOVE TALKING TO YOU ON THE CB, B.J....I'D PREFER US FACE TO FACE.
WE'RE ONLY TWENTY MILES AWAY FROM EACH OTHER.
I KNOW TWENTY MILES MIGHT AS WELL BE A MILLION, GIVEN WHAT'S HAPPENED.
BUT YOU WERE READY BEFORE. YOU'LL BE READY NOW.
IT'S A RISK, BUT IF YOU'RE AS LONELY AS I AM...
BORDER WOMAN
SPINNER-MAN
C-MEN
SPINNER-MAN
SPINNER-MAN
BORDER WOMAN
CAPTAIN MANUEL
...ISN'T IT A RISK WORTH TAKING?

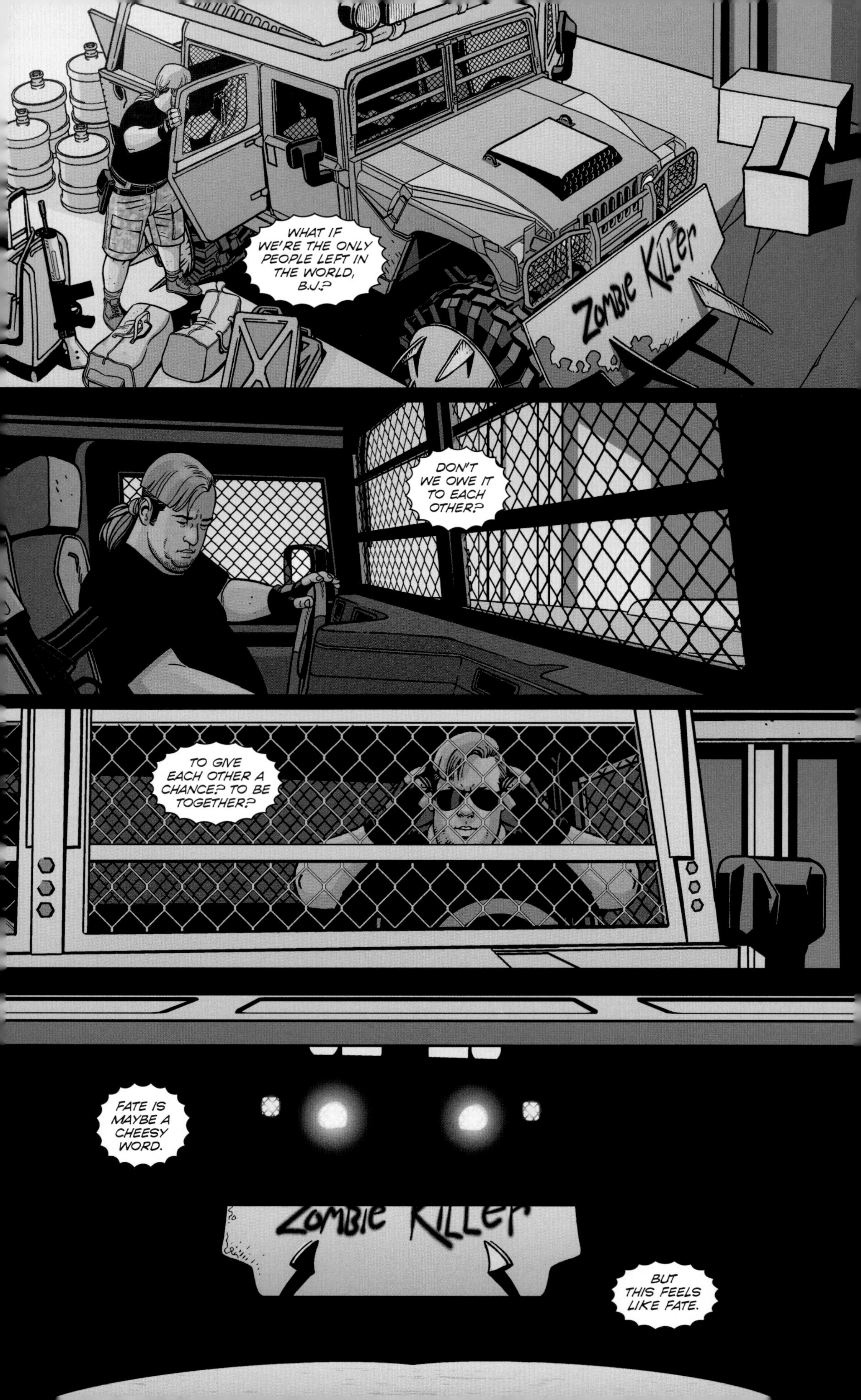
WHAT IF WE'RE THE ONLY PEOPLE LEFT IN THE WORLD, B.J.?
Zombie Killer
DON'T WE OWE IT TO EACH OTHER?
TO GIVE EACH OTHER A CHANCE? TO BE TOGETHER?
FATE IS MAYBE A CHEESY WORD.
Zombie Killer
BUT THIS FEELS LIKE FATE.

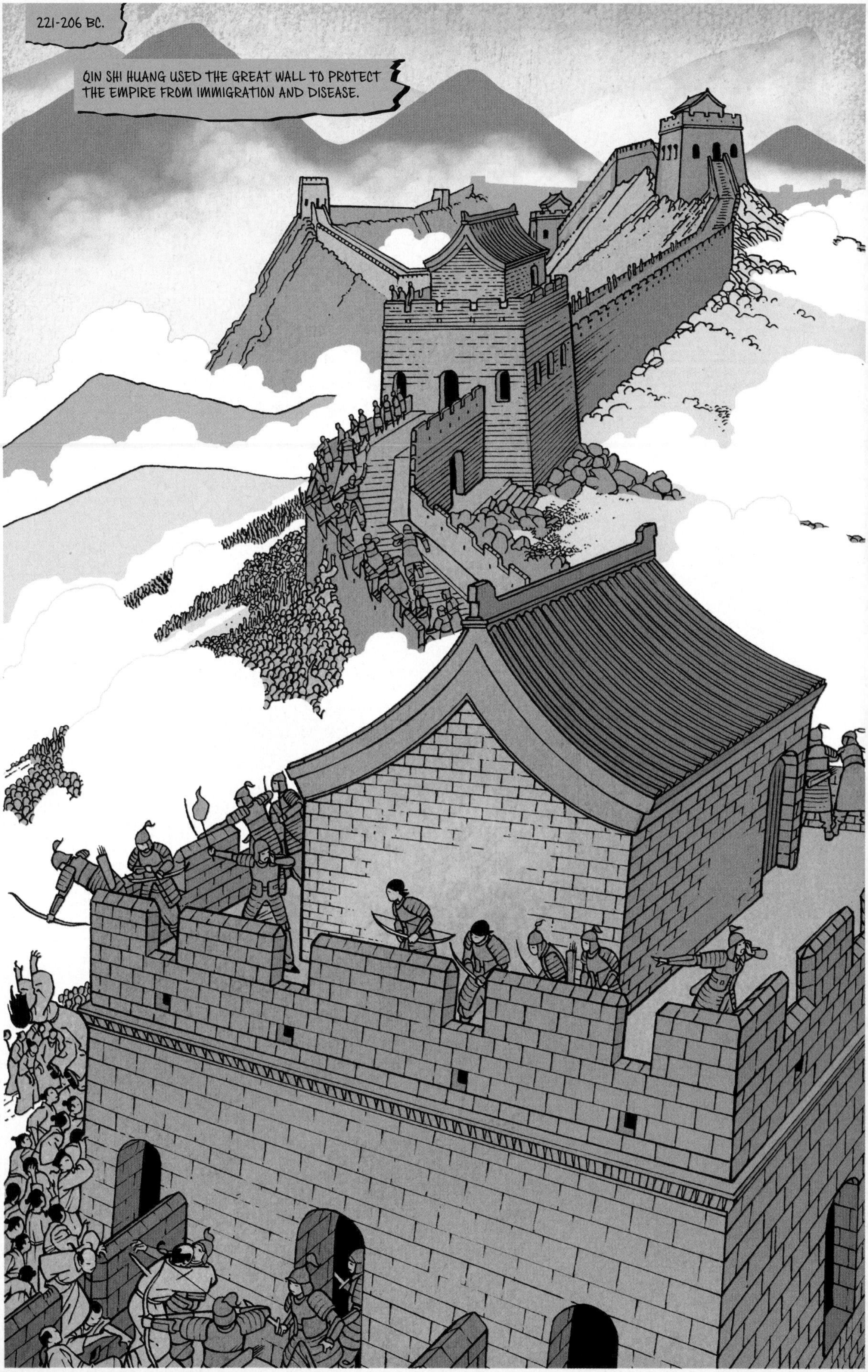
221-206 BC.
QIN SHI HUANG USED THE GREAT WALL TO PROTECT THE EMPIRE FROM IMMIGRATION AND DISEASE.

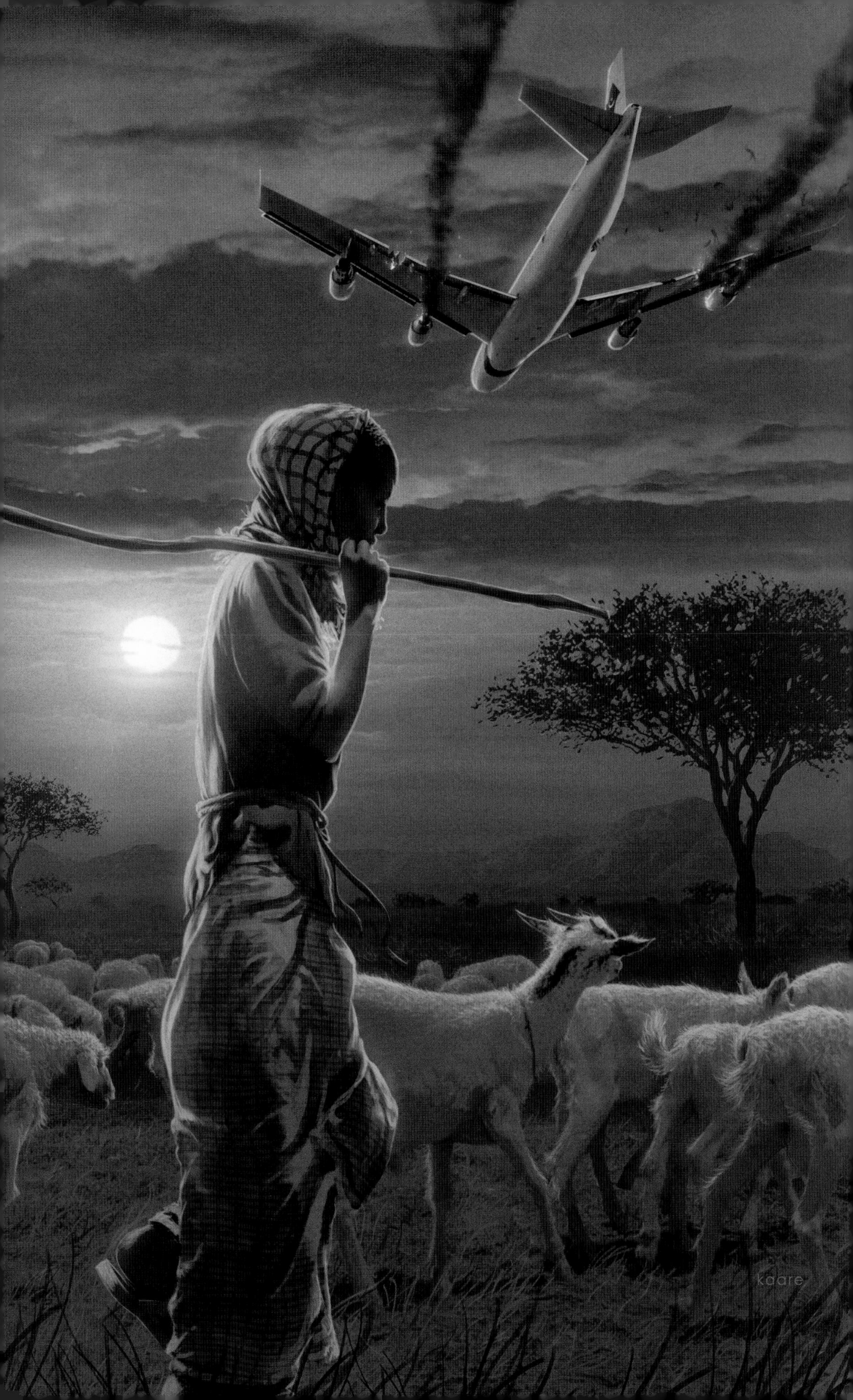
kaare

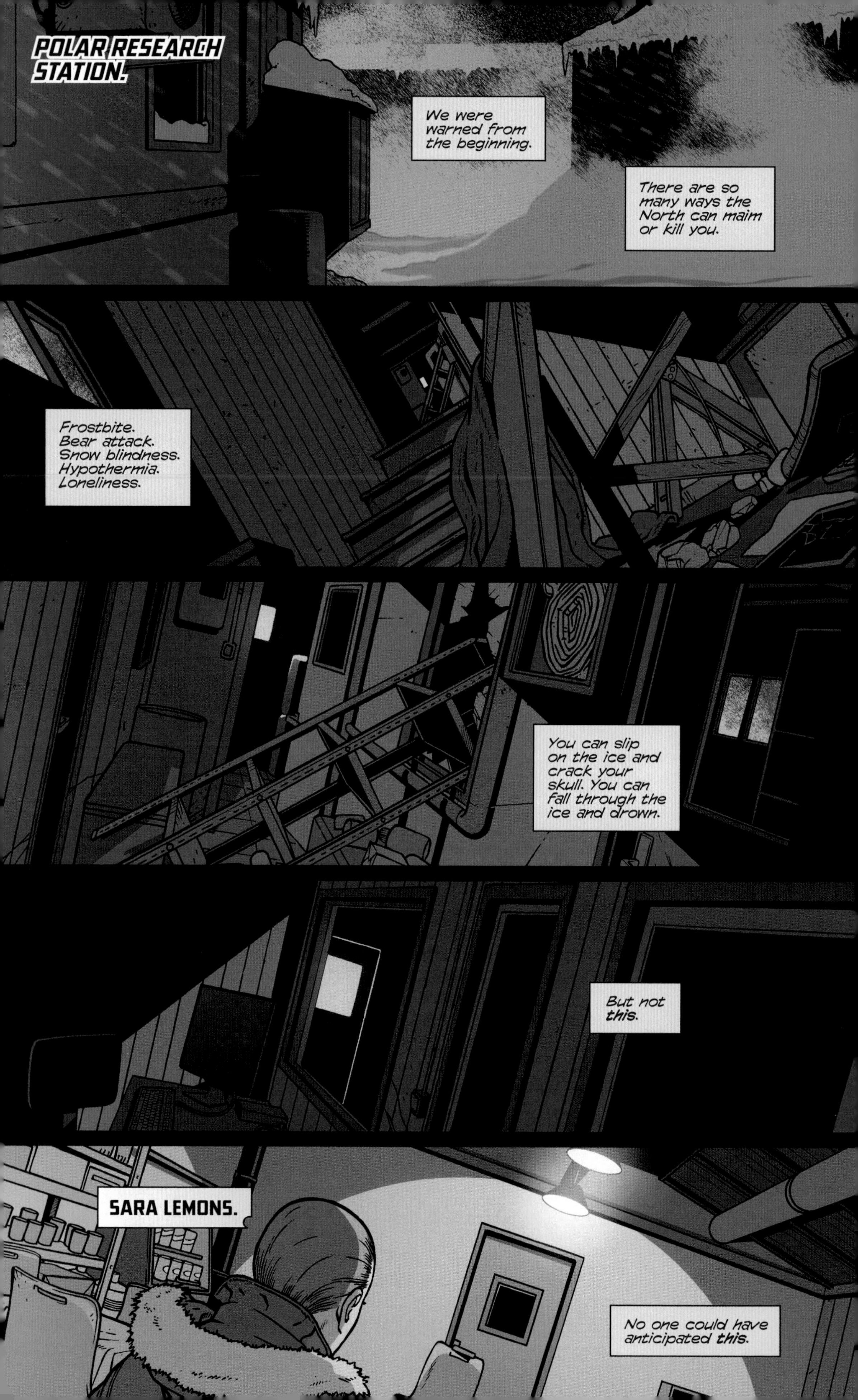
POLAR RESEARCH STATION.
We were warned from the beginning.
There are so many ways the North can maim or kill you.
Frostbite. Bear attack. Snow blindness. Hypothermia. Loneliness.
You can slip on the ice and crack your skull. You can fall through the ice and drown.
But not *this*.
SARA LEMONS.
No one could have anticipated *this*.

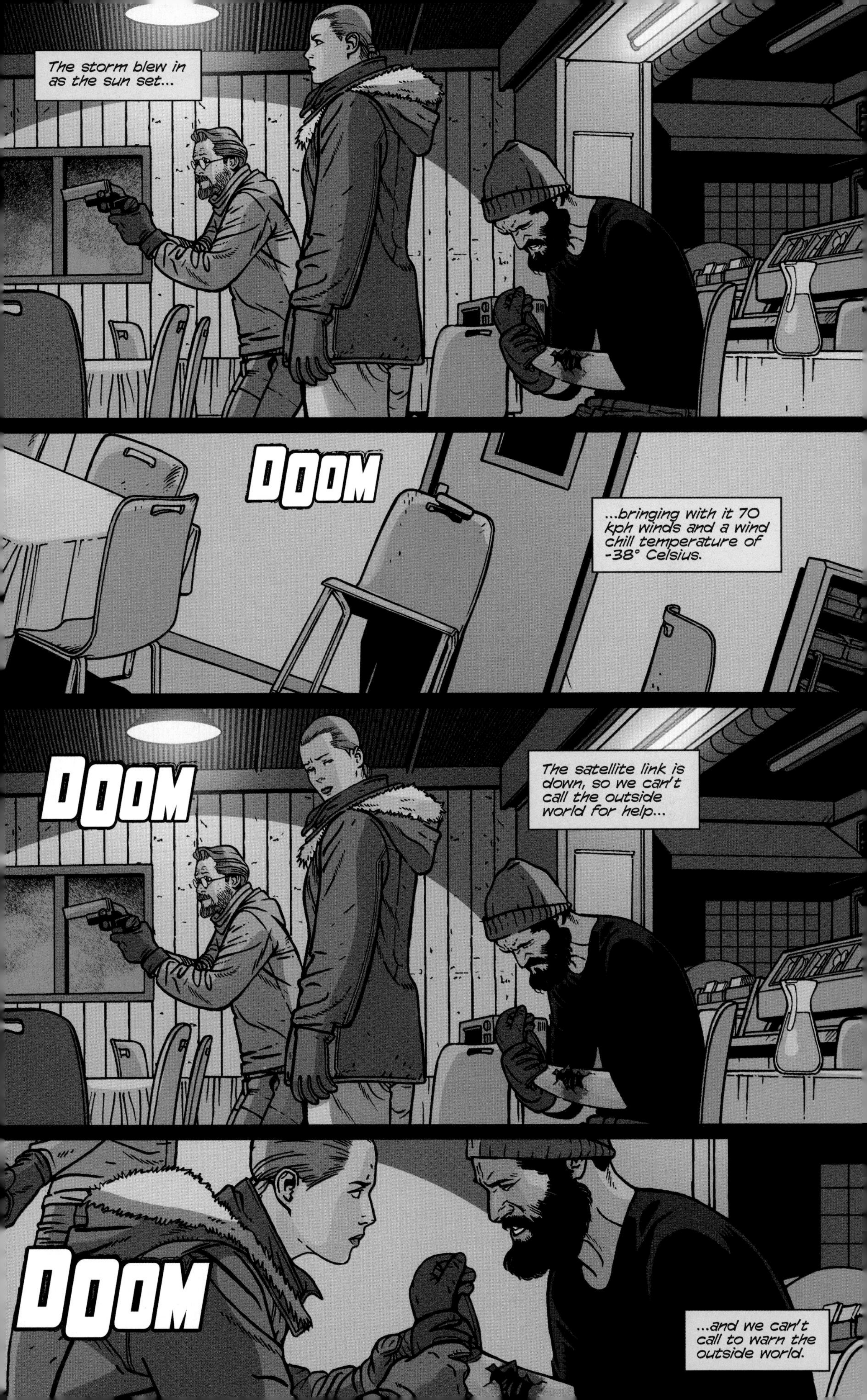
The storm blew in as the sun set...
DOOM
...bringing with it 70 kph winds and a wind chill temperature of -38° Celsius.
DOOM
The satellite link is down, so we can't call the outside world for help...
DOOM
...and we can't call to warn the outside world.

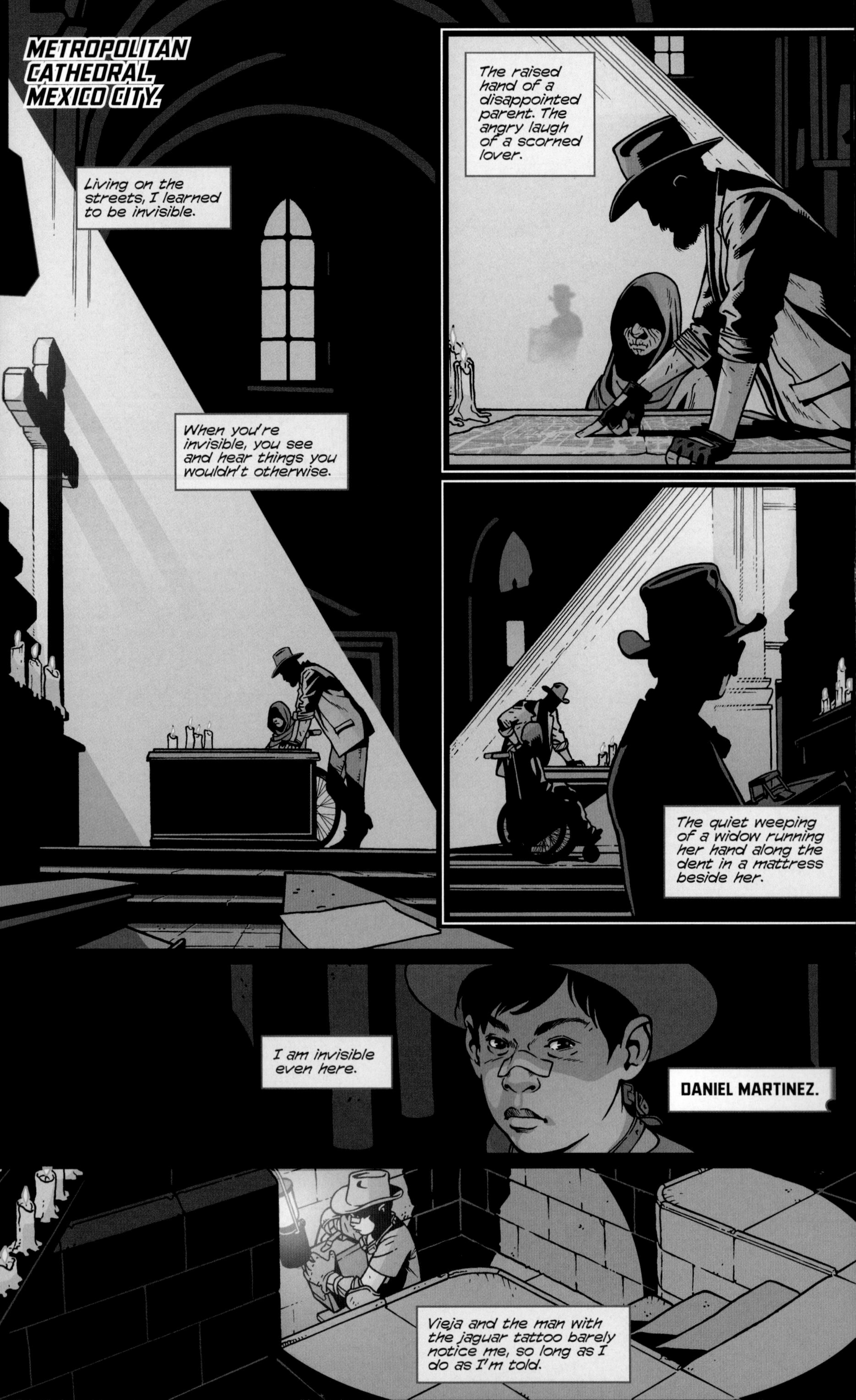
METROPOLITAN CATHEDRAL, MEXICO CITY.
Living on the streets, I learned to be invisible.
When you're invisible, you see and hear things you wouldn't otherwise.
The raised hand of a disappointed parent. The angry laugh of a scorned lover.
The quiet weeping of a widow running her hand along the dent in a mattress beside her.
I am invisible even here.
DANIEL MARTINEZ.
Vieja and the man with the jaguar tattoo barely notice me, so long as I do as I'm told.

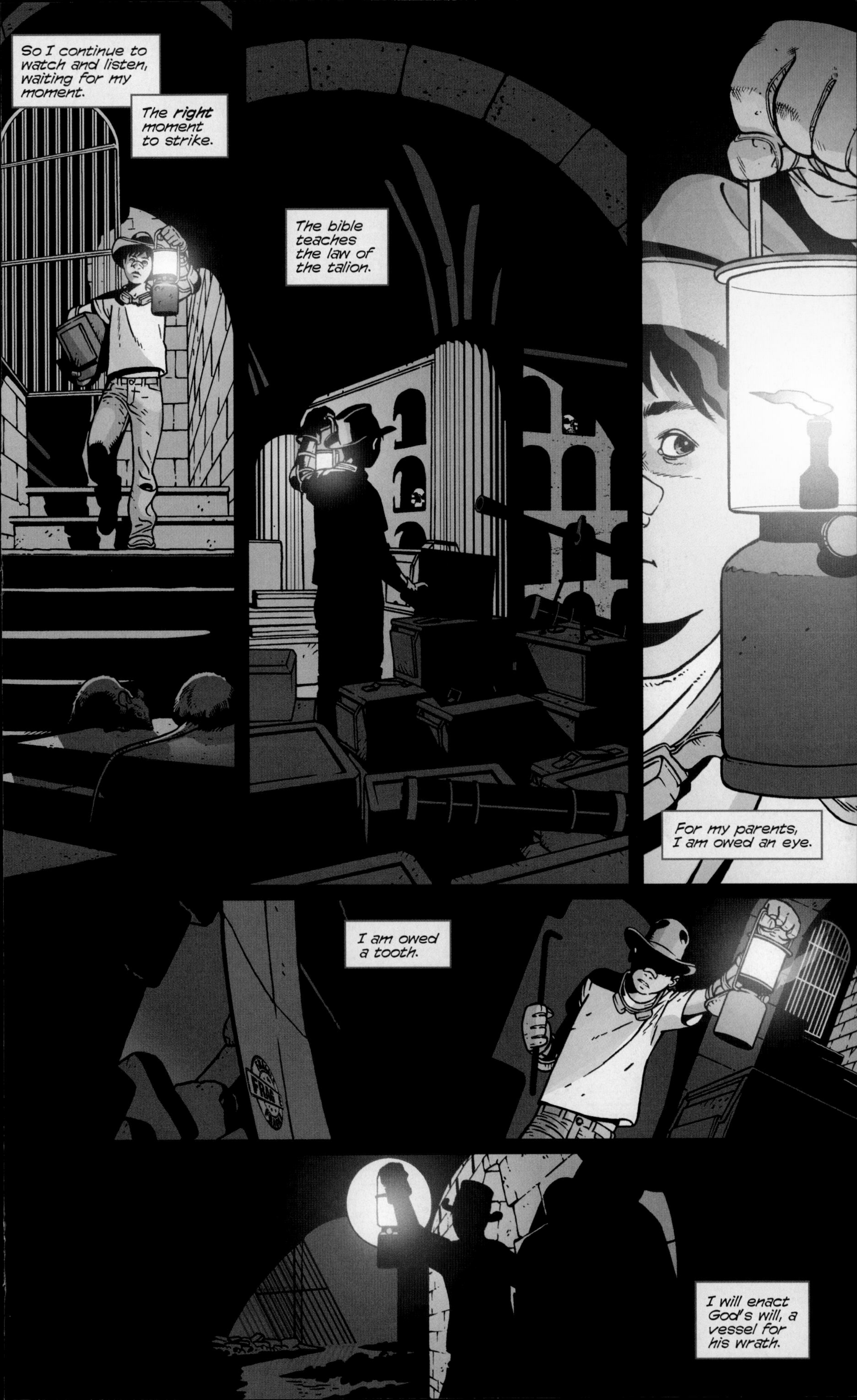
So I continue to watch and listen, waiting for my moment.
The **right** moment to strike.
The bible teaches the law of the talion.
For my parents, I am owed an eye.
I am owed a tooth.
I will enact God's will, a vessel for his wrath.

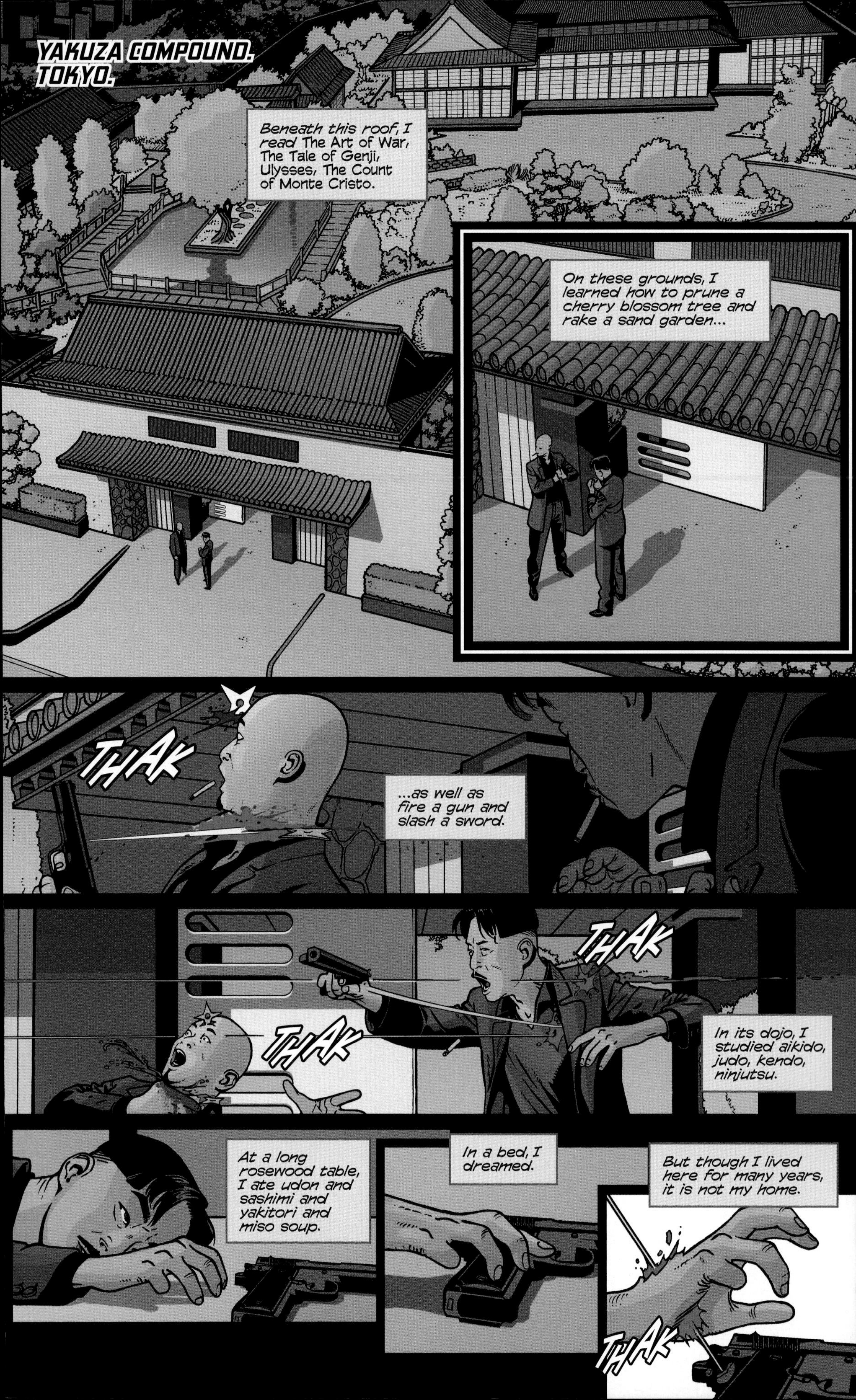
YAKUZA COMPOUND. TOKYO.
Beneath this roof, I read The Art of War, The Tale of Genji, Ulysses, The Count of Monte Cristo.
On these grounds, I learned how to prune a cherry blossom tree and rake a sand garden...
THAK
...as well as fire a gun and slash a sword.
THAK
THAK
In its dojo, I studied aikido, judo, kendo, ninjutsu.
At a long rosewood table, I ate udon and sashimi and yakitori and miso soup.
In a bed, I dreamed.
But though I lived here for many years, it is not my home.
THAK

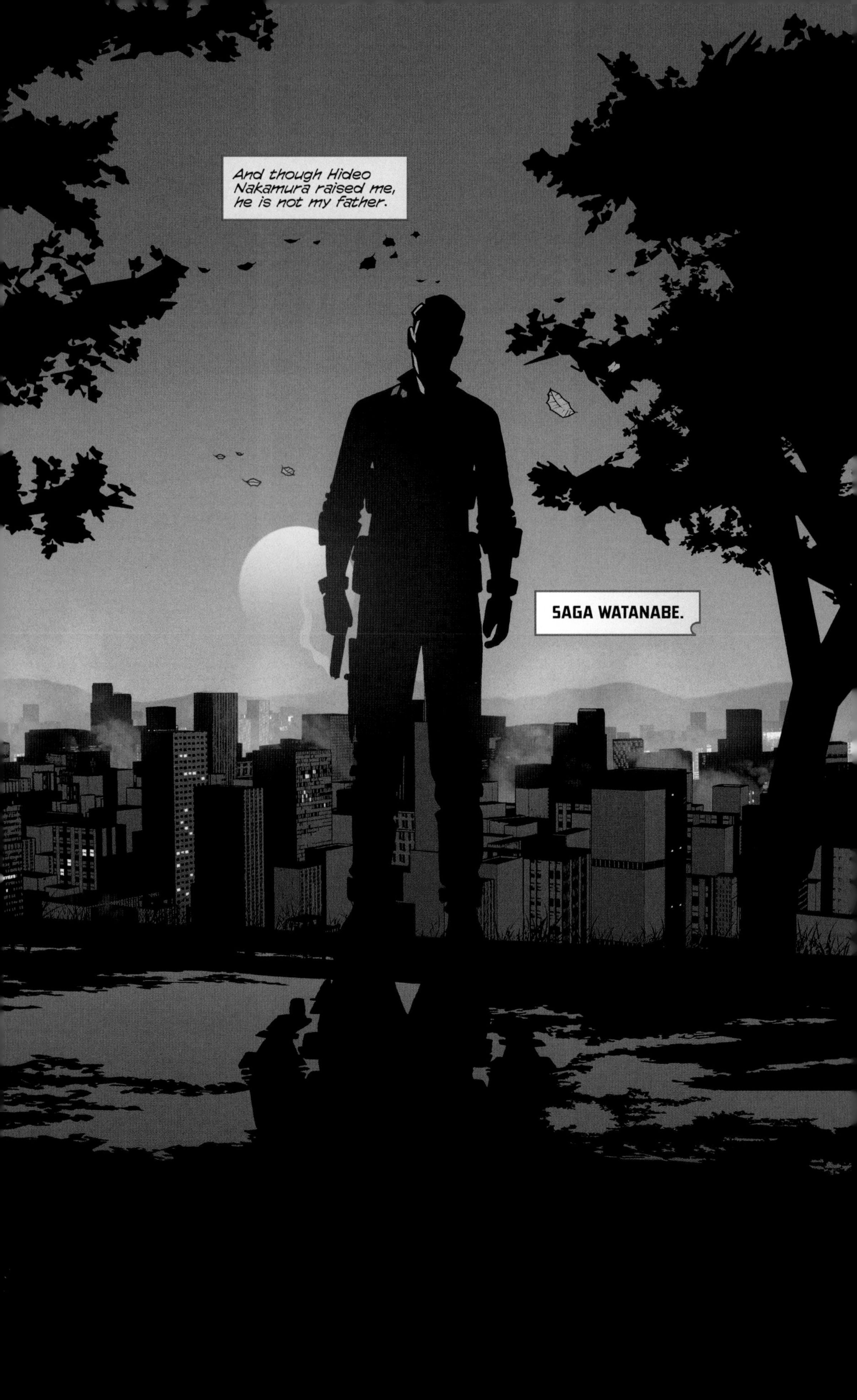
And though Hideo Nakamura raised me, he is not my father.
SAGA WATANABE.

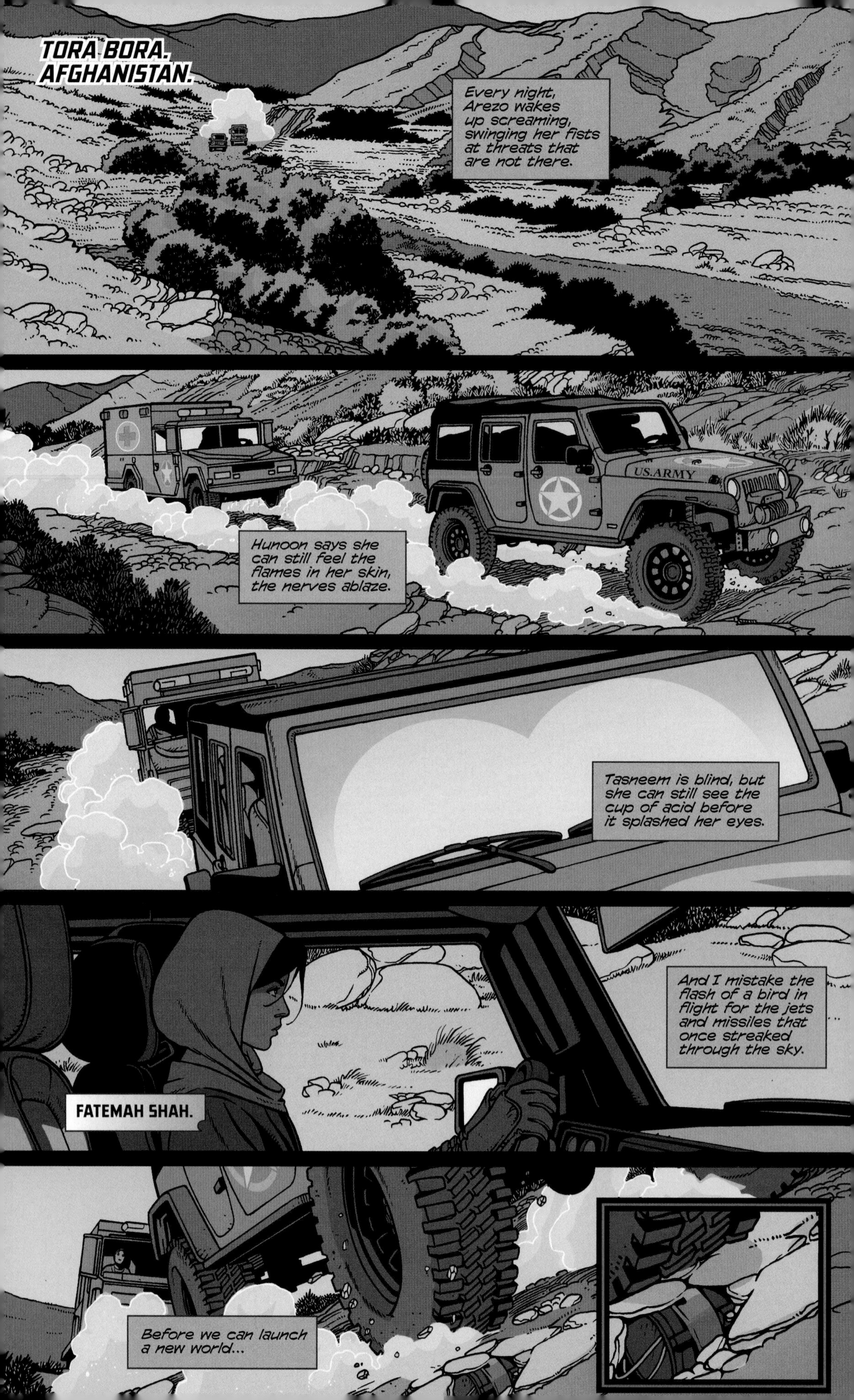
TORA BORA. AFGHANISTAN.
Every night, Arezo wakes up screaming, swinging her fists at threats that are not there.
U.S. ARMY
Hunoon says she can still feel the flames in her skin, the nerves ablaze.
Tasneem is blind, but she can still see the cup of acid before it splashed her eyes.
And I mistake the flash of a bird in flight for the jets and missiles that once streaked through the sky.
FATEMAH SHAH.
Before we can launch a new world...

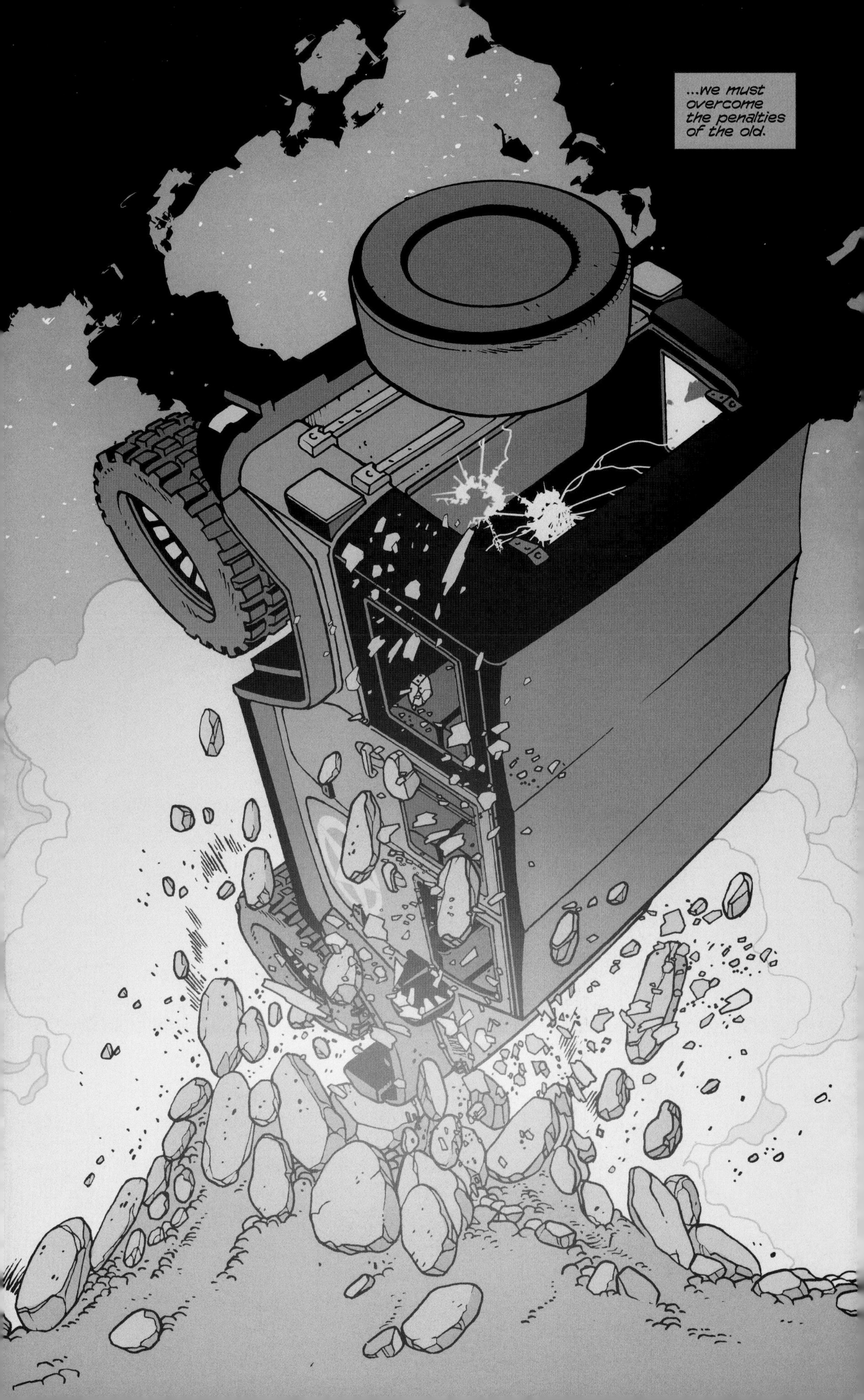
...we must overcome the penalties of the old.

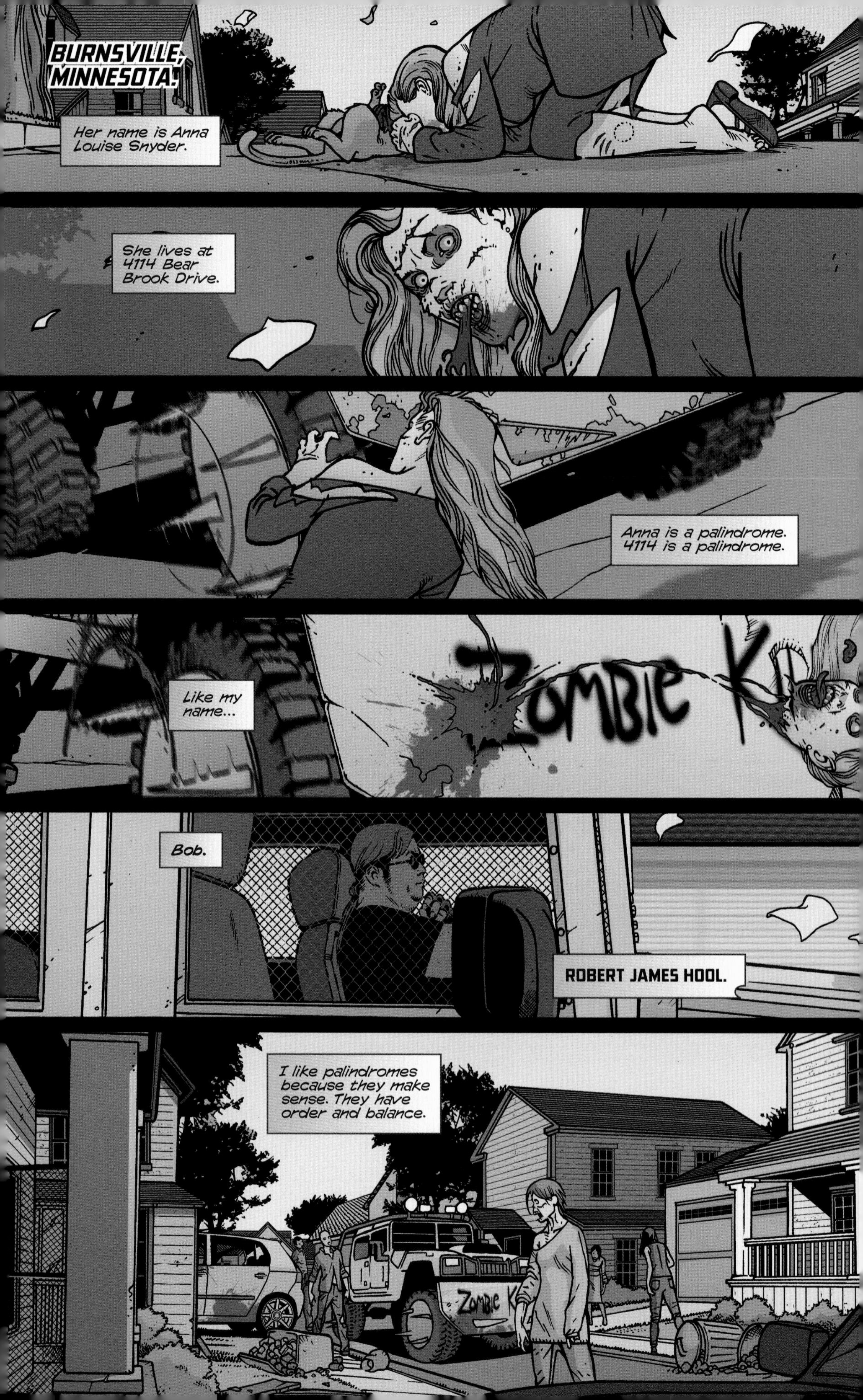
BURNSVILLE, MINNESOTA.
Her name is Anna Louise Snyder.
She lives at 4114 Bear Brook Drive.
Anna is a palindrome. 4114 is a palindrome.
Like my name...
ZOMBIE K
Bob.
ROBERT JAMES HOOL.
I like palindromes because they make sense. They have order and balance.
ZOMBIE K

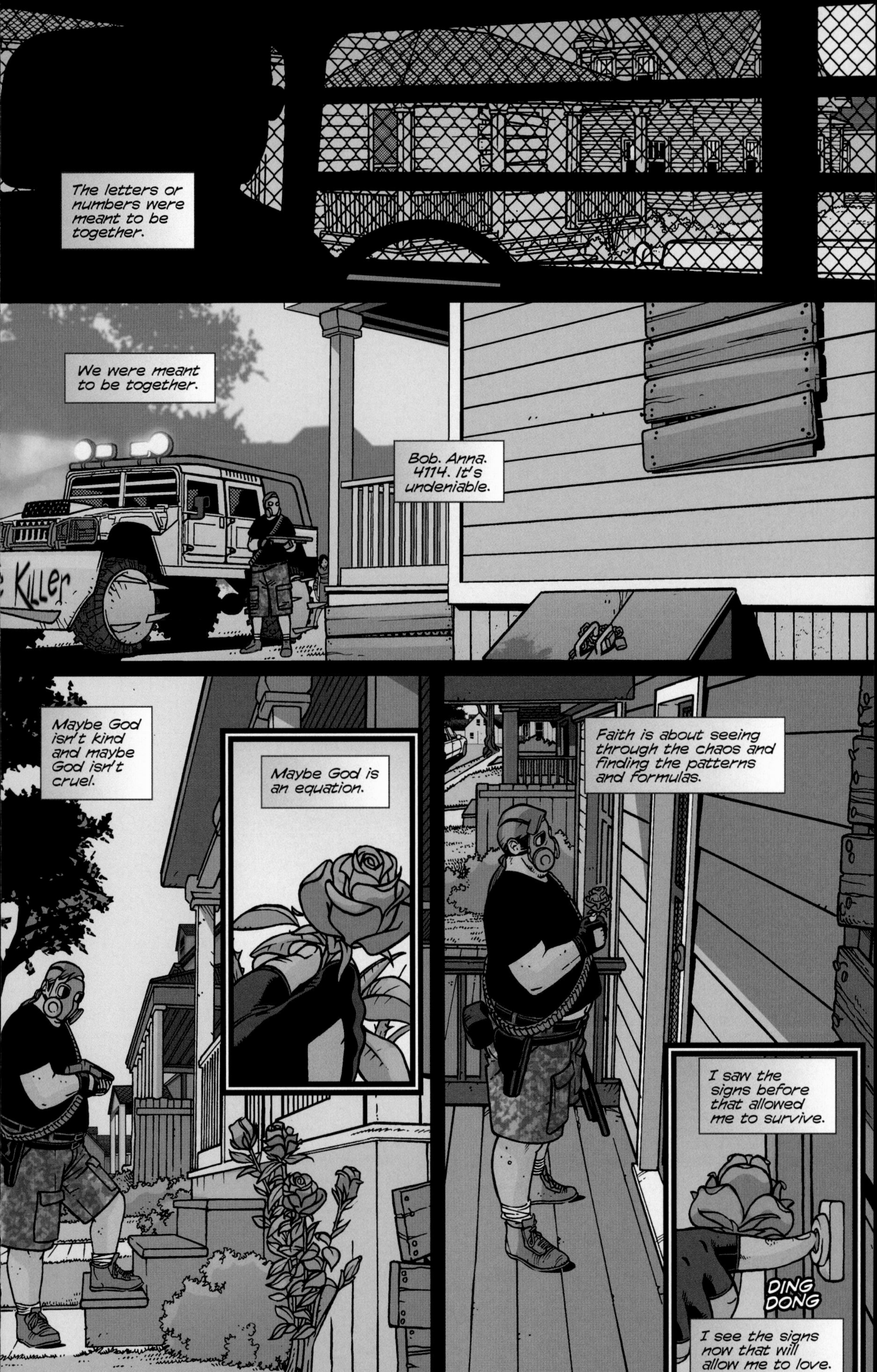
The letters or numbers were meant to be together.
We were meant to be together.
Bob. Anna. 4114. It's undeniable.
Killer
Maybe God isn't kind and maybe God isn't cruel.
Maybe God is an equation.
Faith is about seeing through the chaos and finding the patterns and formulas.
I saw the signs before that allowed me to survive.
DING DONG
I see the signs now that will allow me to love.

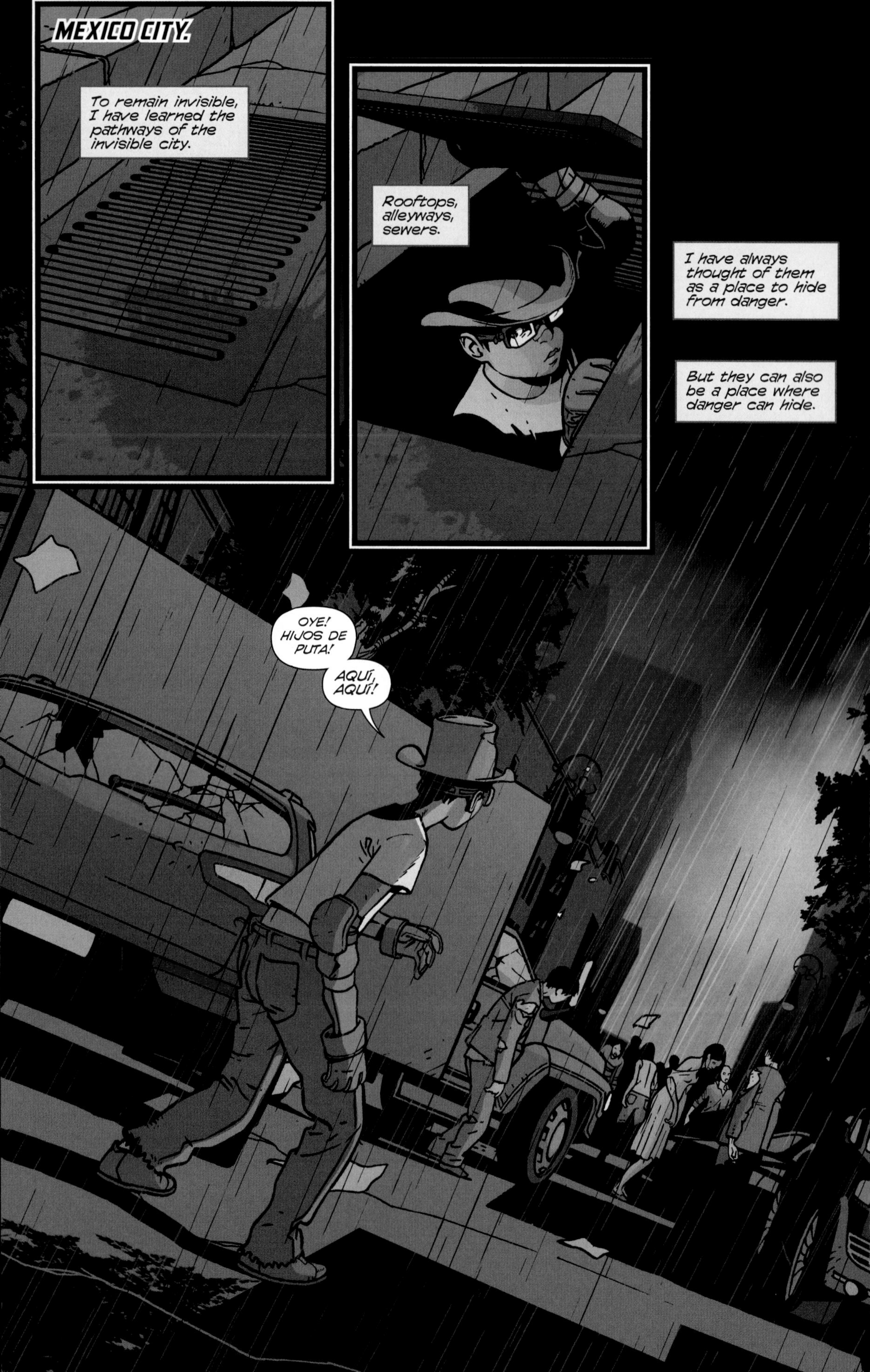
MEXICO CITY.
To remain invisible, I have learned the pathways of the invisible city.
Rooftops, alleyways, sewers.
I have always thought of them as a place to hide from danger.
But they can also be a place where danger can hide.
OYE! HIJOS DE PUTA!
AQUÍ, AQUÍ!

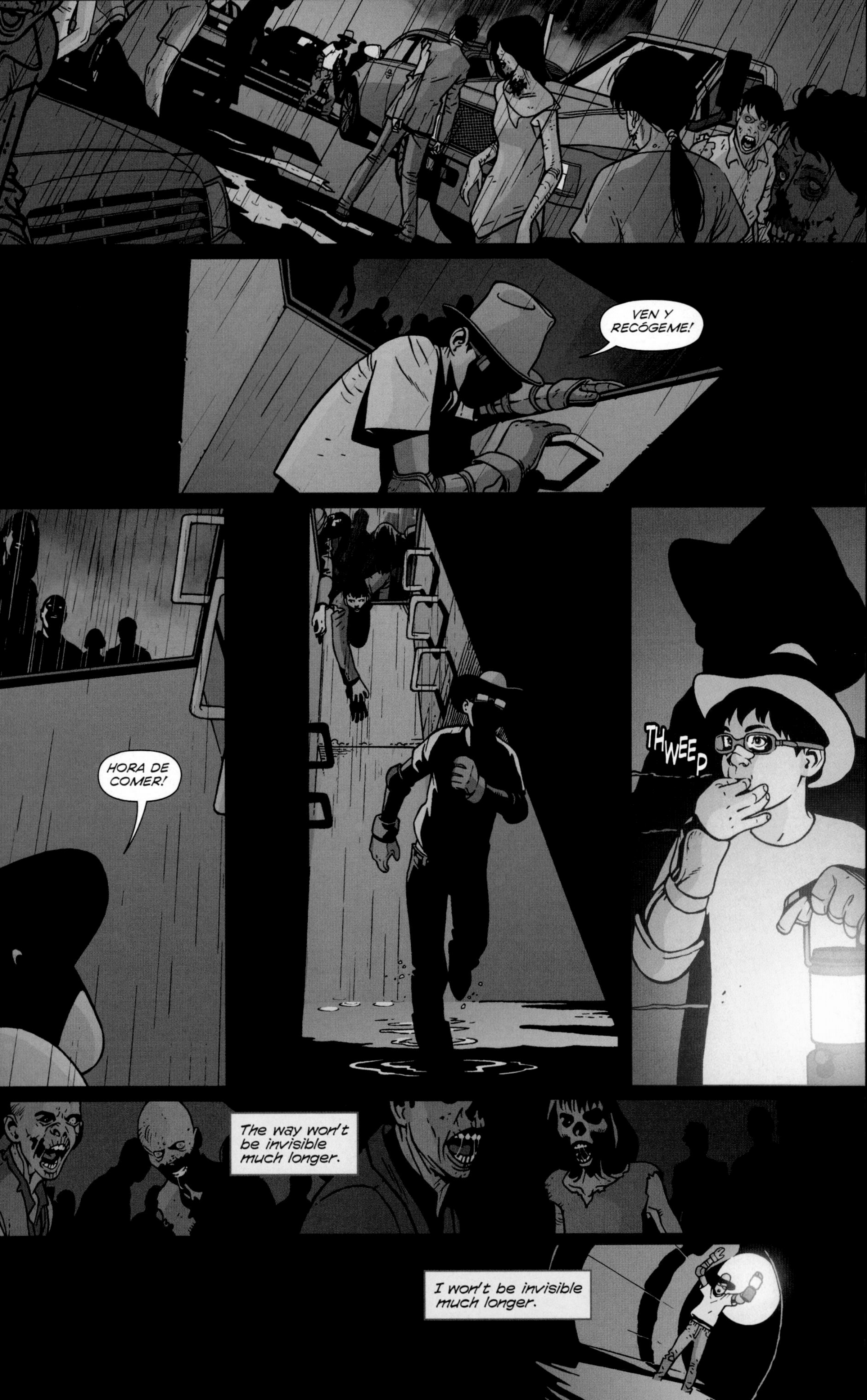
VEN Y
RECÓGEME!
HORA DE
COMER!
THWEEP
The way won't be invisible much longer.
I won't be invisible much longer.

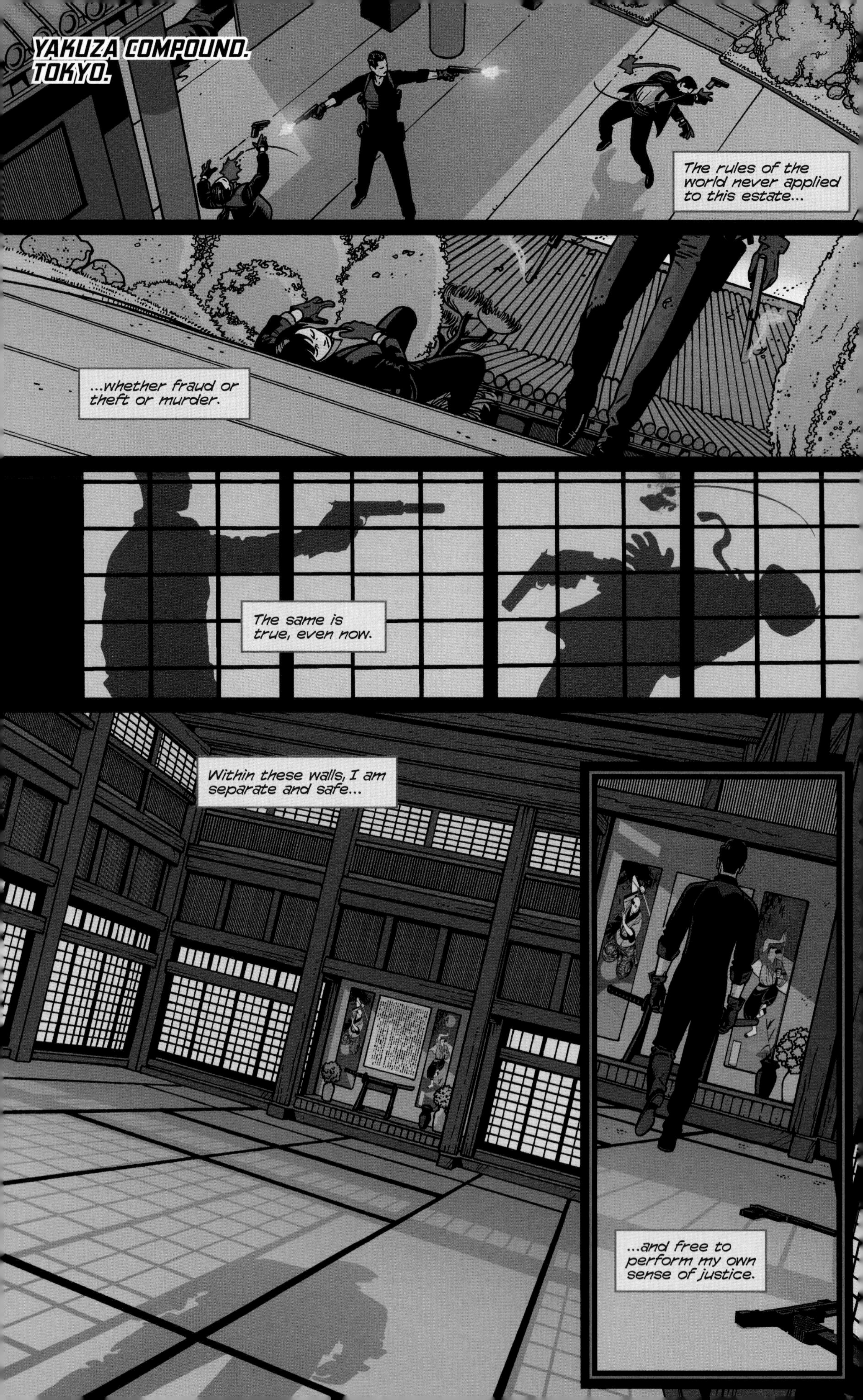
YAKUZA COMPOUND.
TOKYO.
The rules of the world never applied to this estate...
...whether fraud or theft or murder.
The same is true, even now.
Within these walls, I am separate and safe...
...and free to perform my own sense of justice.

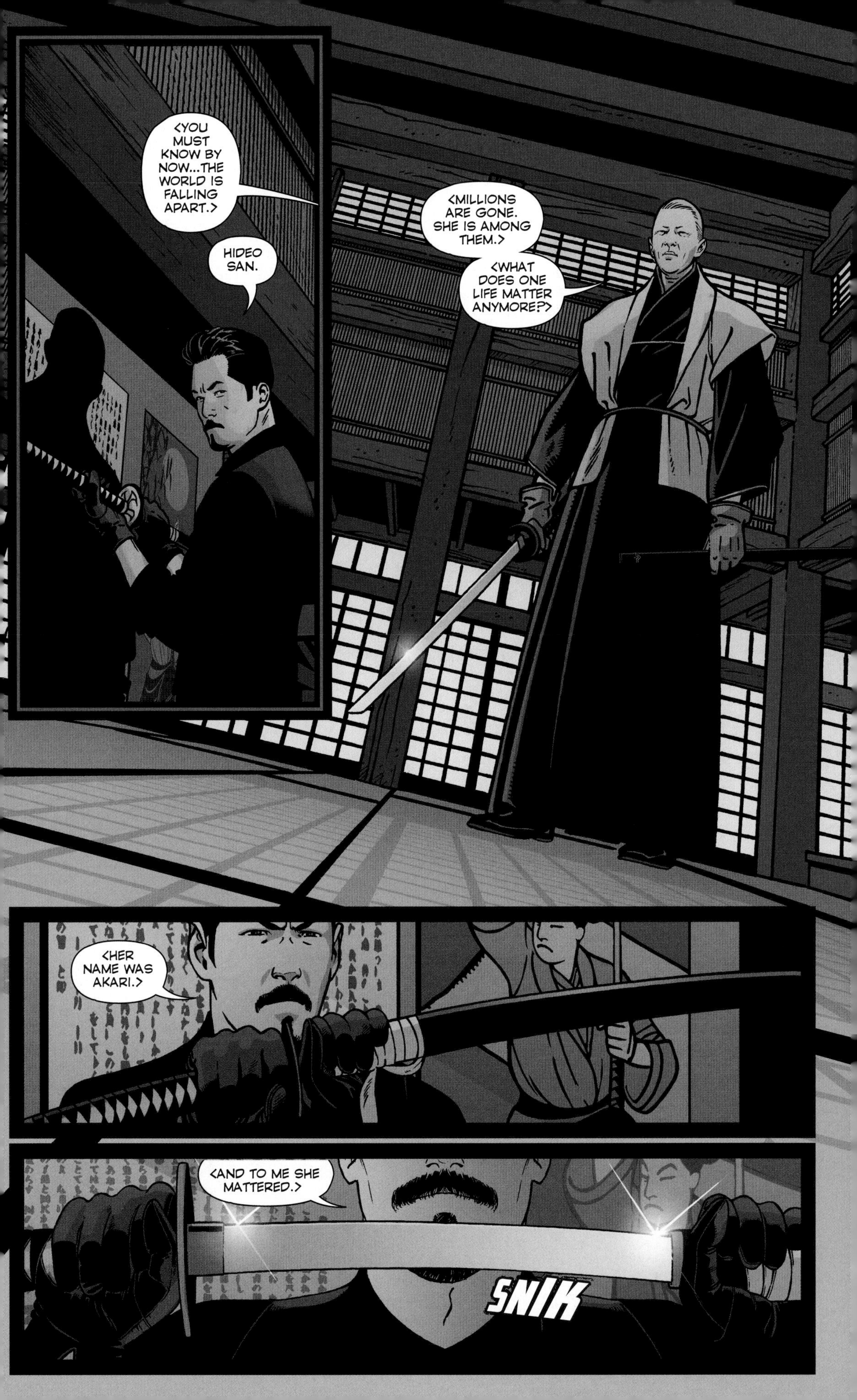
<YOU MUST KNOW BY NOW...THE WORLD IS FALLING APART.>
HIDEO SAN.
<MILLIONS ARE GONE. SHE IS AMONG THEM.>
<WHAT DOES ONE LIFE MATTER ANYMORE?>
<HER NAME WAS AKARI.>
<AND TO ME SHE MATTERED.>
SNIK

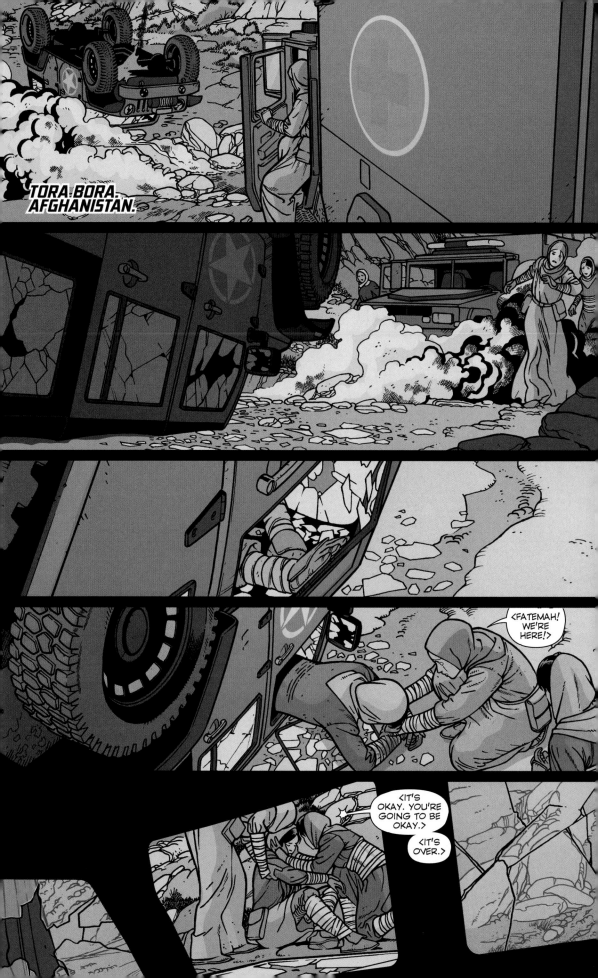

TORA BORA,
AFGHANISTAN.

<FATEMAH! WE'RE HERE!>

<IT'S OKAY. YOU'RE GOING TO BE OKAY.>

<IT'S OVER.>

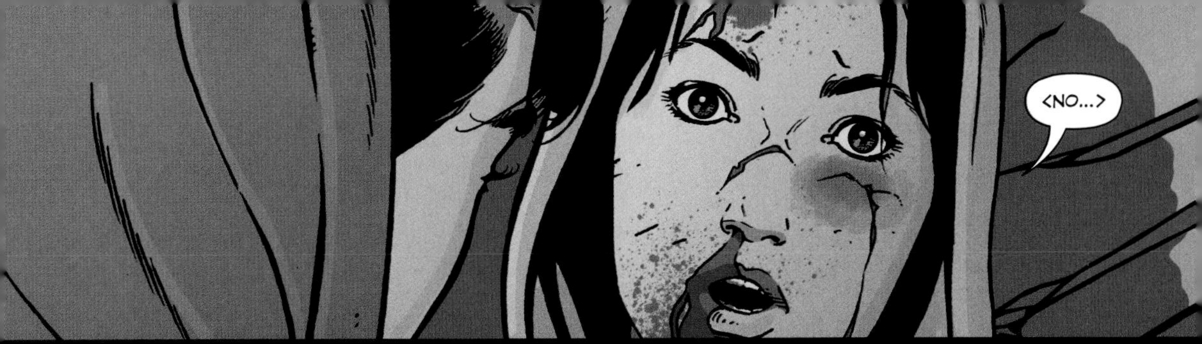
<NO...>

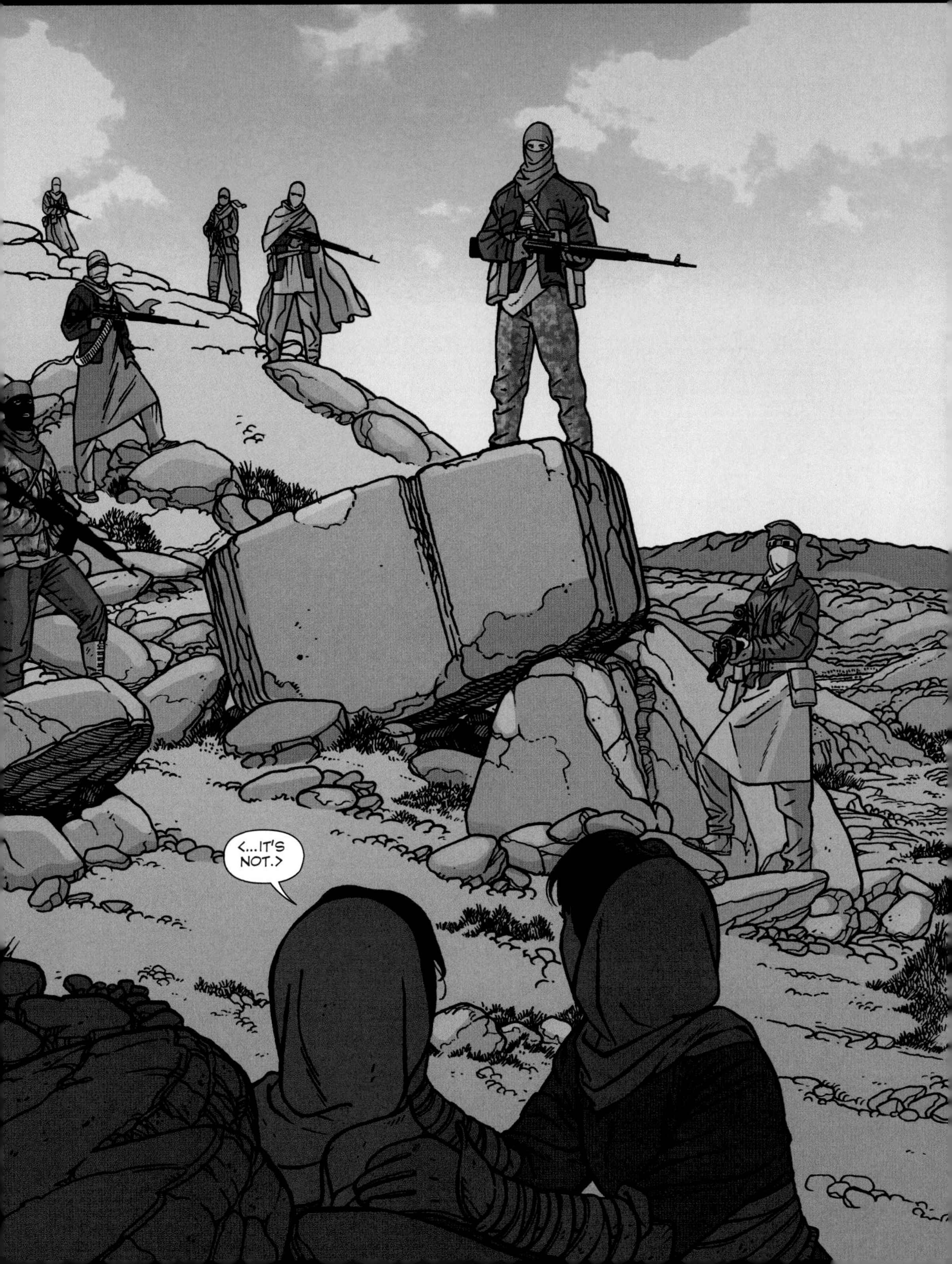
<...IT'S NOT.>

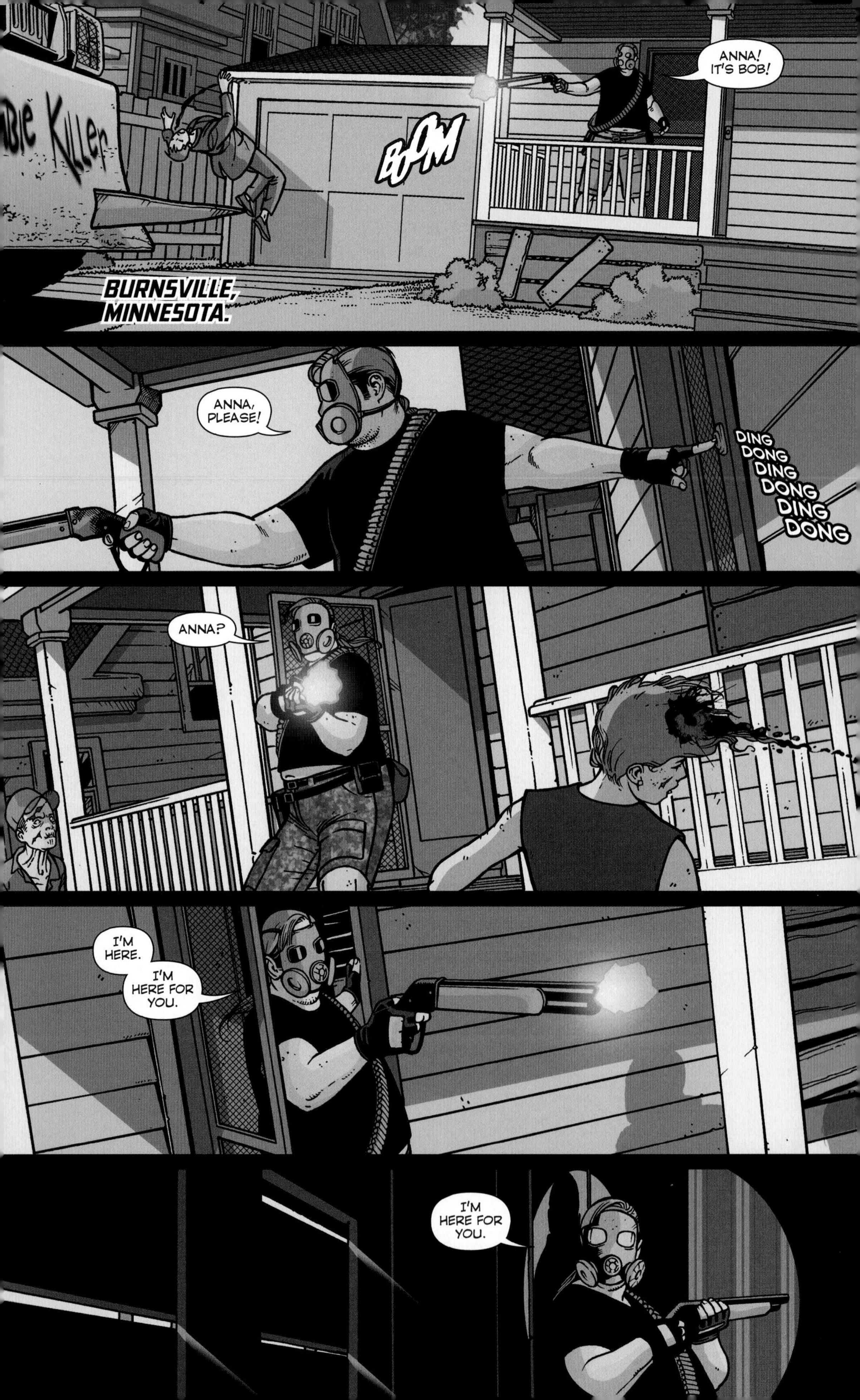
BURNSVILLE, MINNESOTA.
ANNA! IT'S BOB!
BOOM
ANNA, PLEASE!
DING DONG DING DONG DING DONG
ANNA?
I'M HERE.
I'M HERE FOR YOU.
I'M HERE FOR YOU.

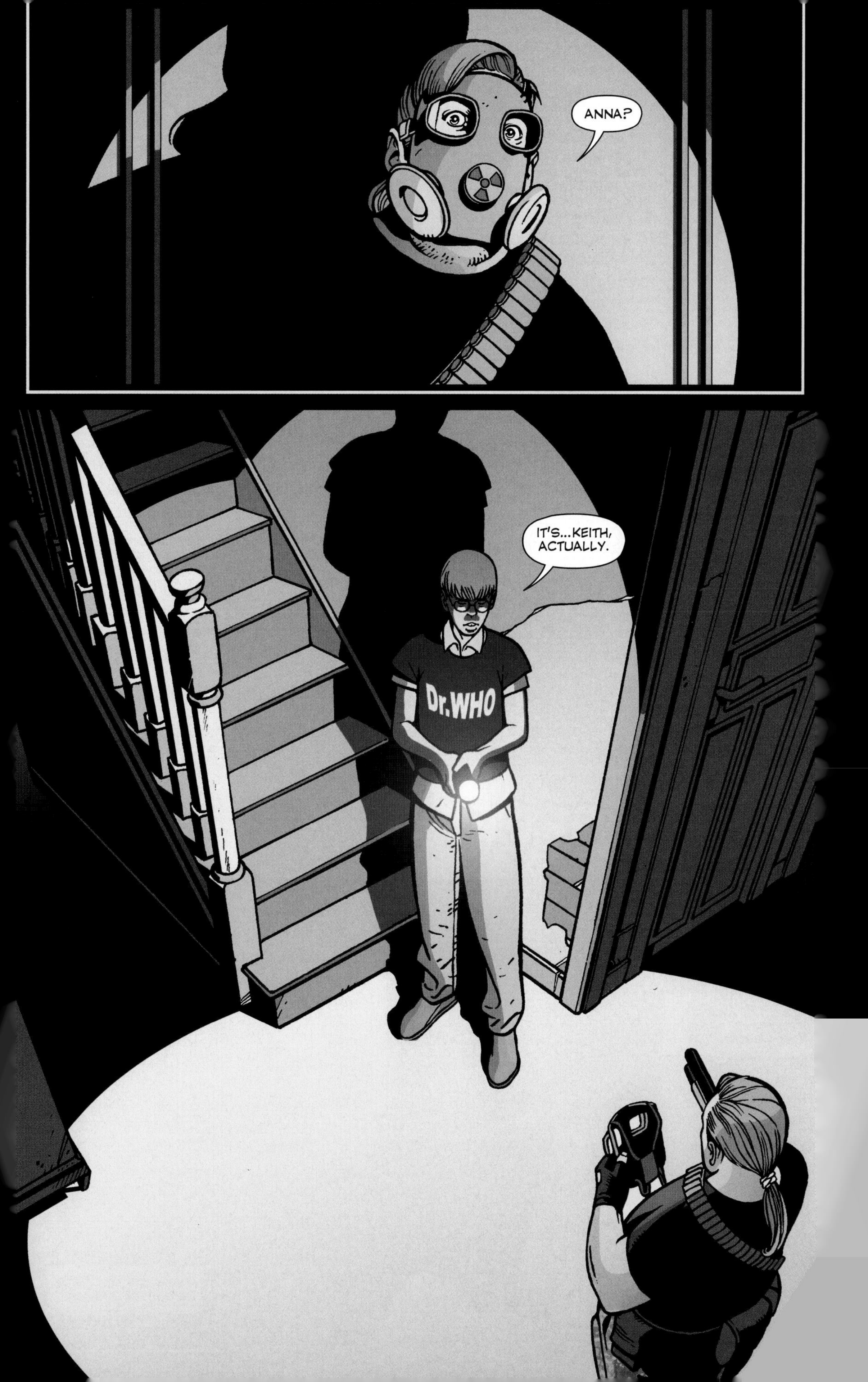
ANNA?
IT'S...KEITH, ACTUALLY.
Dr.WHO

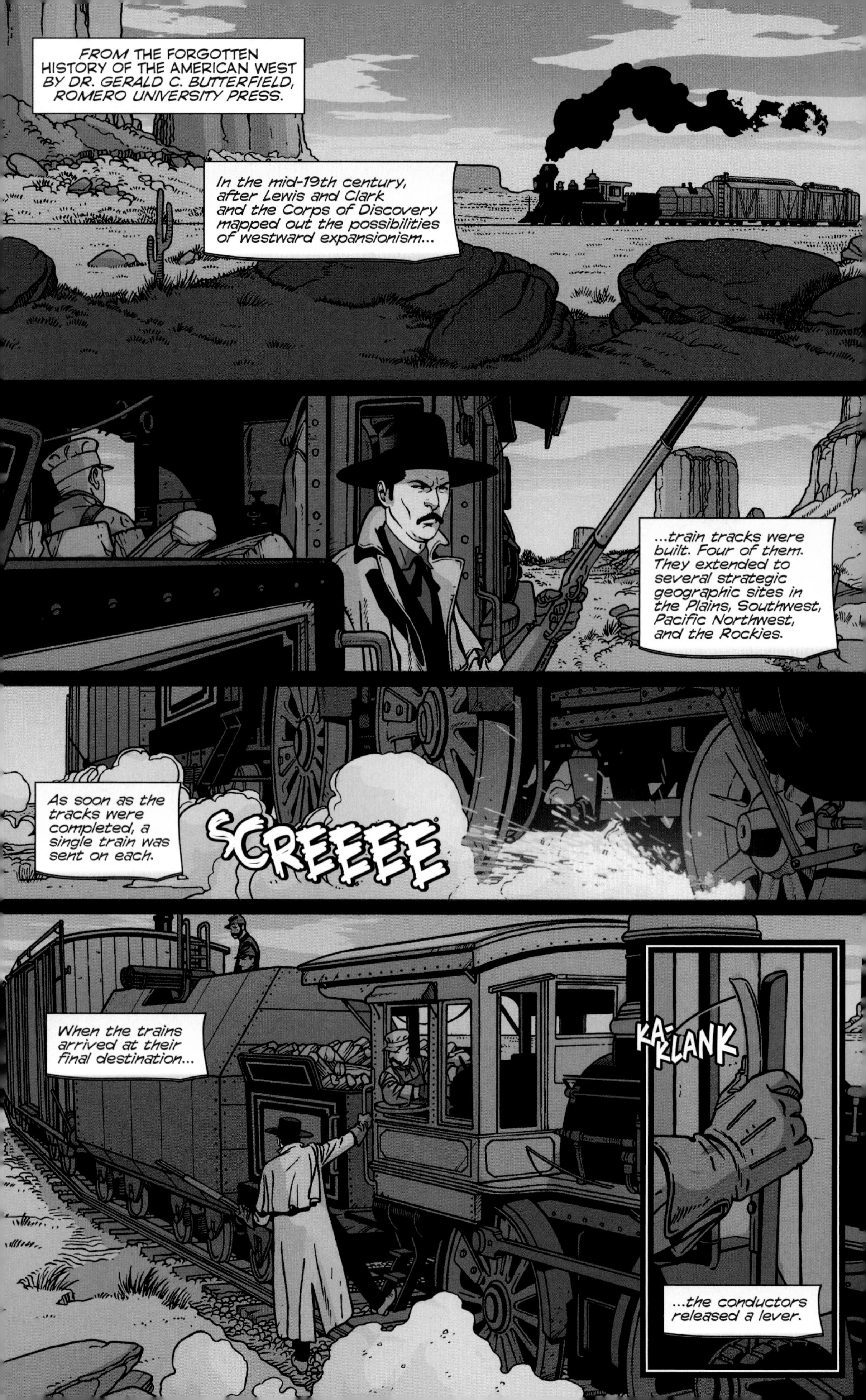
FROM THE FORGOTTEN HISTORY OF THE AMERICAN WEST BY DR. GERALD C. BUTTERFIELD, ROMERO UNIVERSITY PRESS.
In the mid-19th century, after Lewis and Clark and the Corps of Discovery mapped out the possibilities of westward expansionism...
...train tracks were built. Four of them. They extended to several strategic geographic sites in the Plains, Southwest, Pacific Northwest, and the Rockies.
As soon as the tracks were completed, a single train was sent on each.
SCREEEE
When the trains arrived at their final destination...
KA-KLANK
...the conductors released a lever.

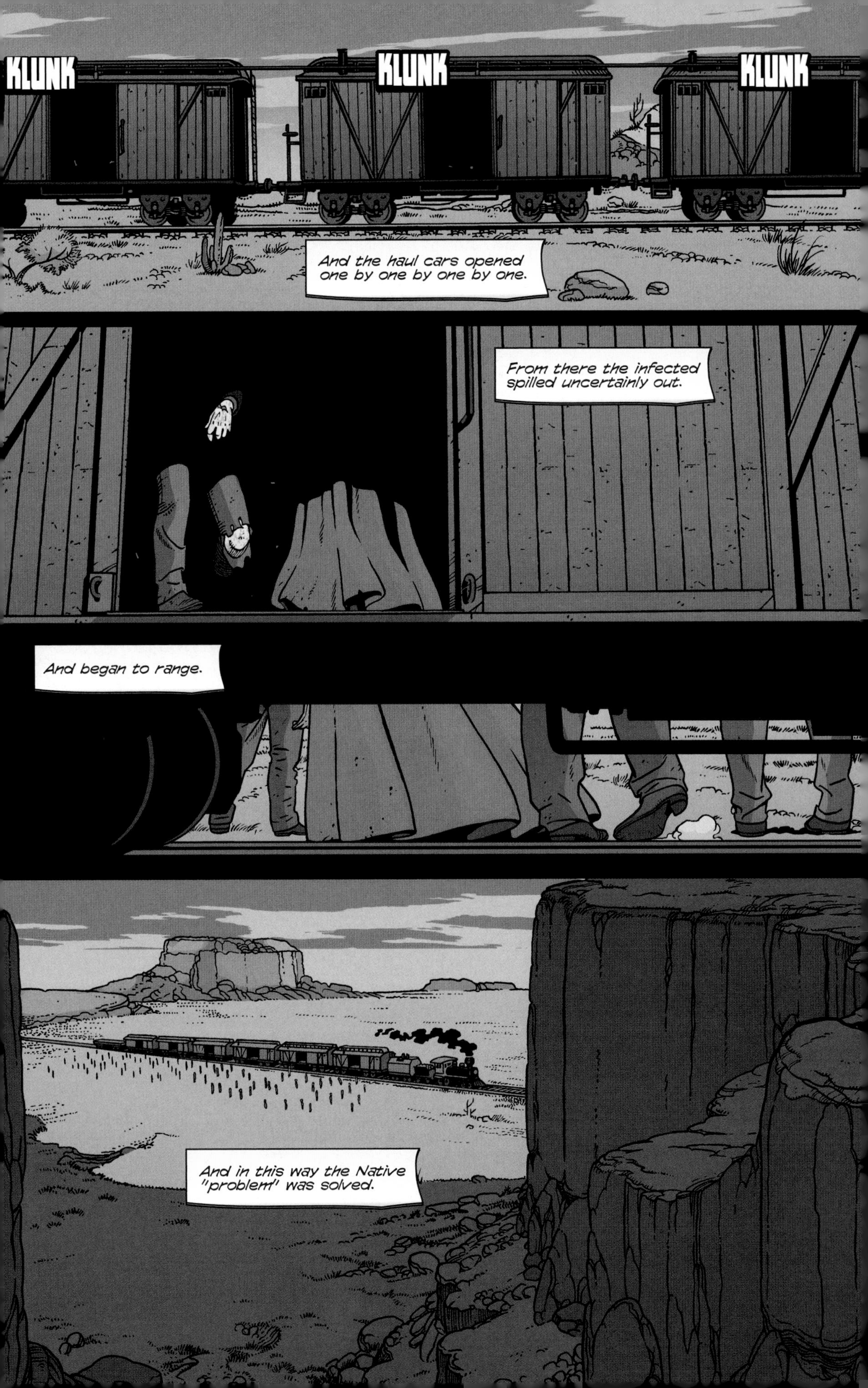
KLUNK
KLUNK
KLUNK
And the haul cars opened one by one by one by one.
From there the infected spilled uncertainly out.
And began to range.
And in this way the Native "problem" was solved.

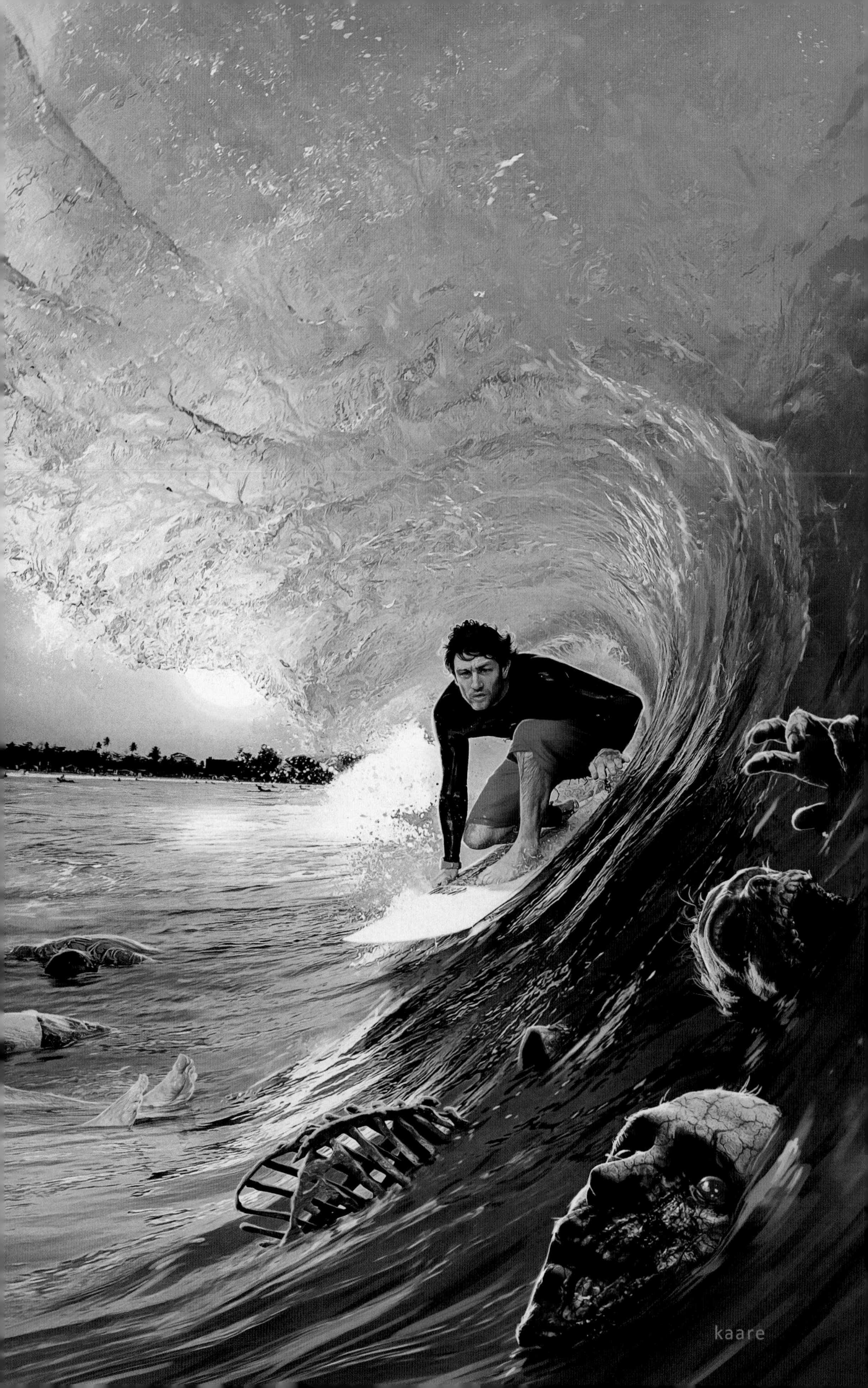
kaare

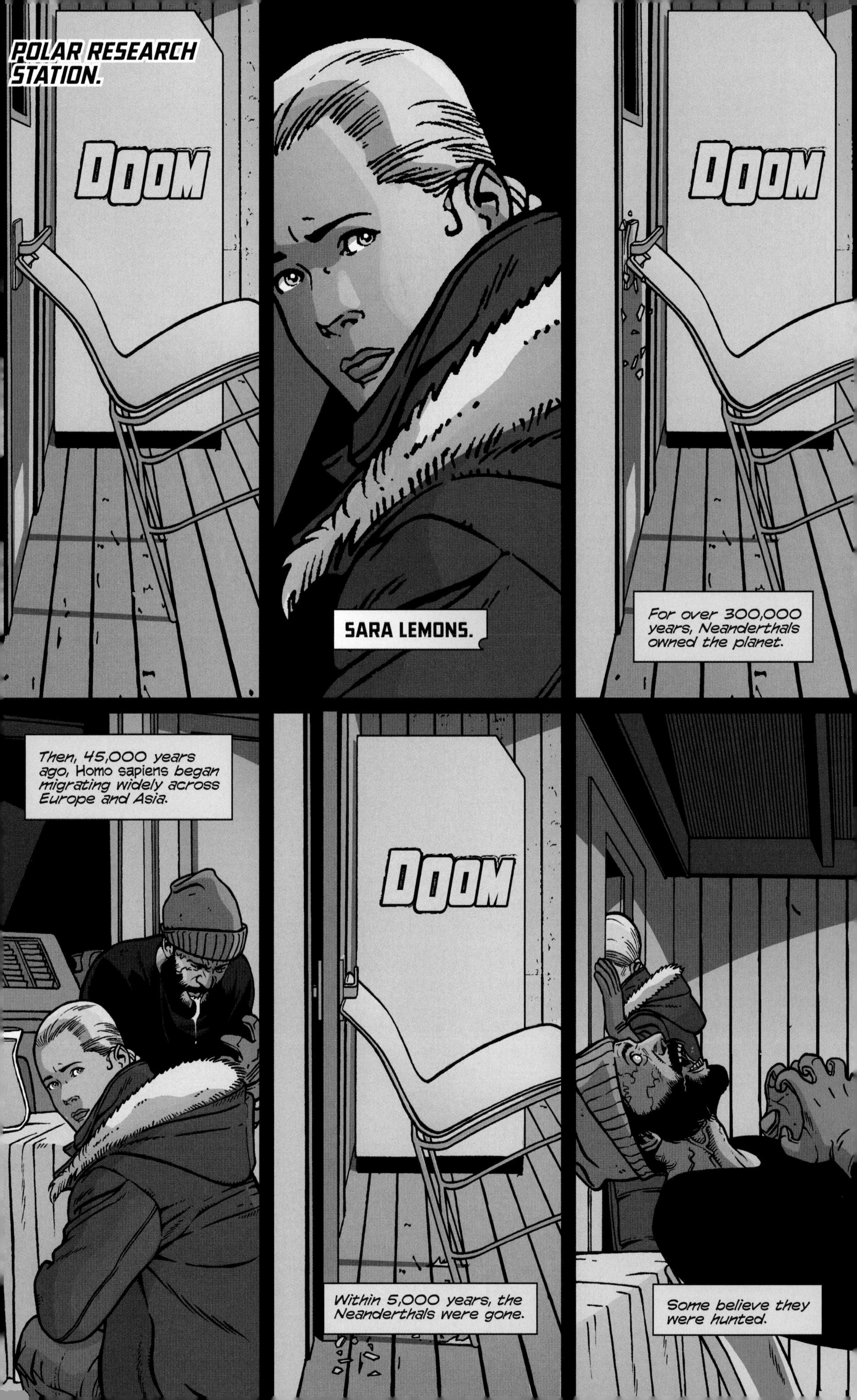
POLAR RESEARCH STATION.
DOOM
SARA LEMONS.
DOOM
For over 300,000 years, Neanderthals owned the planet.
Then, 45,000 years ago, Homo sapiens began migrating widely across Europe and Asia.
DOOM
Within 5,000 years, the Neanderthals were gone.
Some believe they were hunted.

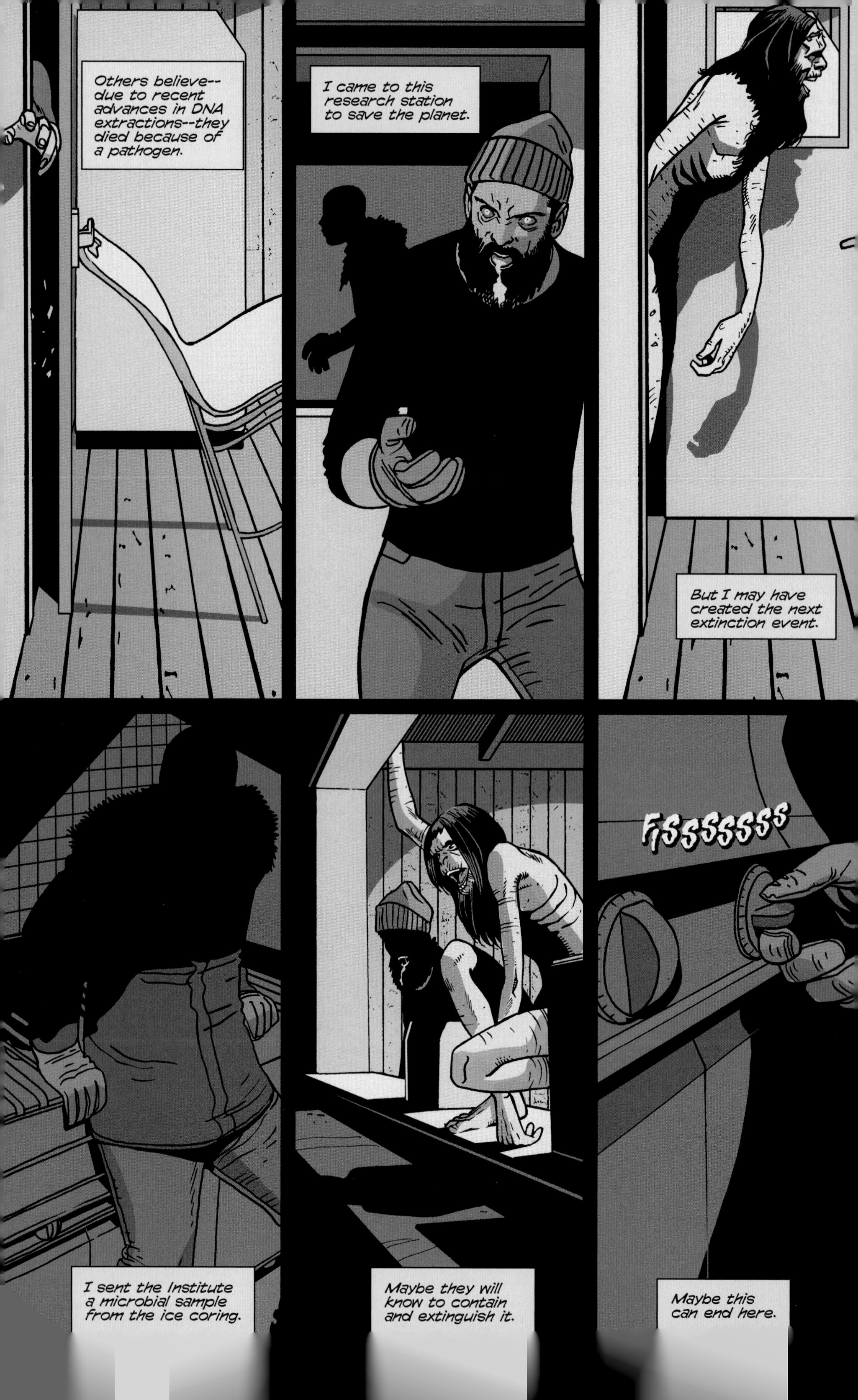
Others believe--due to recent advances in DNA extractions--they died because of a pathogen.
I came to this research station to save the planet.
But I may have created the next extinction event.
I sent the Institute a microbial sample from the ice coring.
Maybe they will know to contain and extinguish it.
FSSSSSSS
Maybe this can end here.

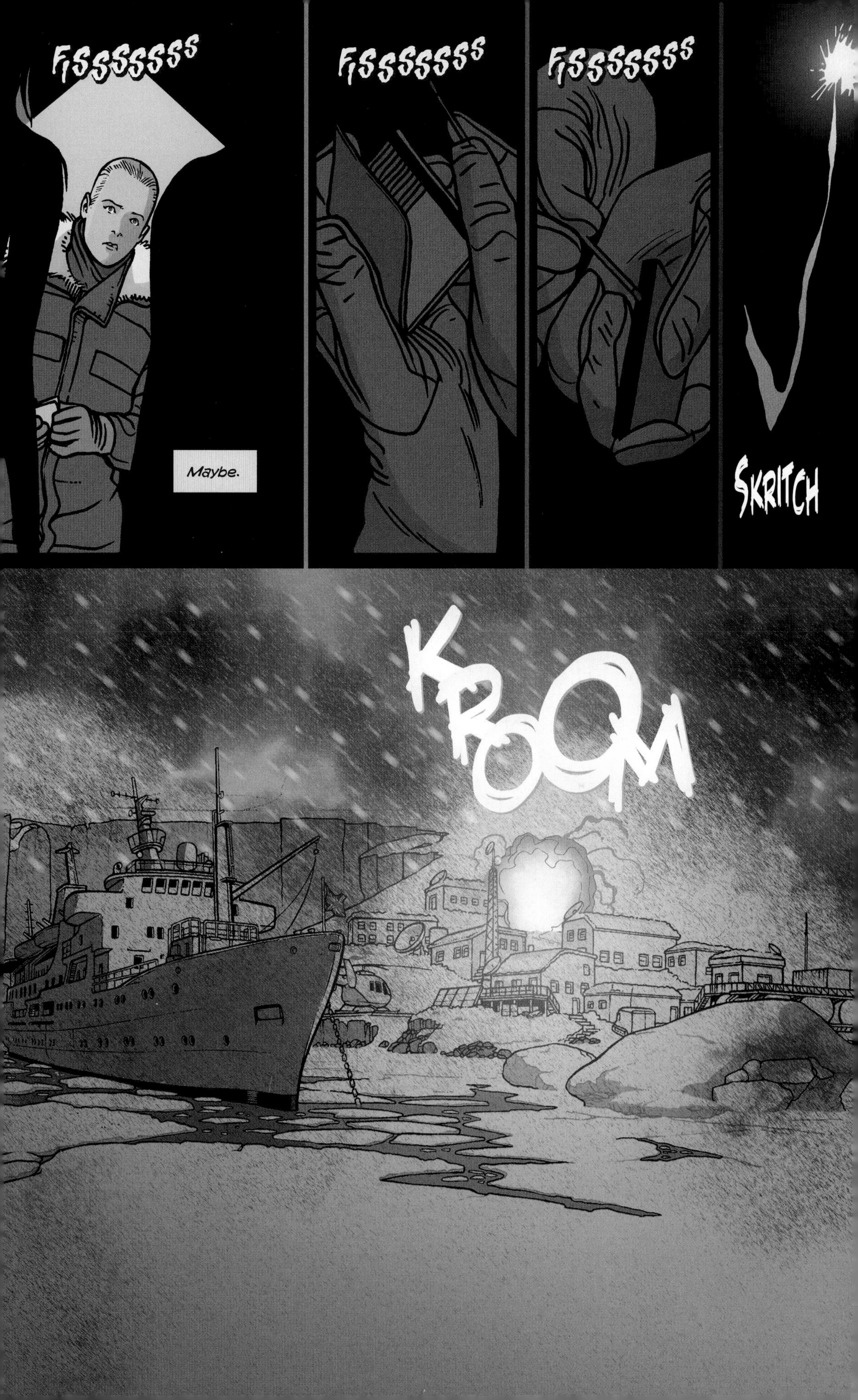
FSSSSSSS
Maybe.
FSSSSSSS
FSSSSSSS
SKRITCH
KROOM

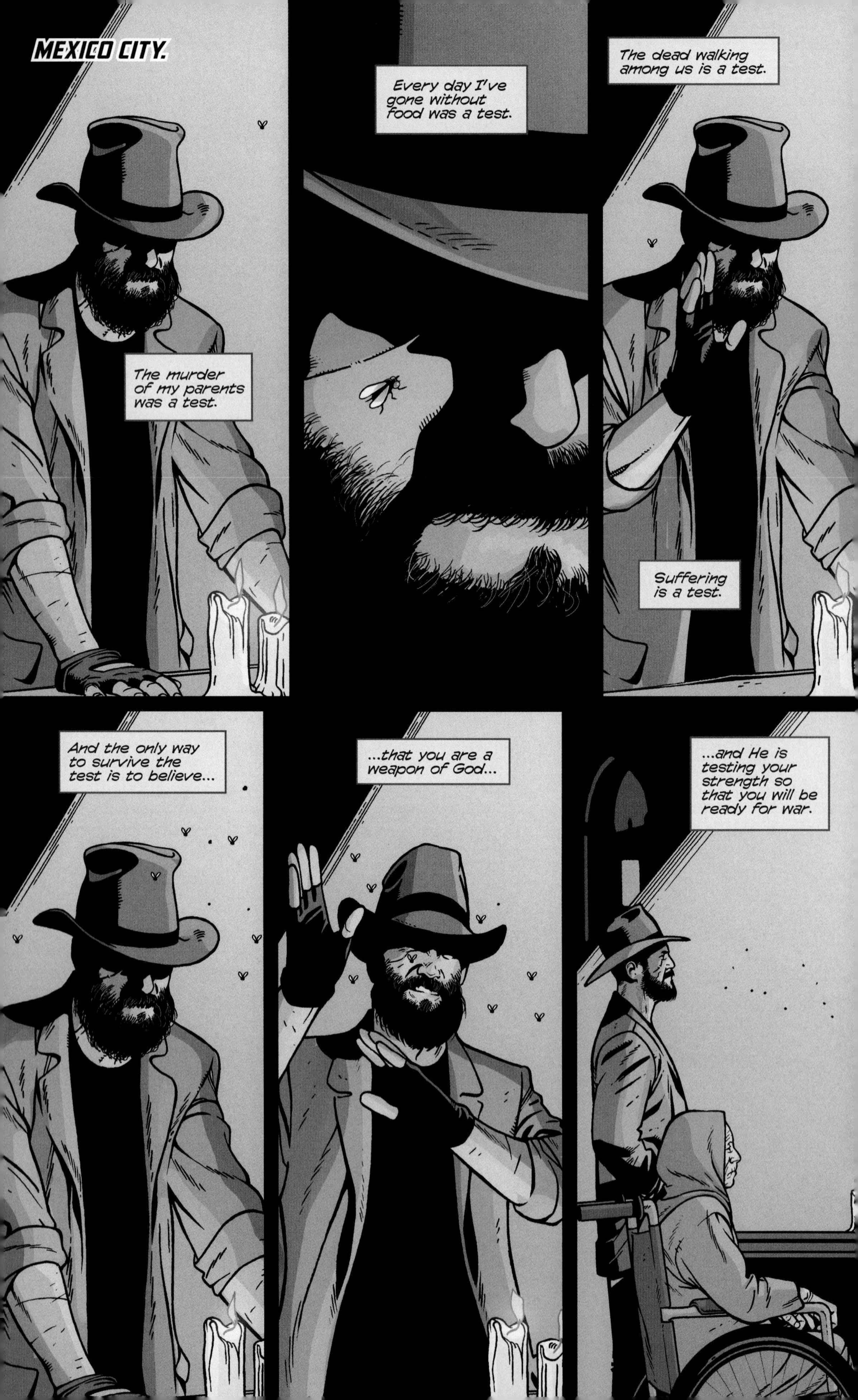
MEXICO CITY.
The murder of my parents was a test.
Every day I've gone without food was a test.
The dead walking among us is a test.
Suffering is a test.
And the only way to survive the test is to believe...
...that you are a weapon of God...
...and He is testing your strength so that you will be ready for war.

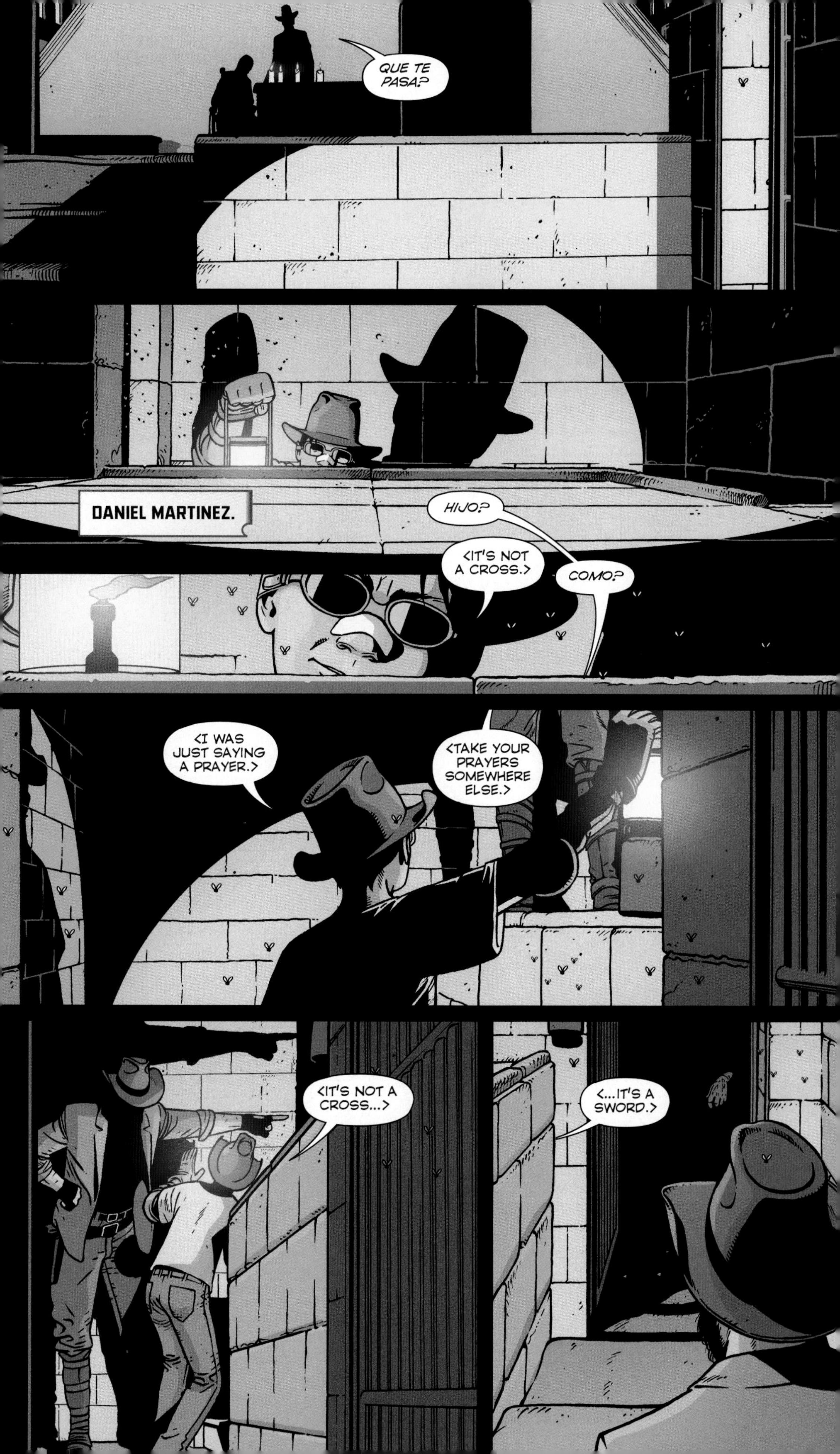
QUE TE PASA?
DANIEL MARTINEZ.
HIJO?
<IT'S NOT A CROSS.>
COMO?
<I WAS JUST SAYING A PRAYER.>
<TAKE YOUR PRAYERS SOMEWHERE ELSE.>
<IT'S NOT A CROSS...>
<...IT'S A SWORD.>

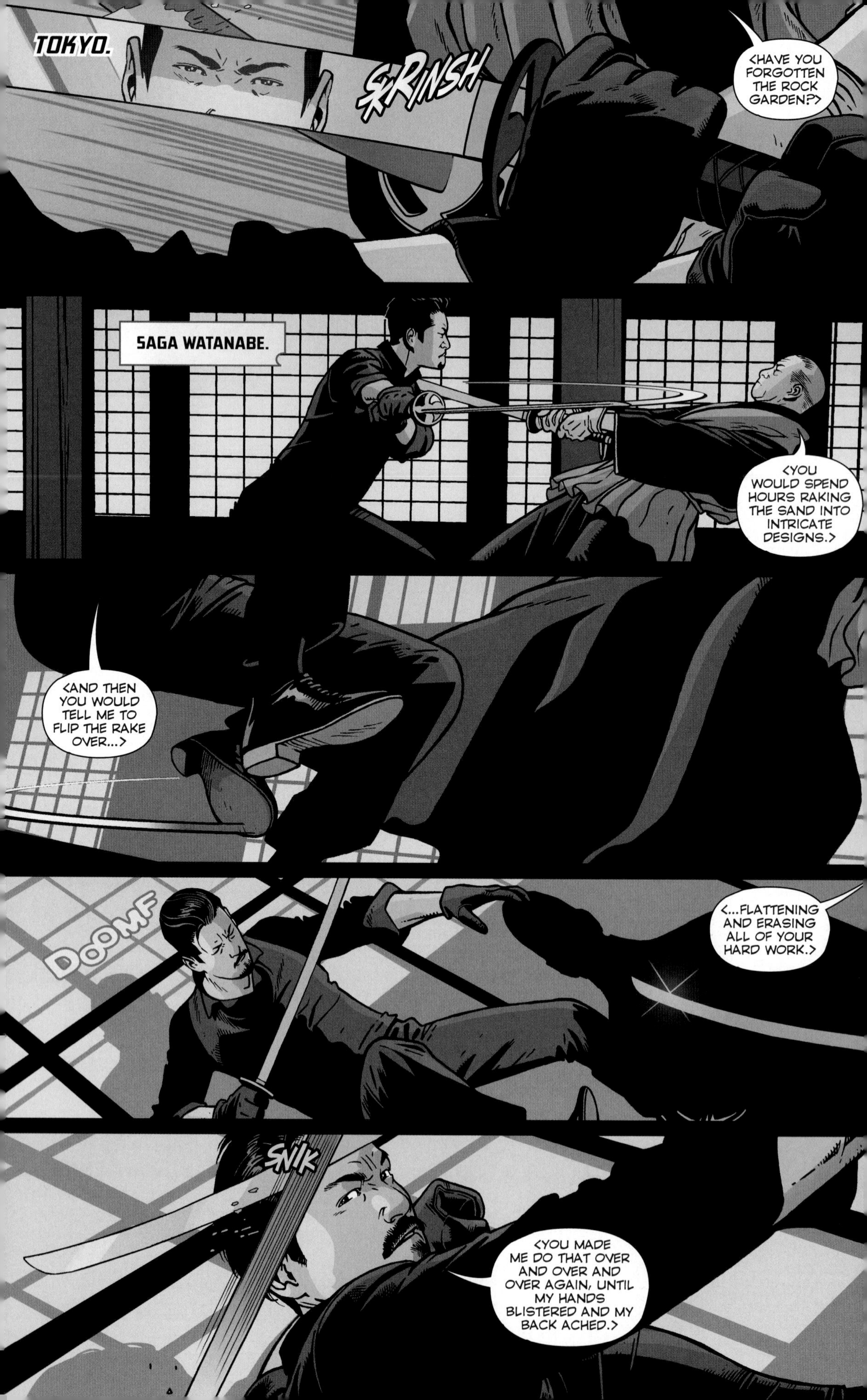
TOKYO.
SKRINSH
<HAVE YOU FORGOTTEN THE ROCK GARDEN?>
SAGA WATANABE.
<YOU WOULD SPEND HOURS RAKING THE SAND INTO INTRICATE DESIGNS.>
<AND THEN YOU WOULD TELL ME TO FLIP THE RAKE OVER...>
DOOMF
<...FLATTENING AND ERASING ALL OF YOUR HARD WORK.>
SNIK
<YOU MADE ME DO THAT OVER AND OVER AND OVER AGAIN, UNTIL MY HANDS BLISTERED AND MY BACK ACHED.>

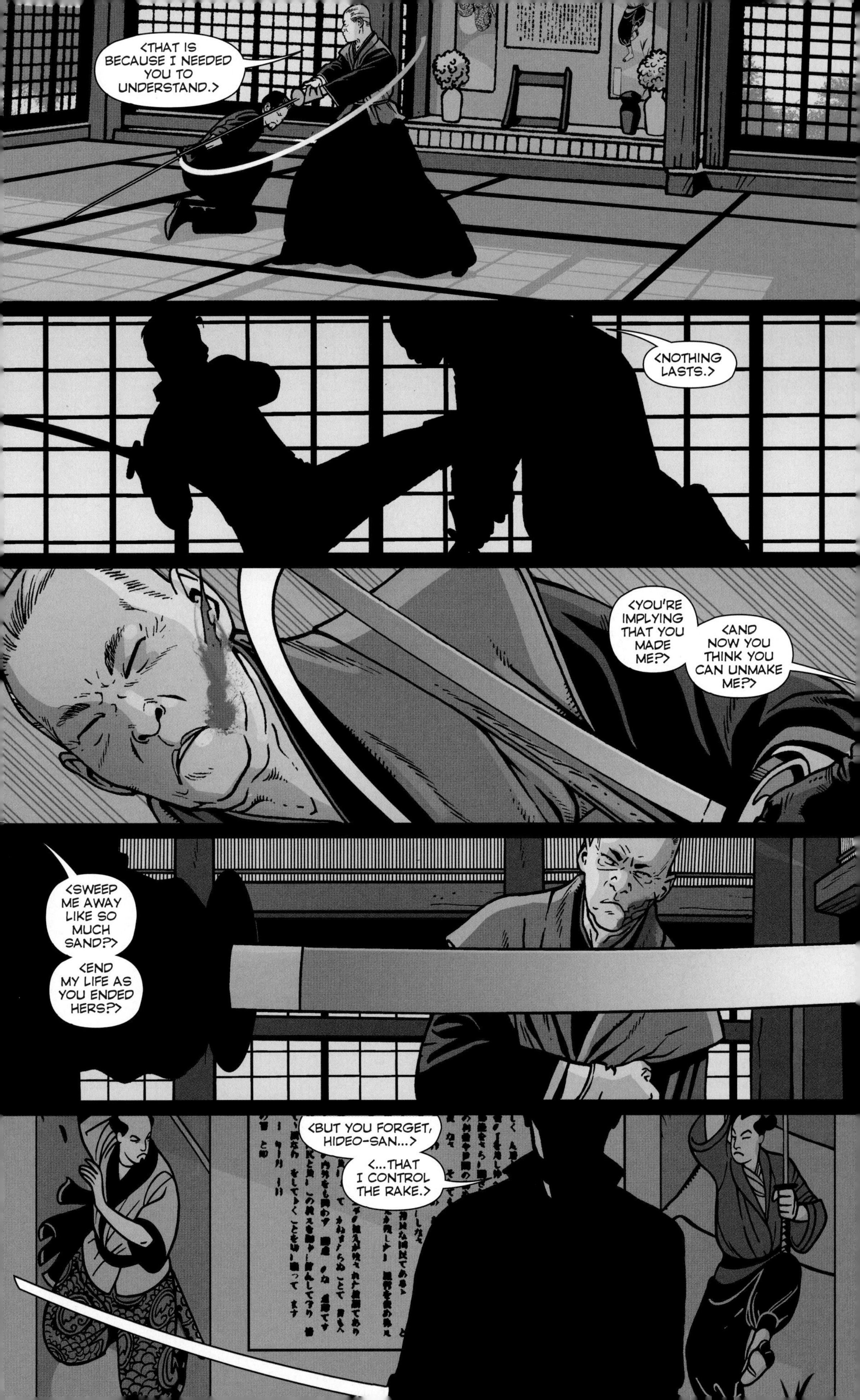
<THAT IS BECAUSE I NEEDED YOU TO UNDERSTAND.>
<NOTHING LASTS.>
<YOU'RE IMPLYING THAT YOU MADE ME?>
<AND NOW YOU THINK YOU CAN UNMAKE ME?>
<SWEEP ME AWAY LIKE SO MUCH SAND?>
<END MY LIFE AS YOU ENDED HERS?>
<BUT YOU FORGET, HIDEO-SAN...>
<...THAT I CONTROL THE RAKE.>

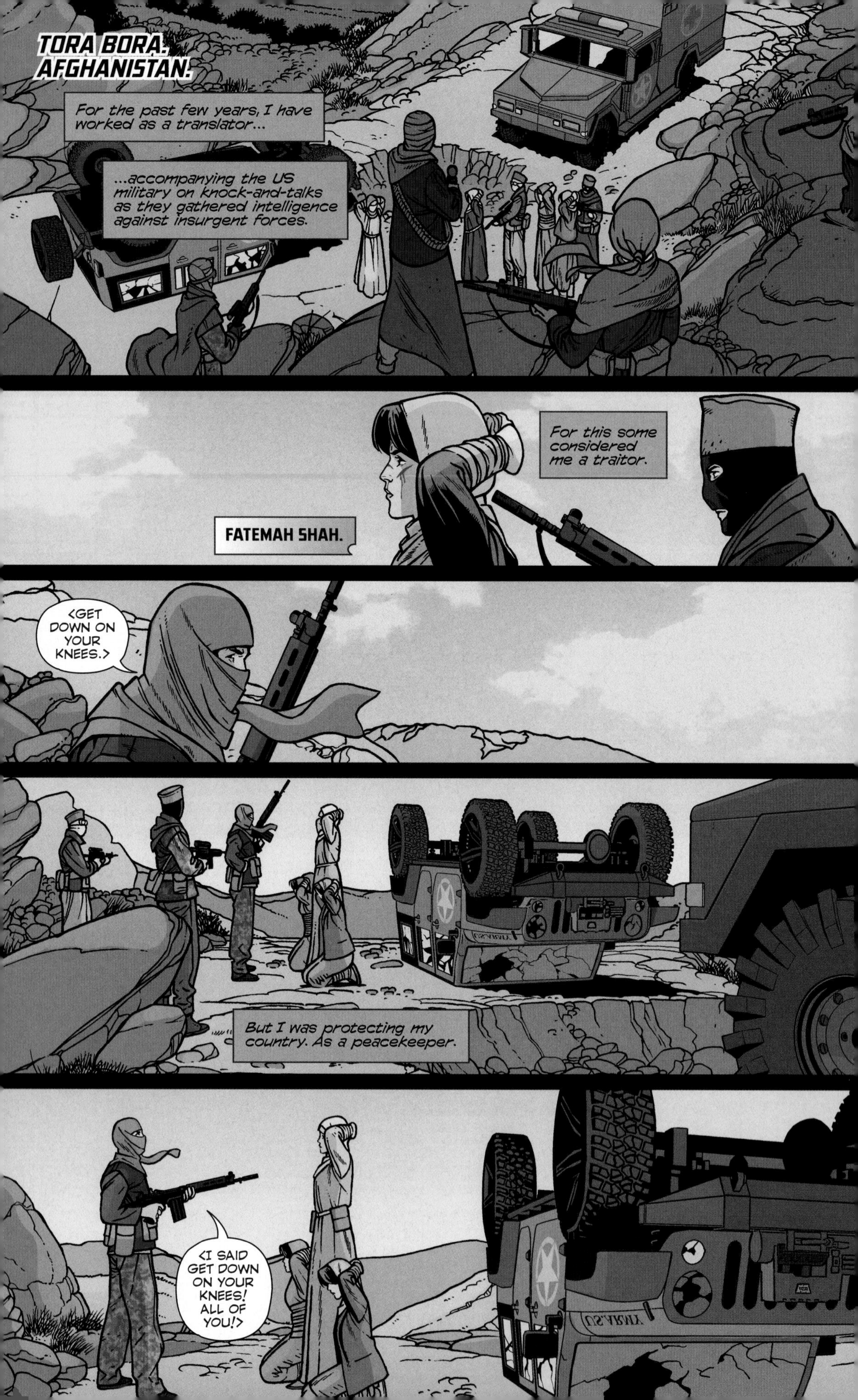

TORA BORA. AFGHANISTAN.
For the past few years, I have worked as a translator...
...accompanying the US military on knock-and-talks as they gathered intelligence against insurgent forces.
For this some considered me a traitor.
FATEMAH SHAH.
<GET DOWN ON YOUR KNEES.>
But I was protecting my country. As a peacekeeper.
<I SAID GET DOWN ON YOUR KNEES! ALL OF YOU!>

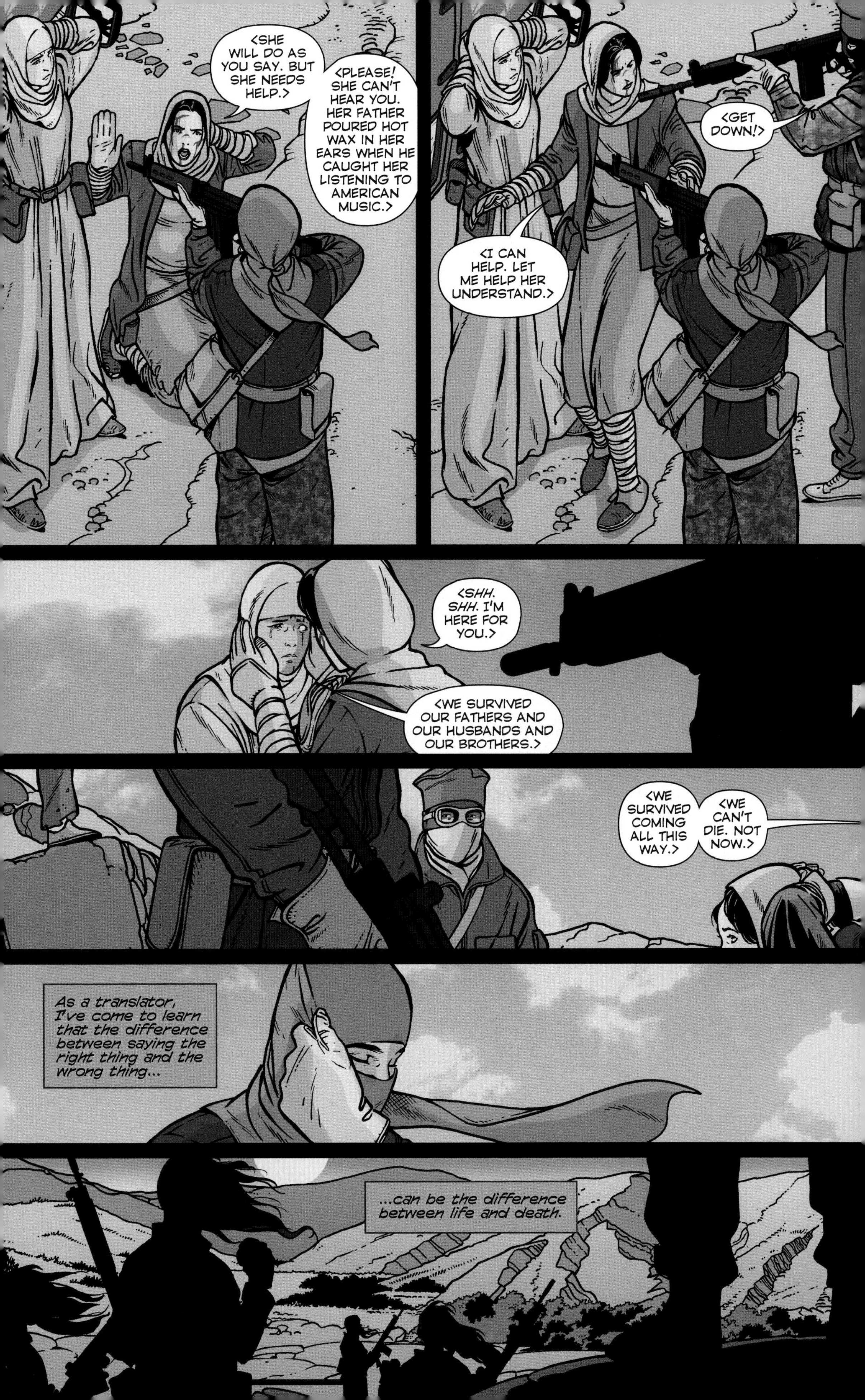
<SHE WILL DO AS YOU SAY. BUT SHE NEEDS HELP.>
<PLEASE! SHE CAN'T HEAR YOU. HER FATHER POURED HOT WAX IN HER EARS WHEN HE CAUGHT HER LISTENING TO AMERICAN MUSIC.>
<GET DOWN!>
<I CAN HELP. LET ME HELP HER UNDERSTAND.>
<SHH. SHH. I'M HERE FOR YOU.>
<WE SURVIVED OUR FATHERS AND OUR HUSBANDS AND OUR BROTHERS.>
<WE SURVIVED COMING ALL THIS WAY.>
<WE CAN'T DIE. NOT NOW.>
As a translator, I've come to learn that the difference between saying the right thing and the wrong thing...
...can be the difference between life and death.

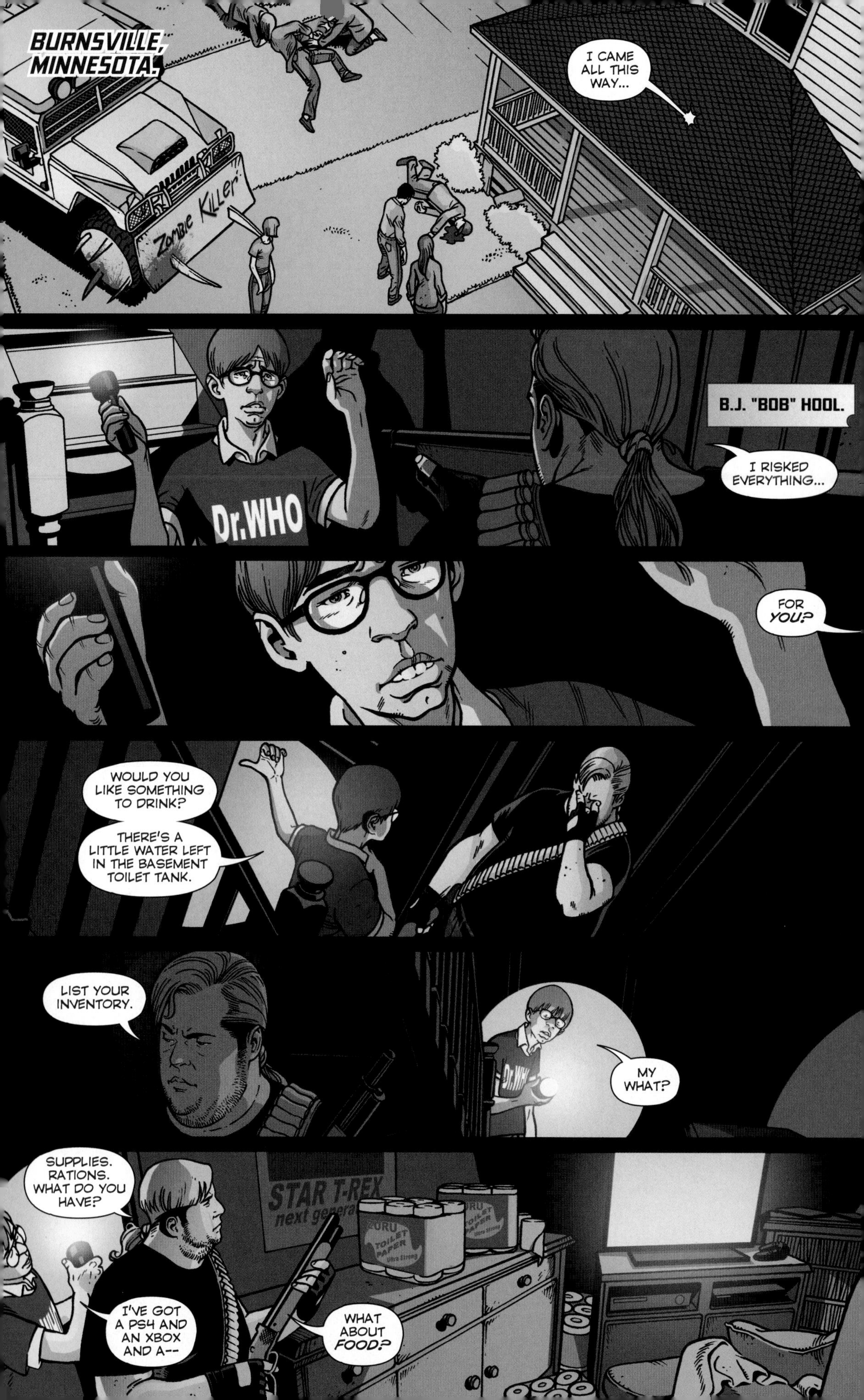
BURNSVILLE, MINNESOTA.
I CAME ALL THIS WAY...
Zombie Killer
B.J. "BOB" HOOL.
I RISKED EVERYTHING...
Dr.WHO
FOR YOU?
WOULD YOU LIKE SOMETHING TO DRINK?
THERE'S A LITTLE WATER LEFT IN THE BASEMENT TOILET TANK.
LIST YOUR INVENTORY.
MY WHAT?
SUPPLIES. RATIONS. WHAT DO YOU HAVE?
STAR T-REX
I'VE GOT A PS4 AND AN XBOX AND A--
WHAT ABOUT FOOD?

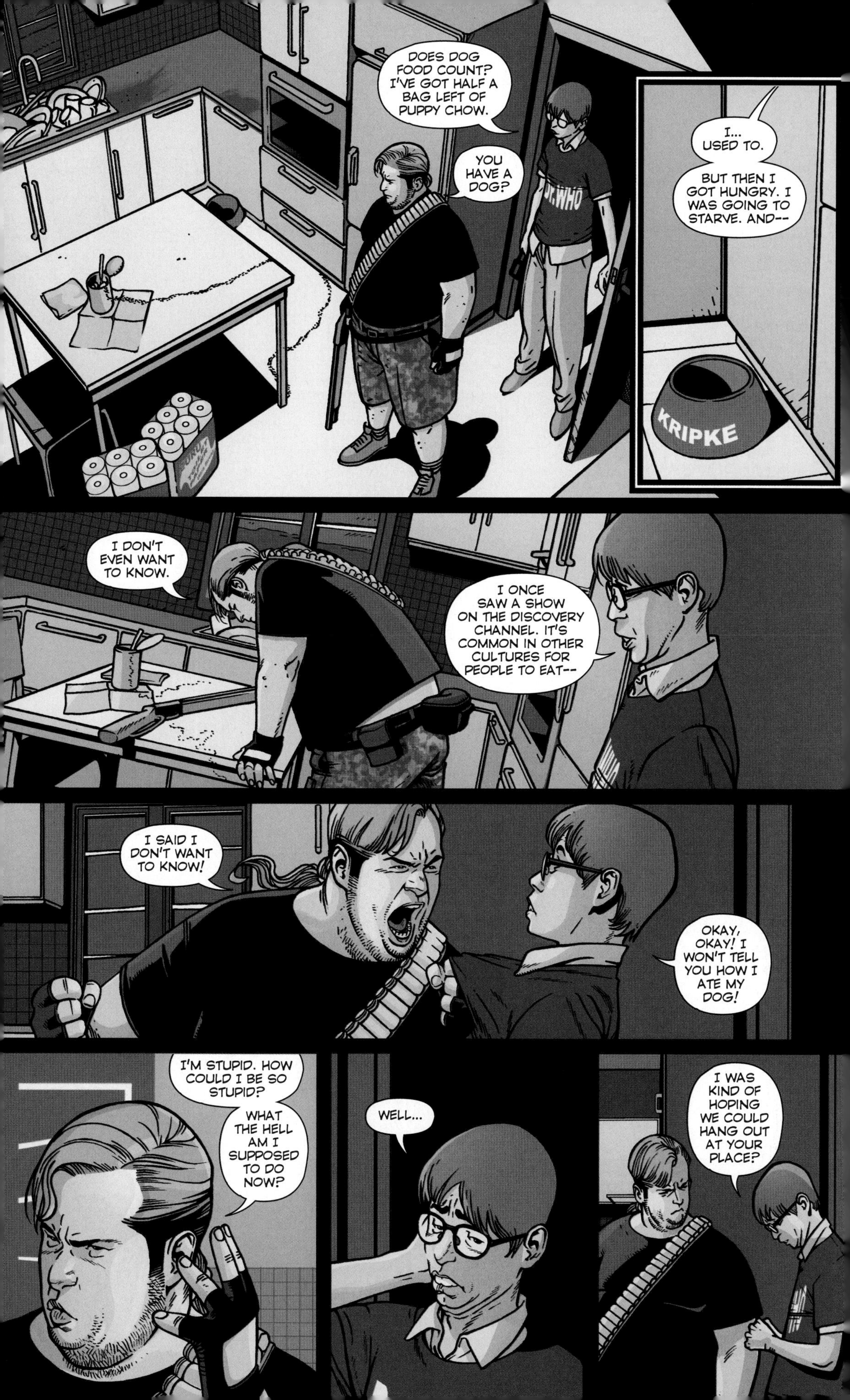
DOES DOG FOOD COUNT? I'VE GOT HALF A BAG LEFT OF PUPPY CHOW.
YOU HAVE A DOG?
Dr.WHO
I... USED TO.
BUT THEN I GOT HUNGRY. I WAS GOING TO STARVE. AND--
KRIPKE
I DON'T EVEN WANT TO KNOW.
I ONCE SAW A SHOW ON THE DISCOVERY CHANNEL. IT'S COMMON IN OTHER CULTURES FOR PEOPLE TO EAT--
I SAID I DON'T WANT TO KNOW!
OKAY, OKAY! I WON'T TELL YOU HOW I ATE MY DOG!
I'M STUPID. HOW COULD I BE SO STUPID?
WHAT THE HELL AM I SUPPOSED TO DO NOW?
WELL...
I WAS KIND OF HOPING WE COULD HANG OUT AT YOUR PLACE?

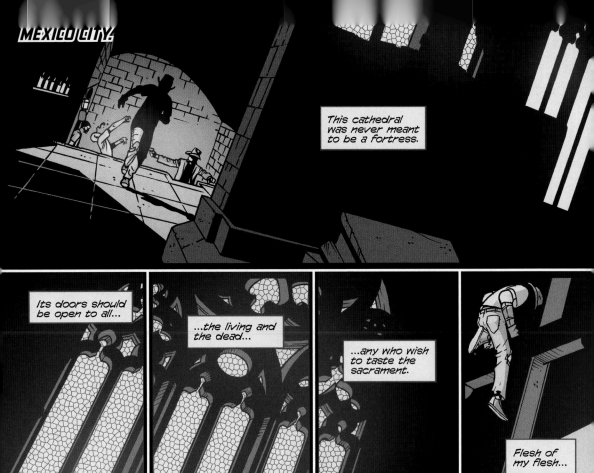

This cathedral was never meant to be a fortress.

Its doors should be open to all...

...the living and the dead...

...any who wish to taste the sacrament.

Flesh of my flesh...

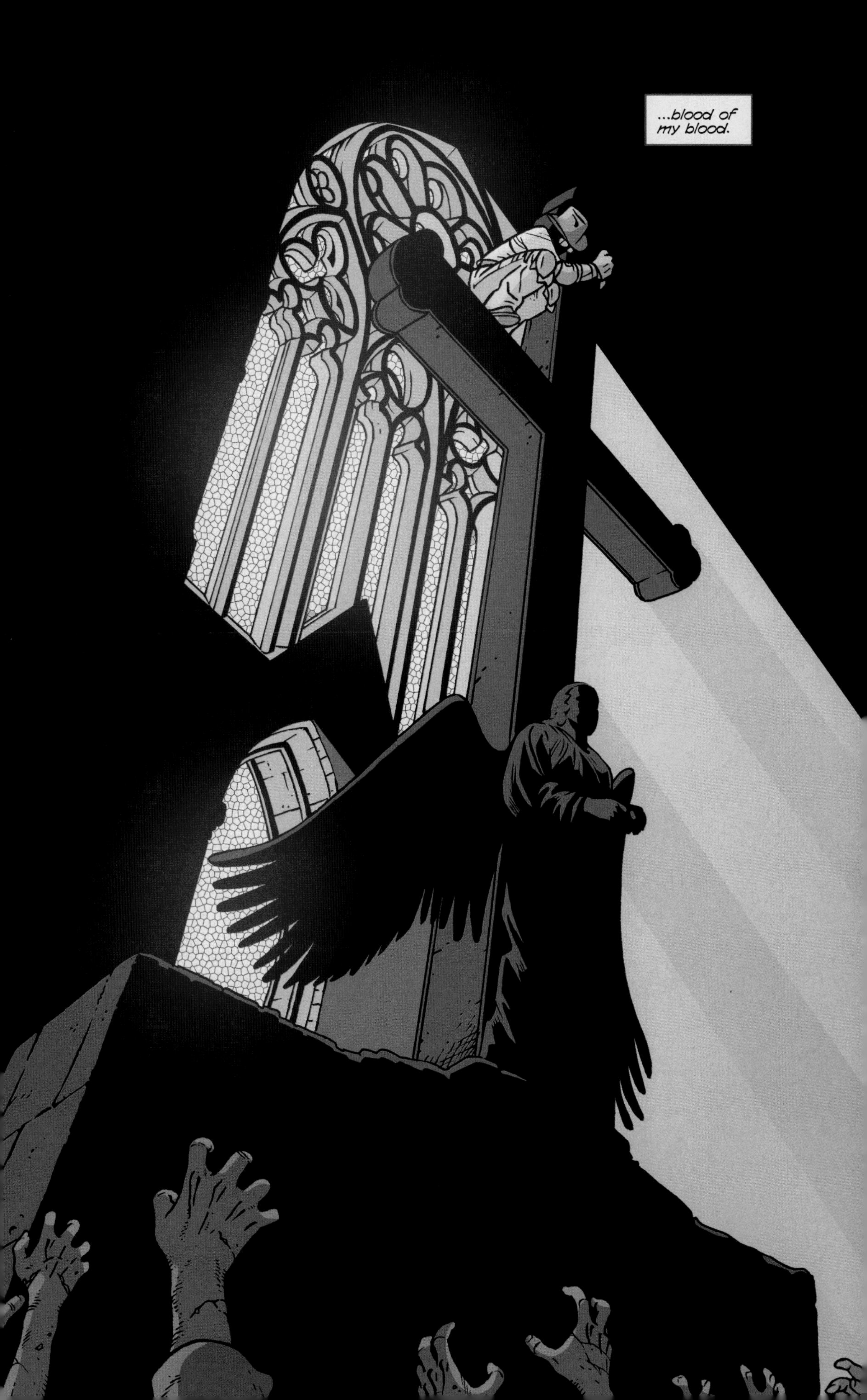
...blood of my blood.

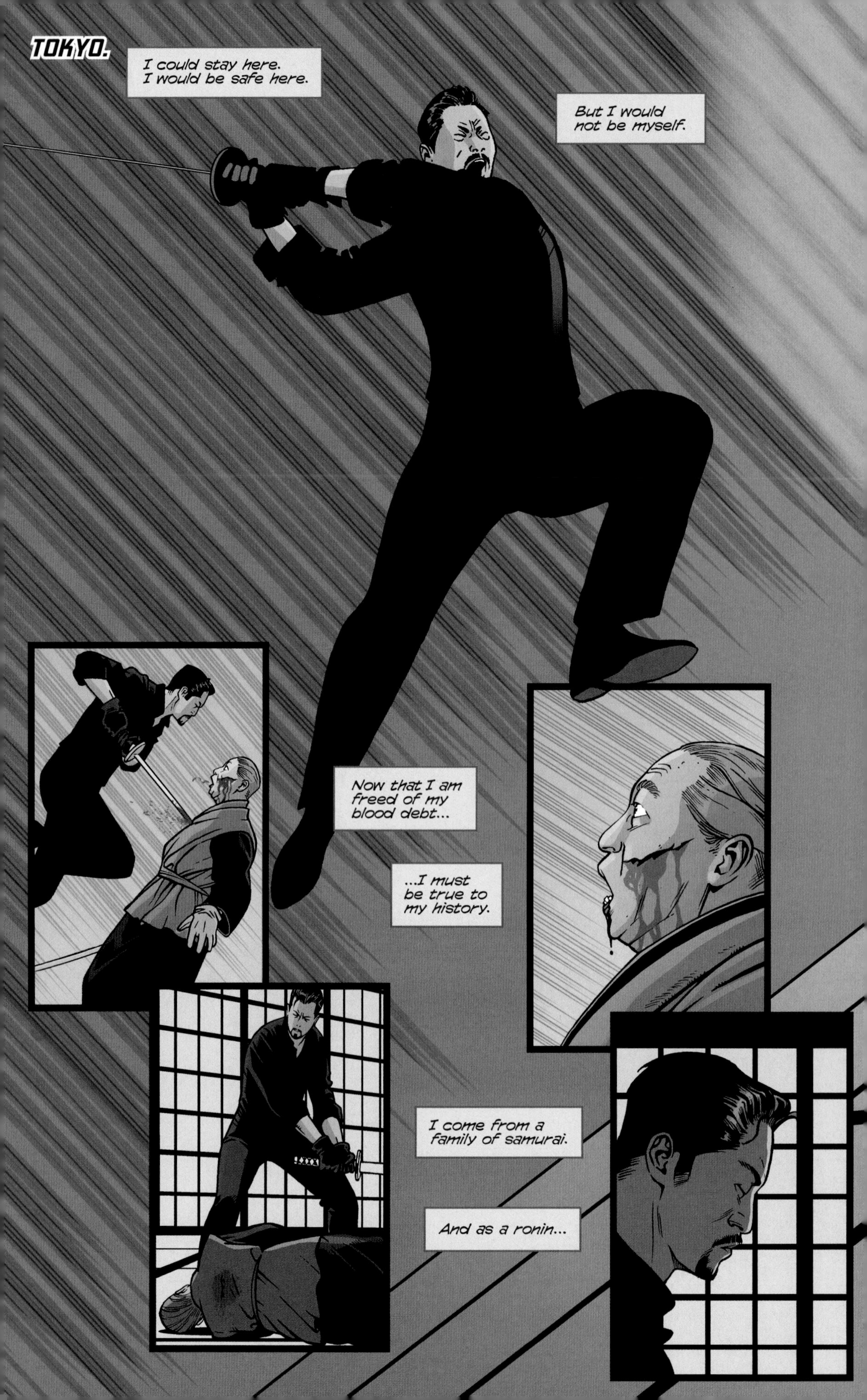
TOKYO.
I could stay here.
I would be safe here.
But I would
not be myself.
Now that I am
freed of my
blood debt...
...I must
be true to
my history.
I come from a
family of samurai.
And as a ronin...

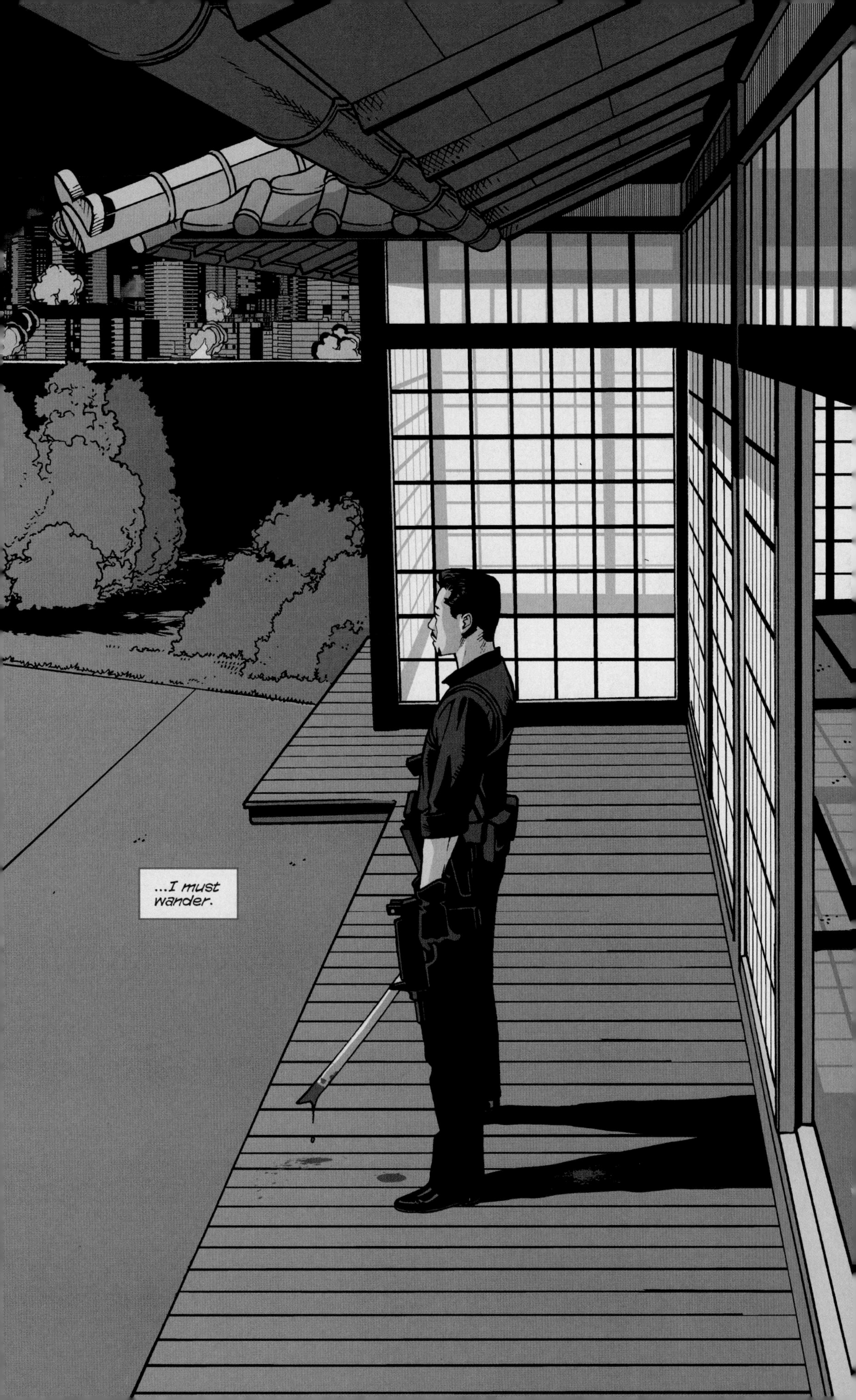
...I must wander.

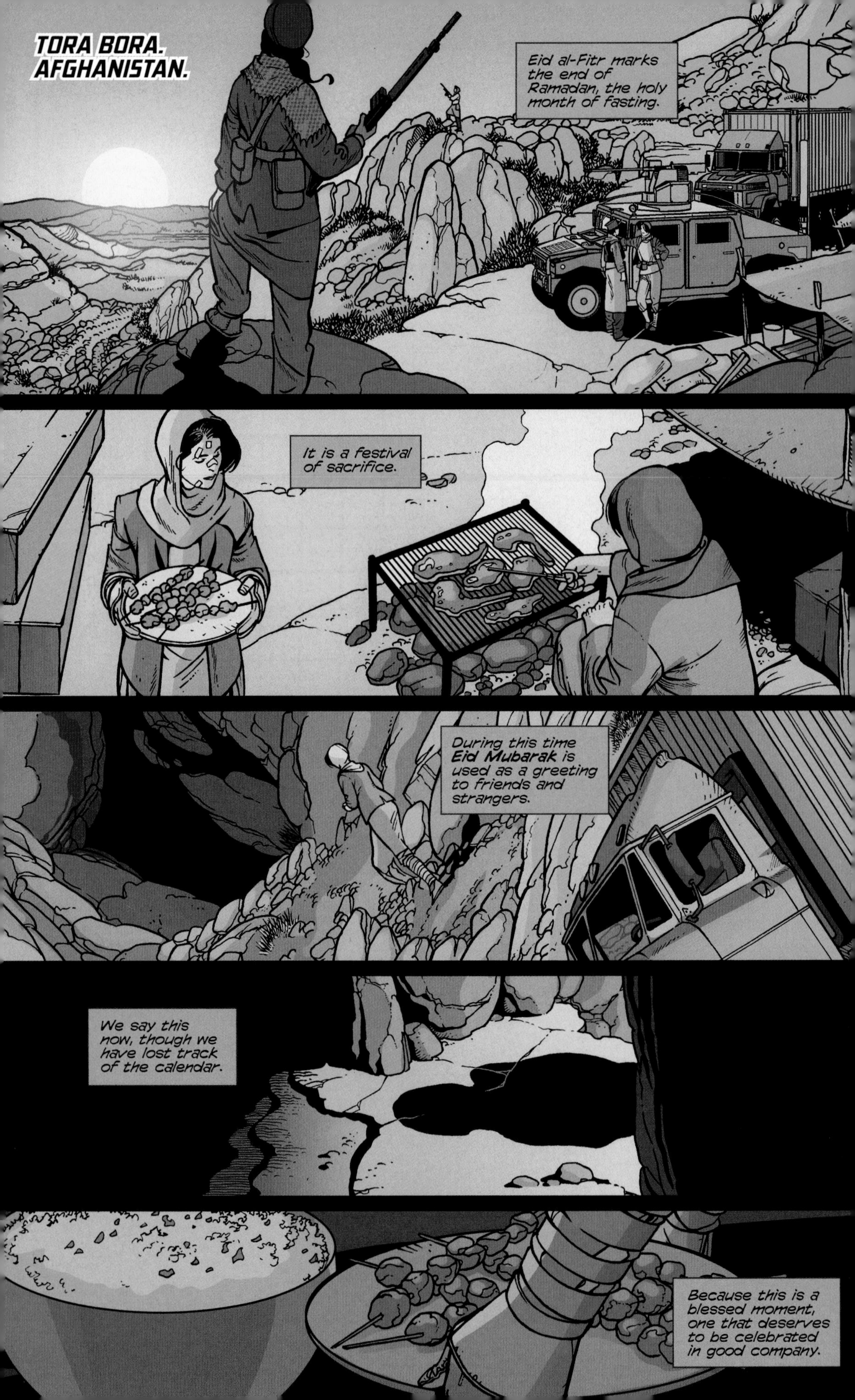

TORA BORA. AFGHANISTAN.
Eid al-Fitr marks the end of Ramadan, the holy month of fasting.
It is a festival of sacrifice.
During this time Eid Mubarak is used as a greeting to friends and strangers.
We say this now, though we have lost track of the calendar.
Because this is a blessed moment, one that deserves to be celebrated in good company.

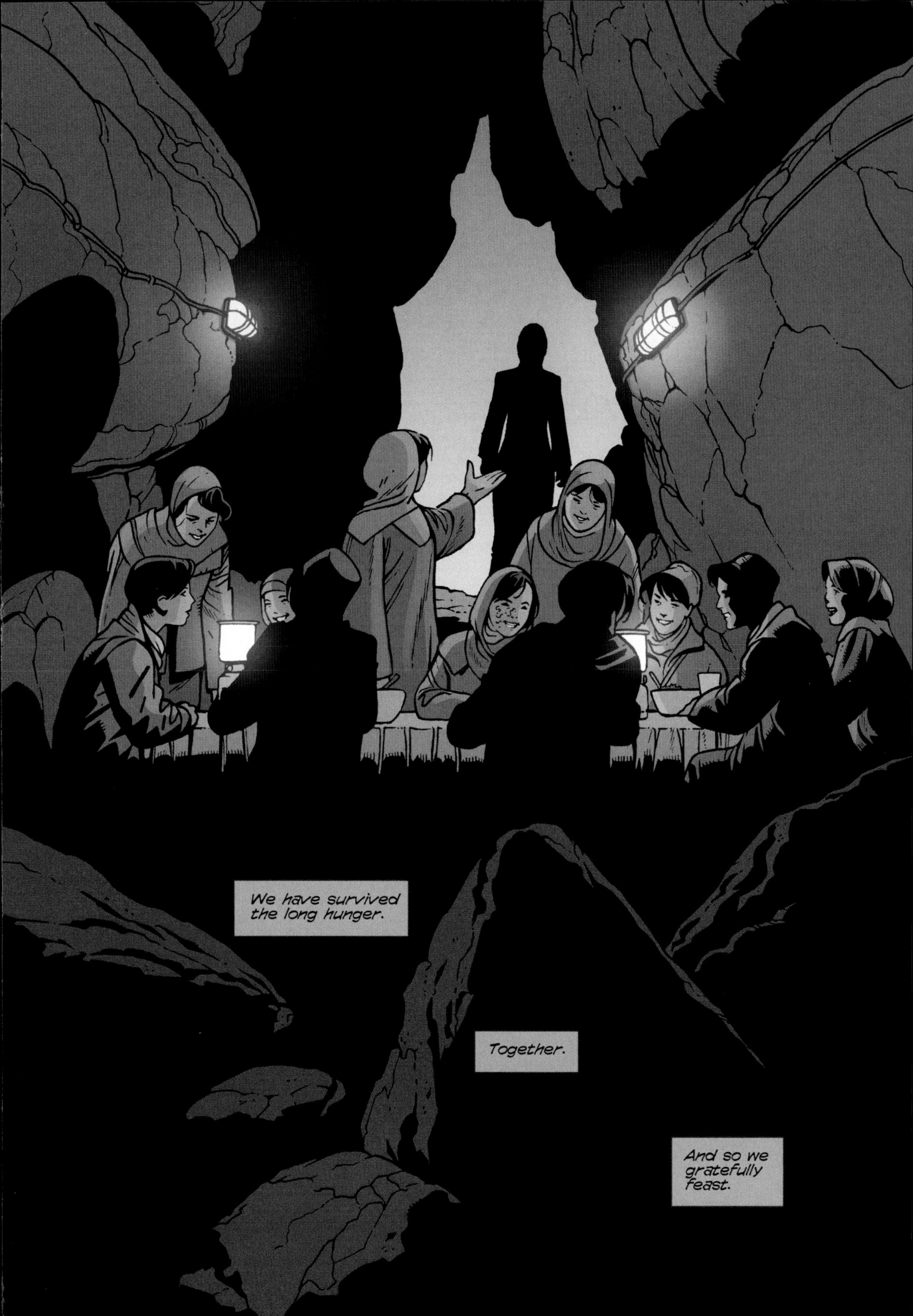
We have survived the long hunger.
Together.
And so we gratefully feast.

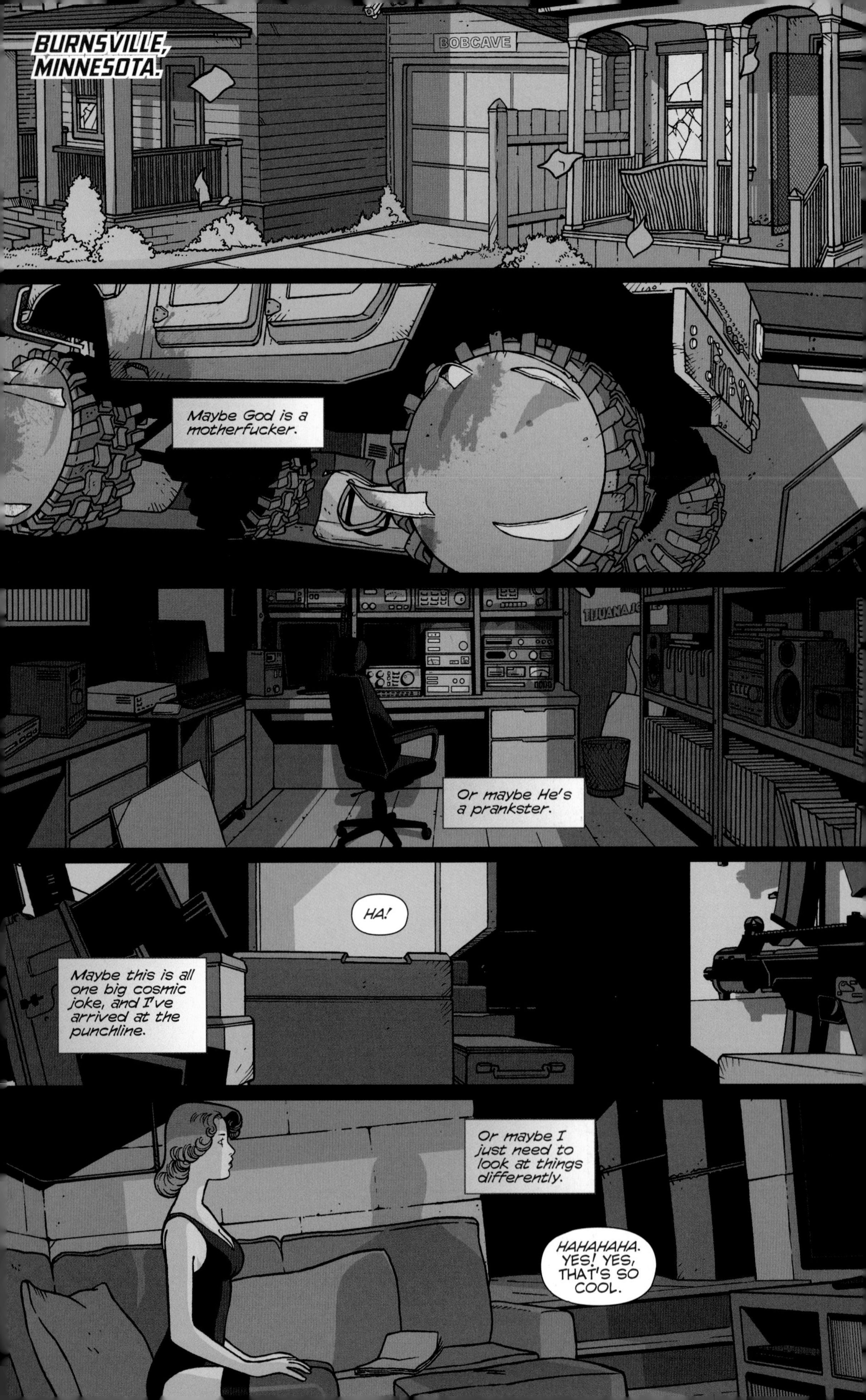
BURNSVILLE, MINNESOTA.
BOBCAVE
Maybe God is a motherfucker.
TIJUANA
Or maybe He's a prankster.
HA!
Maybe this is all one big cosmic joke, and I've arrived at the punchline.
Or maybe I just need to look at things differently.
HAHAHAHA. YES! YES, THAT'S SO COOL.

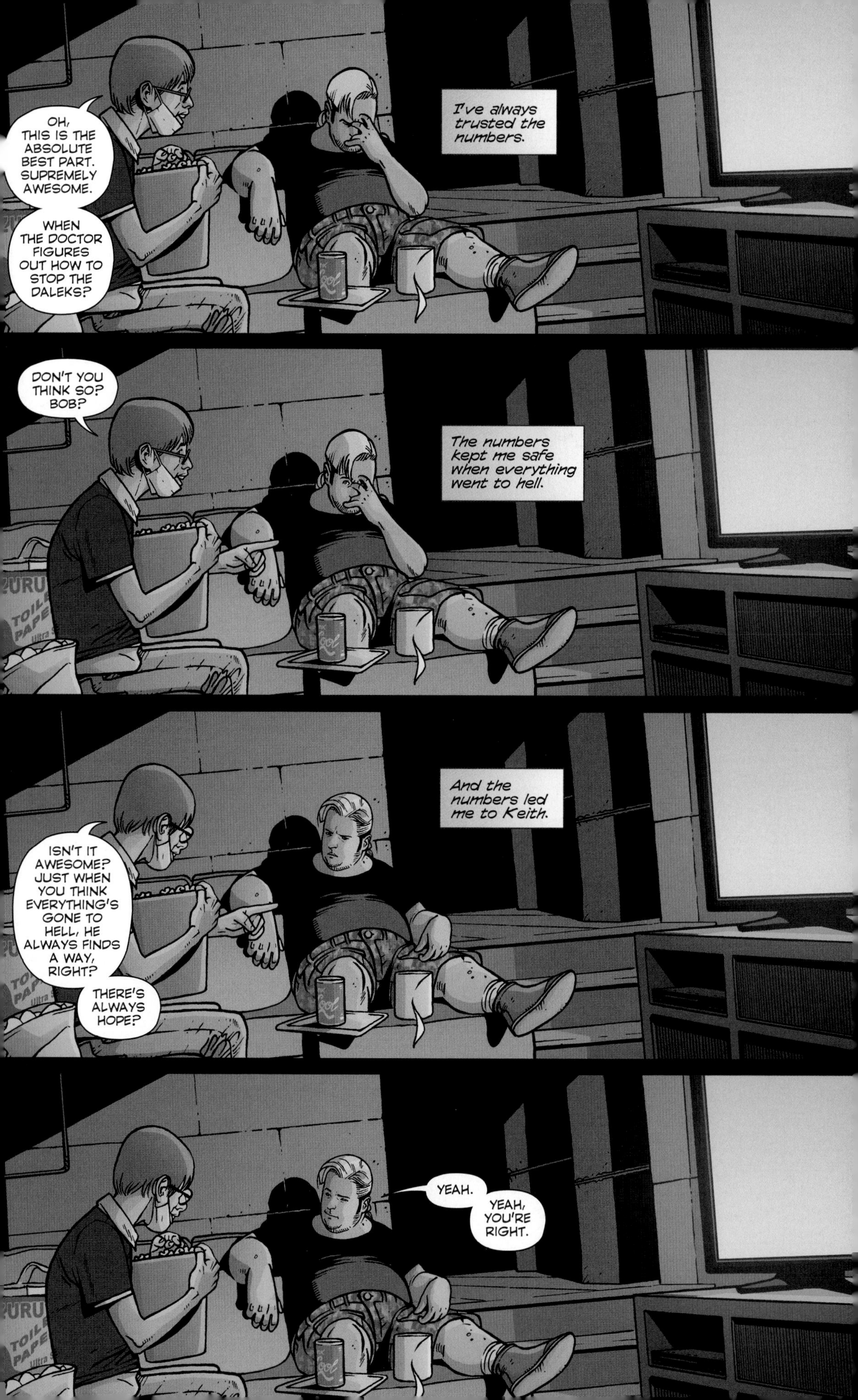
OH, THIS IS THE ABSOLUTE BEST PART. SUPREMELY AWESOME.
WHEN THE DOCTOR FIGURES OUT HOW TO STOP THE DALEKS?
I've always trusted the numbers.
DON'T YOU THINK SO? BOB?
The numbers kept me safe when everything went to hell.
And the numbers led me to Keith.
ISN'T IT AWESOME? JUST WHEN YOU THINK EVERYTHING'S GONE TO HELL, HE ALWAYS FINDS A WAY, RIGHT?
THERE'S ALWAYS HOPE?
YEAH.
YEAH, YOU'RE RIGHT.

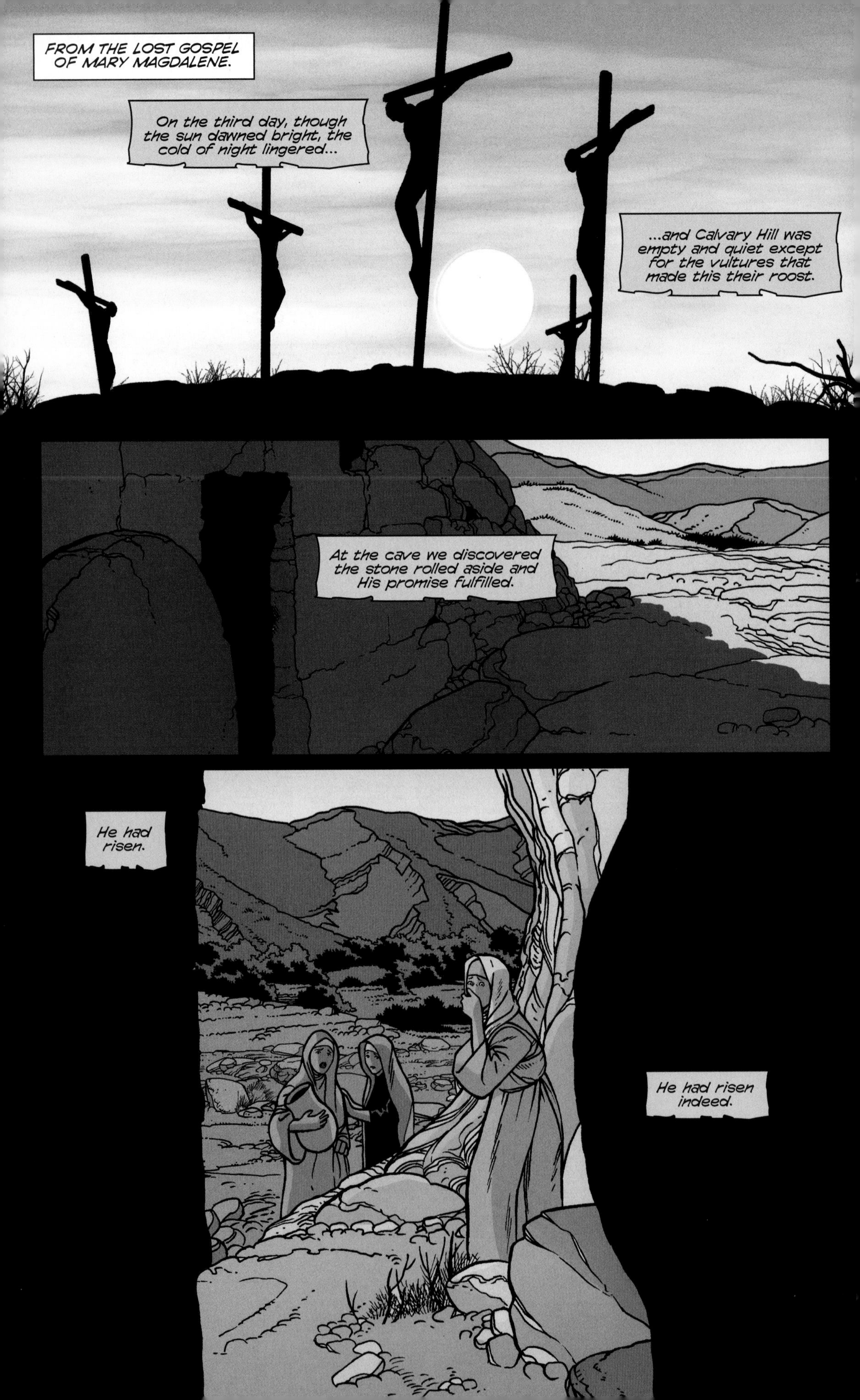
FROM THE LOST GOSPEL OF MARY MAGDALENE.
On the third day, though the sun dawned bright, the cold of night lingered...
...and Calvary Hill was empty and quiet except for the vultures that made this their roost.
At the cave we discovered the stone rolled aside and His promise fulfilled.
He had risen.
He had risen indeed.

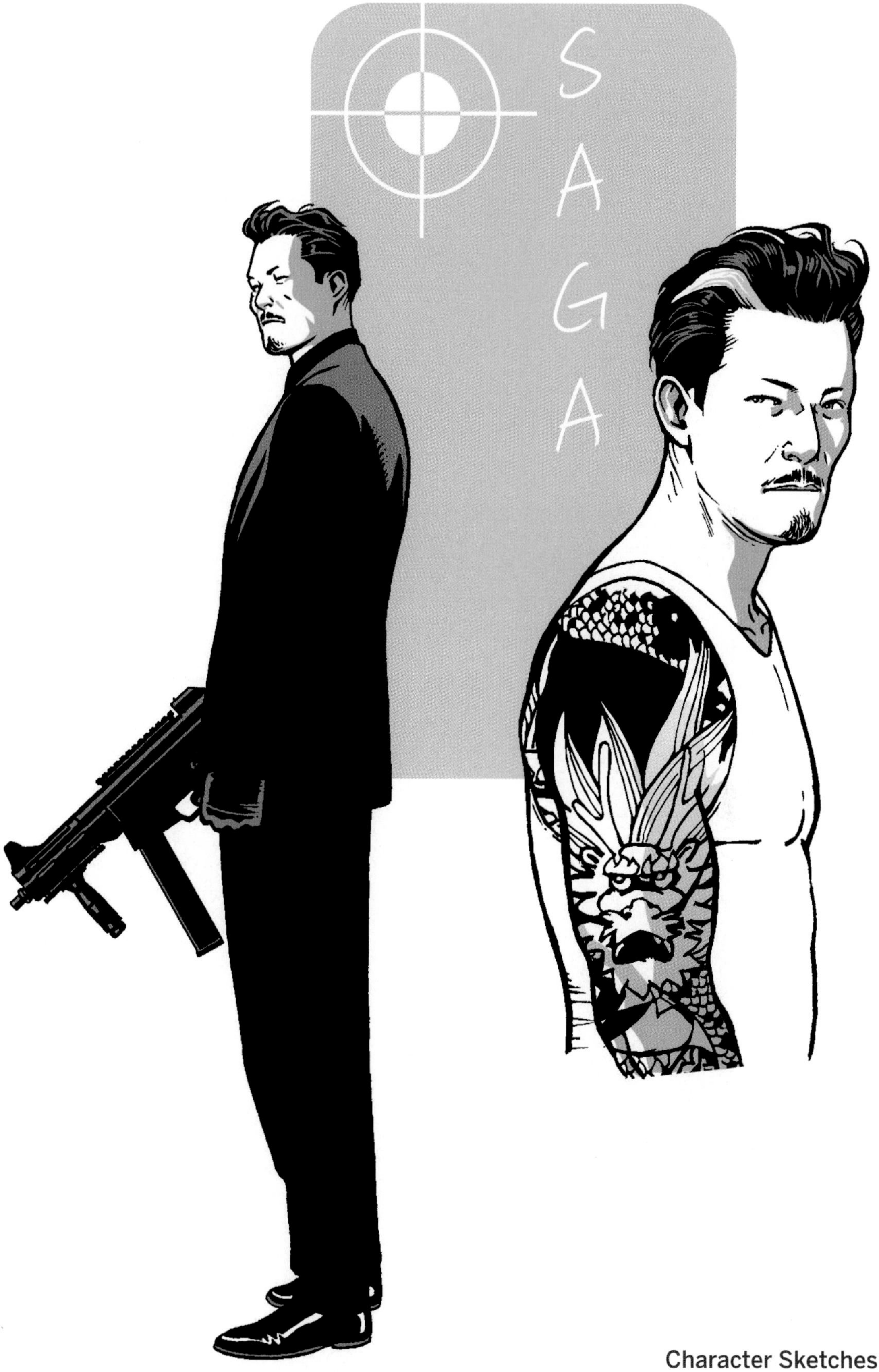
SAGA

Character Sketches
by Ramon Rosanas

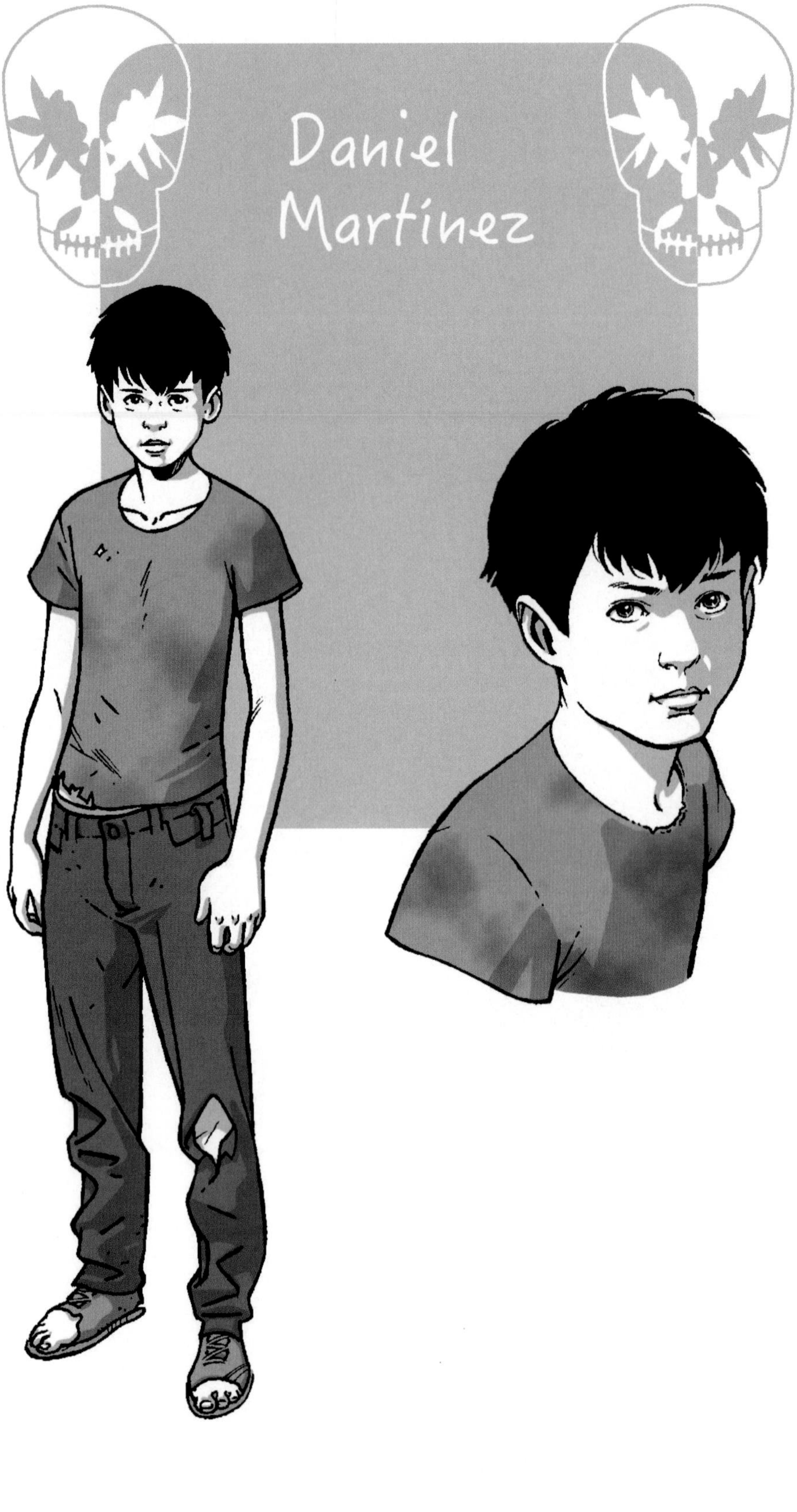
Daniel
Martínez

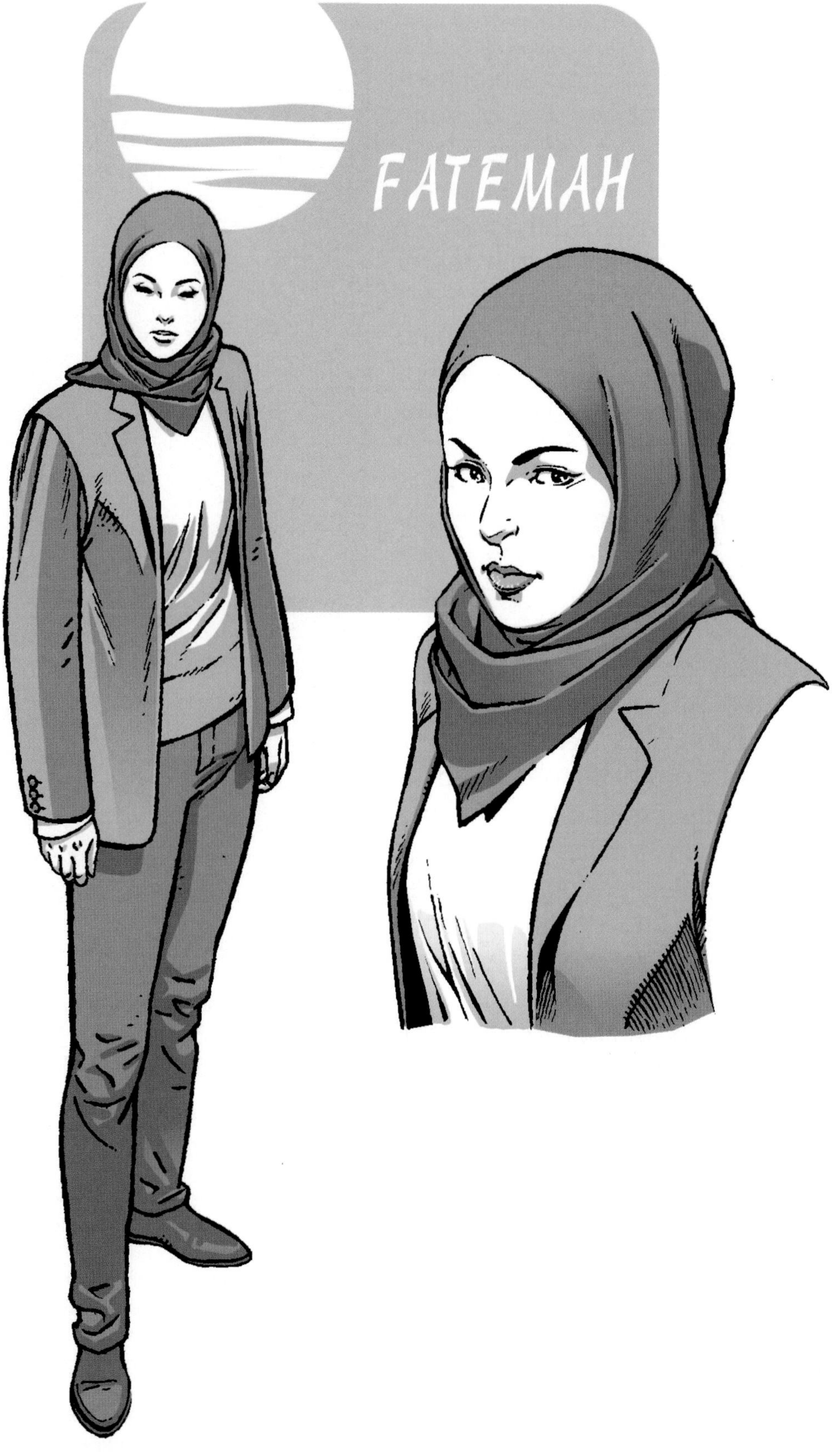
FATEMAH

A LETTER FROM THE CREATOR OF
YEAR ZERO

Horror offers a cracked-mirror version of reality—and political, cultural and environmental unease often finds a reflection in the genre. Look at how *Frankenstein* rose out of the Industrial Revolution, informed by the fear of science and technology, of man playing God. Look at how *Godzilla* was born out of post-atomic anxieties. Look at how *Invasion of the Body Snatchers* aligned with McCarthyism and the Red Scare, the dread of an enemy living invisibly among us.

People say we're in a golden age of horror—the likes of which we haven't seen since the Cold War paranoia of the eighties. Look at the news and it's not hard to understand why. Australia is burning and Venice is drowning. Yet another mass shooting bloodies the headlines. Presidential hopefuls are arguing, and everything is simultaneously a truth and a lie. North Korea is readying another missile test. Hong Kong is rioting. Oh, and not only has flu season been especially nasty, the corona pandemic is just getting started.

I could go on. But you already understand. Because you feel the same creeping anxiety every time you knob on the radio or log on to social media. Destroying the world has never been more popular—in film, tv, comics, novels—because destroying the world has never felt more probable.

We're all one cough or missile strike away from Year Zero…

You're of course familiar with Romero's *Night of the Living Dead* and Kirkman's *The Walking Dead*—but unlike these franchises, we're not focusing in on a group of survivors in a basement or a troupe of misfits wandering the countryside. *Year Zero* isn't about the micro—it's the macro. A global account of a world in ruin.

Here is a scientist at a polar research station. Here is a street urchin in Mexico City. Here is a Yakuza hitman in Tokyo. Here is a military translator in Kabul. Here is a prepper in suburban America. And here, too, in every issue, is a fragment of history (a medieval tapestry, a Chinese scroll, scraps of da Vinci's notebook, etc.) that will inform and revise your understanding of the virus's origins.

I often approach a project with a stylistic goal. In this case, I wanted the form to serve the function. The world is shattered, so the design should be as well.

We found a great partner in Ramon Rosanas. His art is wonderfully cinematic, and he's done a brilliant job bringing this dead planet to life. Not only did he research each setting—in order to capture it authentically on a granular level—but the colorist Lee Loughridge joined forces with him and differentiated the color palette of each character, a masterly touch. I'm lucky to be working with them both.

Now here I am talking about headline news and global anxiety and taking a knife to the nerve of the moment, but it's also true that writers are often wrestling with their own worries on the page. Consider Cormac McCarthy. One night he woke up in a hotel with his son lying beside him in the bed. He thought he heard drumming and he pulled off his sheets and approached the window and looked out on the black hills humped in the distance. That seemed to be the source of the sound, and he imagined them then as war drums and the red glow of dawn made the land appear as if it was catching flame. From this moment came the idea for *The Road*, which is one of the most terrifying novels I've ever read—because it's all about a father trying to keep his son safe.

As you move from story to story, you will fit the shards together into a mosaic that will ultimately give you a fresh understanding of what it means to be human in a post-human world. You'll find stories of hope and sacrifice…and you'll find stories of the abyss.

We all know zombies best from film, but film has limits. There's only so much you can do with the budget and the time and the camera. But comics are limitless. I wanted to take advantage of the medium and really blow the doors off. Why limit ourselves to a house or a mall or a lab, when we could go anywhere (at any time)? I like to think *Year Zero* takes horror to a new, epic level by taking advantage of the freedom ink and paper offer.

And Axel Alonso encouraged this from the very beginning. He pushed for risk and ambition and literary smarts alongside the pyrotechnic action and heart-stopping fear. He didn't just want me to write another zombie story. He wanted me to write the definitive zombie story.

In the same way, *Year Zero* is a personal story. You'll see me struggling with questions of love and faith and fear and paranoia. Writing a horror comic is a little like braving a roller coaster or a haunted house. You dare the nightmare and emerge out the other side with a little less poison in your system. Because you survived the worst.

I grew up a horror fiend—snorting Stephen King and guzzling *Fangoria* and injecting John Carpenter—and it's my absolute pleasure to share that addiction with you now, as we bring this monster of a story to stumbling, teeth-gnashing life. Thanks for reading.

Benjamin Percy
Minnesota
March 03, 2020

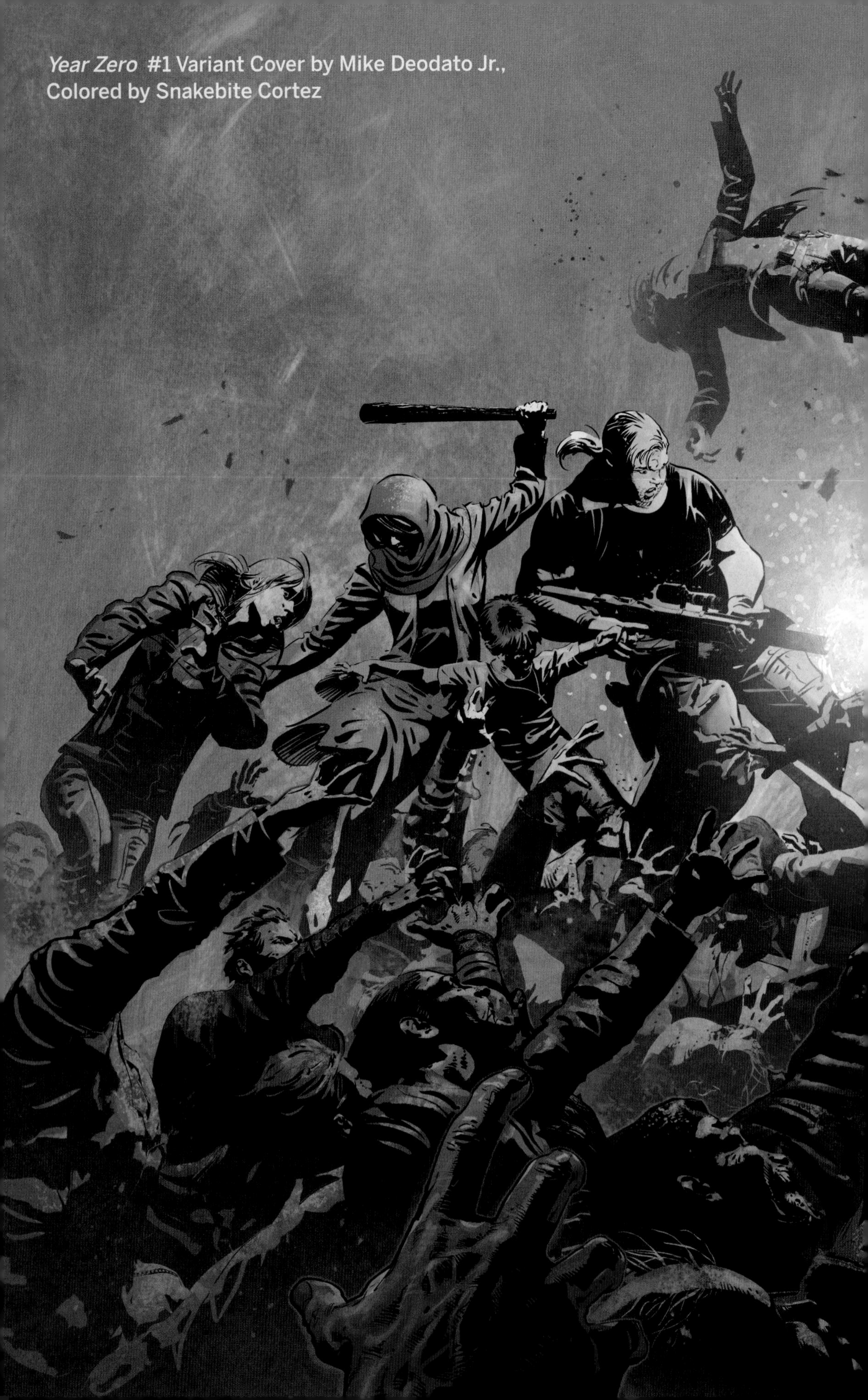

Year Zero #1 Variant Cover by Mike Deodato Jr., Colored by Snakebite Cortez

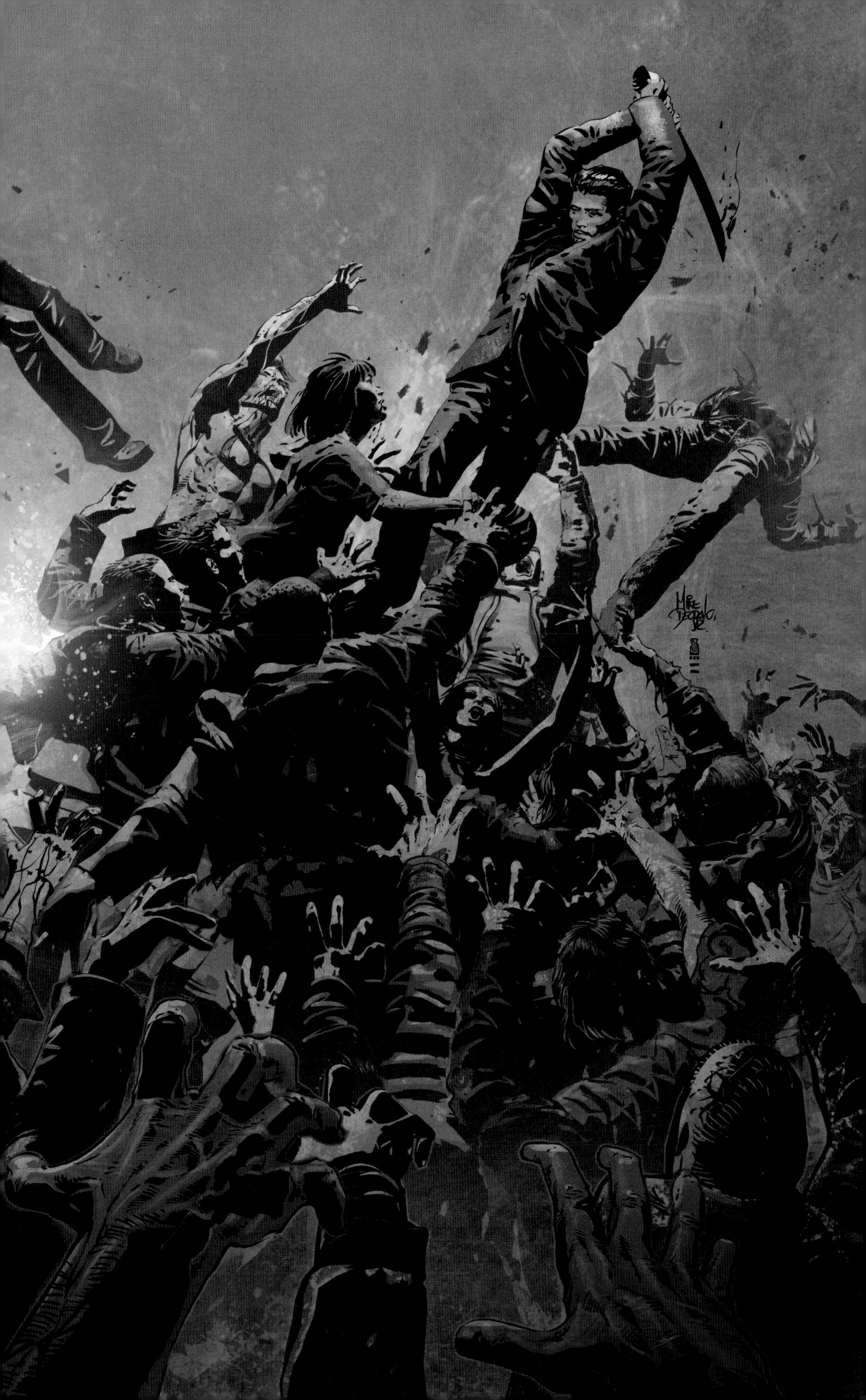

Panel 1
Establishing shot of Tokyo skyline. Day.

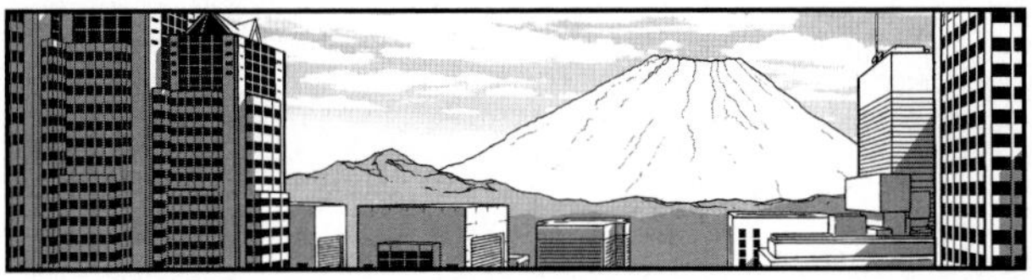

CAPTION: NOW. TOKYO.

SAGA (CAP:) Buddhists believe there are six realms of being.

Panel 2
Interior. SAGA WATANABE (Japanese, eerly 40s, think Ken Watanabe. Immaculate, precise in his manner as well as his dress. Black suit, no tie.) walks down the hall of a luxury hotel, pulling a small suitcase. He wears a black suit with no tie that can't hide his athletic build. His every movement is meticulous, trained, efficient. We don't know this yet, but he's a Yakuza assassin. Think of him as Japanese Bond. In his other hand, he holds his keycard.

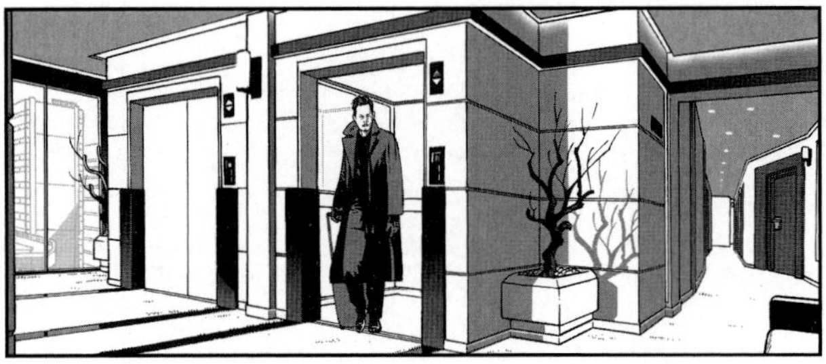

CAPTION: SAGA WATANABE.

SAGA (CAP): Heaven, Asura, humankind, animals, hungry ghosts, and hell.

Panel 3
As he keys open his room…he notices a housekeeper nearby. Her cart is in the hall. But she stands in the open doorway of a room. Her attitude cautious.

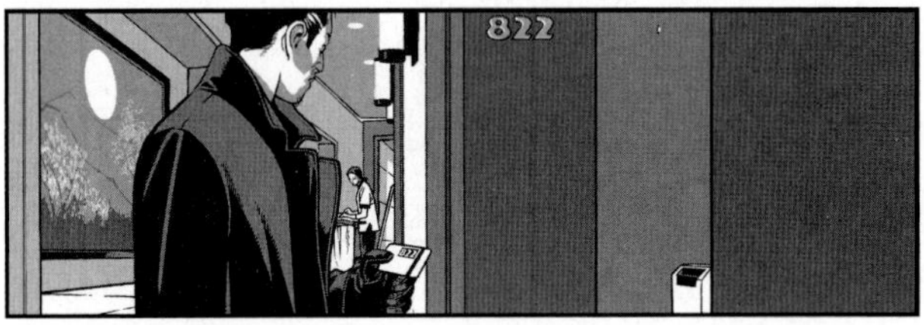
822

SAGA (CAP): Within the realms, we are reborn, over and over and over.

Panel 4
Maybe we just get a glimpse of what she finds inside… overturned furniture, a handprint of blood on the wall…

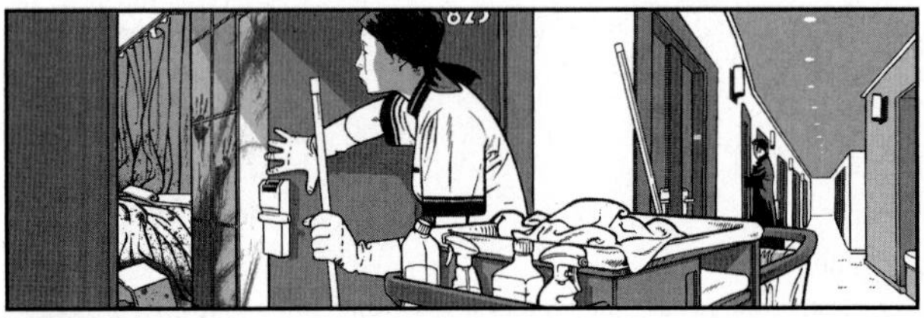

HOUSEKEEPER: <Hello? Housekeeping?>

Panel 5
Saga puts up the "Do Not Disturb" sign as he enters his own room.

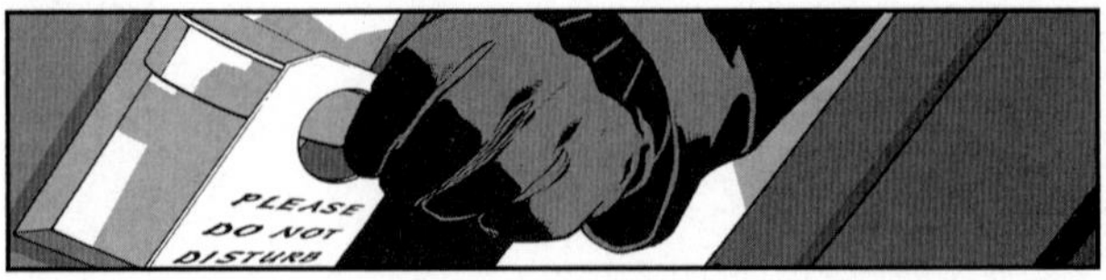
PLEASE
DO NOT
DISTURB

SAGA (CAP): Nothing is permanent.

Panel 1
Wide view of Saga's hotel room. In the foreground, his
suitcase sits on the bed. In the background he is looking
out the window, his back to us.

SAGA (CAP):   The whole of your behavior deter-
                    mines a sliding scale of punishment
                    and reward.

Panel 2
Close on his wrist as he pushes back his sleeve and
looks at his watch (to indicate he knows what's going
to transpire any second now). It's not the watch of a
businessman. It's the watch of a spy. Depth gauges. Too
many dials and buttons. Small panel.

SAGA (CAP):   Maybe I play a role in all of this.

Panel 3
From his POV, we see that that across the street, in a
futuristic business tower, a group of seemingly powerful
men and women have filed into a meeting room.

Panel 4
Close on his hands as he opens his suitcase..

SAGA (CAP):   I might pull the trigger…

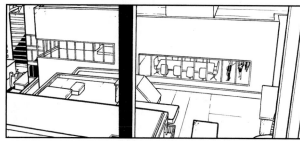

Panel 5
And we reveal a sniper's rifle, tucked into
compartments, which has not yet been assembled.

SAGA (CAP):   …or slide the knife….

Panel 6
He snaps together the pieces of his sniper rifle. Again,
there is a clinical, unemotional quality to everything he
does. We can imagine him slitting someone's throat with
the same expression that he spreads butter on toast.

SAGA (CAP):   …or prime the detonator.

Panel 7
There is a panicked knocking at his door.

SFX: THUD THUD THUD

Panel 1
Saga has ignored the knocking, thinking (rightly) that it is the housekeeper. He is using a 007-esque device (suction cup and laser) to carve out a circle of glass in the window.

SAGA (CAP:)   But you determine your destiny.

Panel 2
Saga has now angled the rifle through the freshly cut hole in the glass and brought the scope to his eye.

SAGA (CAP:)   You get what you deserve.

Panel 3
Looking from Saga's POV through the scope: He studies his target in the digital crosshairs. High-tech readings as it zooms in on one man – an older Asian gentleman with silver hair. Give him a distinct look.

SAGA (CAP:)   I merely help you attain it.

Panel 4
The knocking at the door returns and now grows more extreme.

SFX: THUD THUD THUD

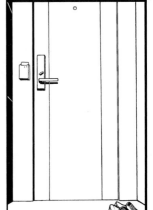

Panel 5
Saga pulls his eye away from the scope and turns his head…listening.

SAGA (CAP:)   You are impermanent.

Panel 6
As he does, our point of view goes deep inside the room, so we see him at the window….
…as a body plunges silently through the air behind him. Surrounded by a sparkling nest of broken glass. But he never sees this, his attention on the rattling doorknob. Wide panel.

SAGA (CAP:)   And I am karma.

This page is a 9-panel grid.

Panel 1
Cut: Back to Tokyo. Saga's eyes narrow of over the scope of his rifle. He needs to focus on his hit. But the desperate knocking continues outside his door.

CAPTION: NOW. TOKYO.

HOUSEKEEPER (OFF): Please! Please!

Panel 2
Saga stands and turns fully around now, with desperate annoyance.

SFX: THUD THUD THUD

SAGA (NARRATION): In the West, people think about time horizontally.

Panel 3
He walks to the door, gun at his side.

SAGA (NARRATION): Ancestors are tracked by their movement, as each generation chases greater fortunes.

Panel 4
Close on his eye as he looks through the keyhole…

SAGA (NARRATION): But in the East, time is vertical.

Panel 5
His POV through keyhole: Nothing out of the ordinary. Just a hallway with a housekeeping cart in it.

SAGA (NARRATION): The past is ever-present—in tea ceremonies, in the offerings on the first day of Obon, in the shrines tucked between skyscrapers…

Panel 6
Close on his ear, as he presses it to the door, listening.

SAGA (NARRATION): …and in the burden of familial legacy.

Panel 7
He walks back to the window.

SAGA (NARRATION): My family tracks back to the samurai.

Panel 8
And looks through the scope..

SAGA (NARRATION): And the samurai were known for their meticulous preparation.

Panel 9
And his eyes go suddenly wide with shock.

SAGA (NARRATION): Not just for victory on the battlefield.

PAGE 19

Panel 1
Wide panel. From Saga's view through the scope, a wide shot reveal that everyone in the boardroom is dead. Blood everywhere.

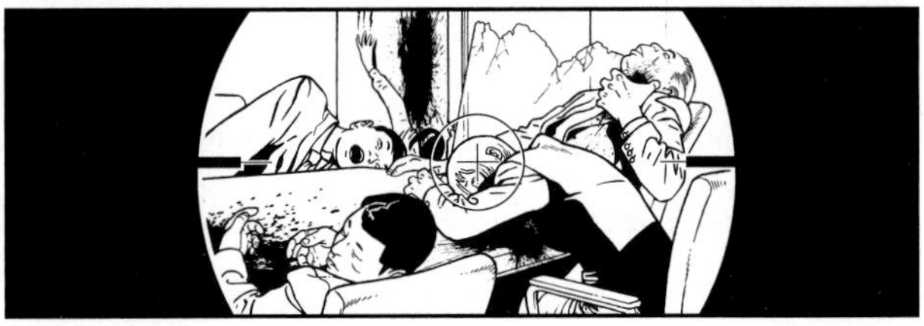

SAGA (NARRATION): But for failure.

SAGA (NARRATION): They were ready to fail.

Panel 2
Saga lifts his face away from the scope. He is going through a series of mental calculations—shifting gears here. As he looks out over the city. Small panel. Maybe an inset between Panels 1 and 3.

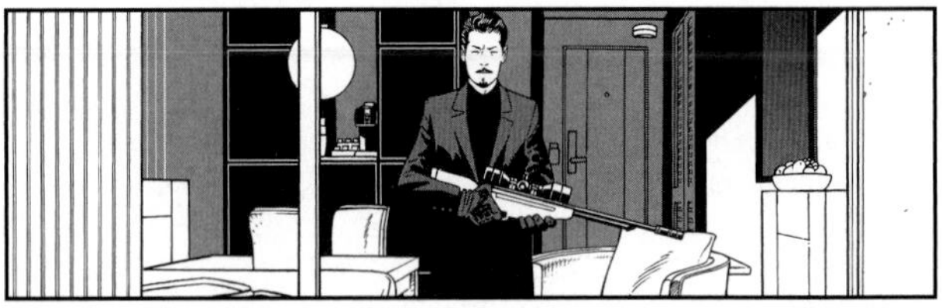

SAGA (NARRATION): Before a battle, they would anticipate every worst-case scenario.

Panel 3
BIG PANEL. Our point of view is over his shoulder. A building explodes in the distance. A helicopter wasps through the sky. There is smoke on the horizon. Anything you can envision that implies a…blooming chaos.

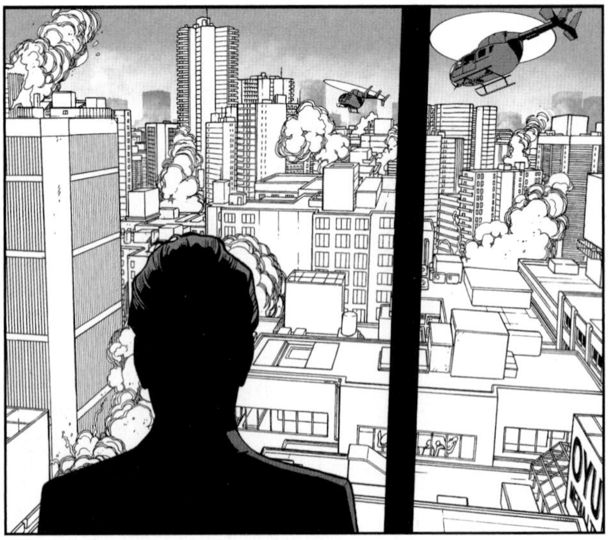

SAGA (NARRATION): A broken sword, a muddy field, sun in their eyes, a gashed tendon.

PAGE 20

Panel 1
Saga goes back to the door, rifle at the ready.

SAGA (NARRATION): That way, when something went wrong, they would remain calm—and their response would be immediate because it was preconceived.

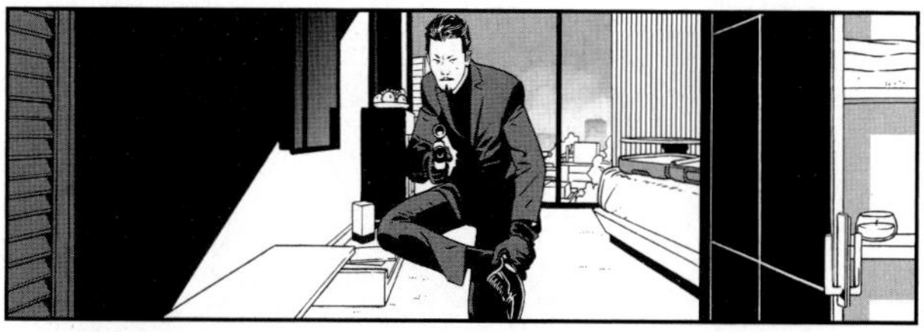

Panel 2
He opens the door.

SAGA (NARRATION): My name is Saga Watanabe. I come from the tradition of the samurai.

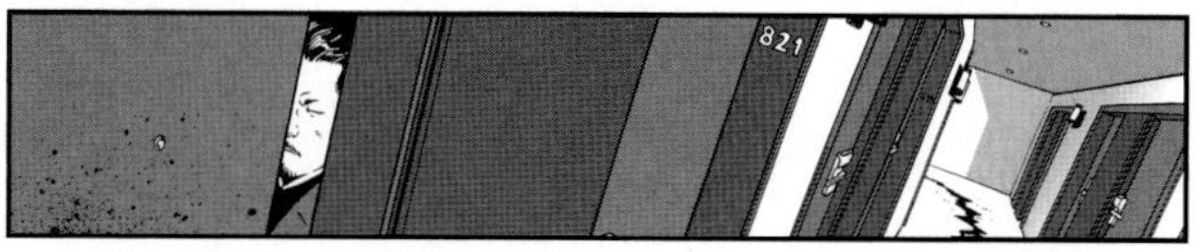
821

Panel 3
…and finds the hallway empty … except for the now overturned housekeeping cart…and a long slug's trail of blood leading down the hall and around the corner.

SAGA (NARRATION): And now the worst is happening.

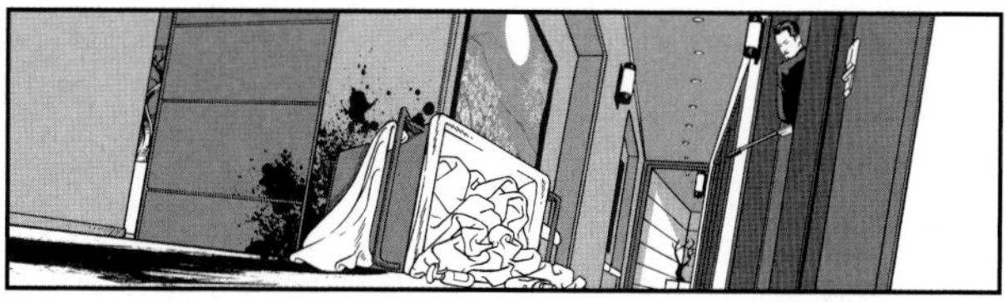

Panel 4
He hurries back to the bed, to his suitcase.

SAGA (NARRATION): The worst is here.

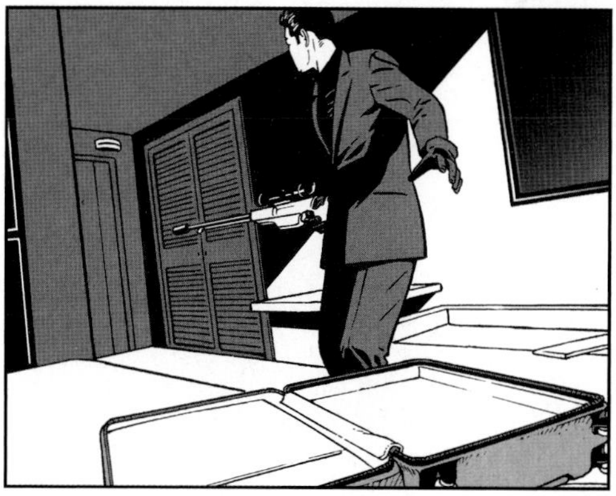

Panel 5
He opens another compartment in it.

SAGA (NARRATION): And I…

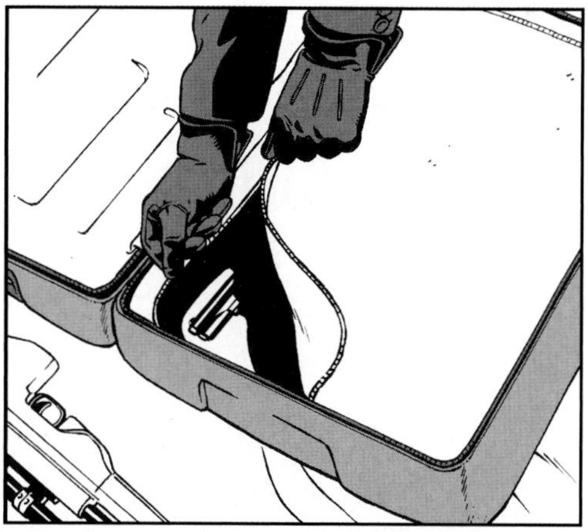

Panel 6
This reveals a whole host of weapons: sidearms, grenades, knives. He is a warrior… he recognizes a fight is coming.

SAGA (NARRATION): …am ready.

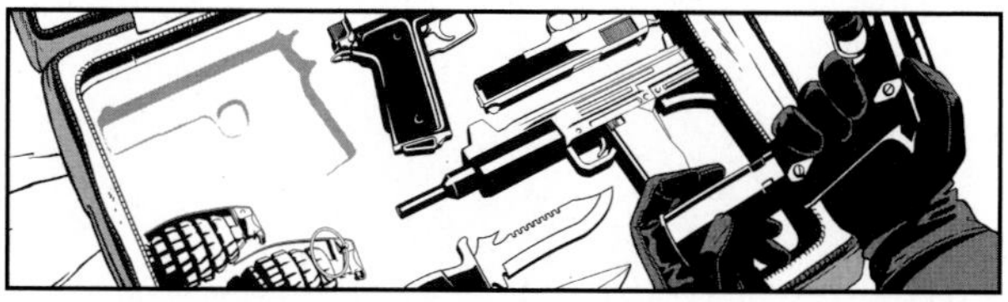

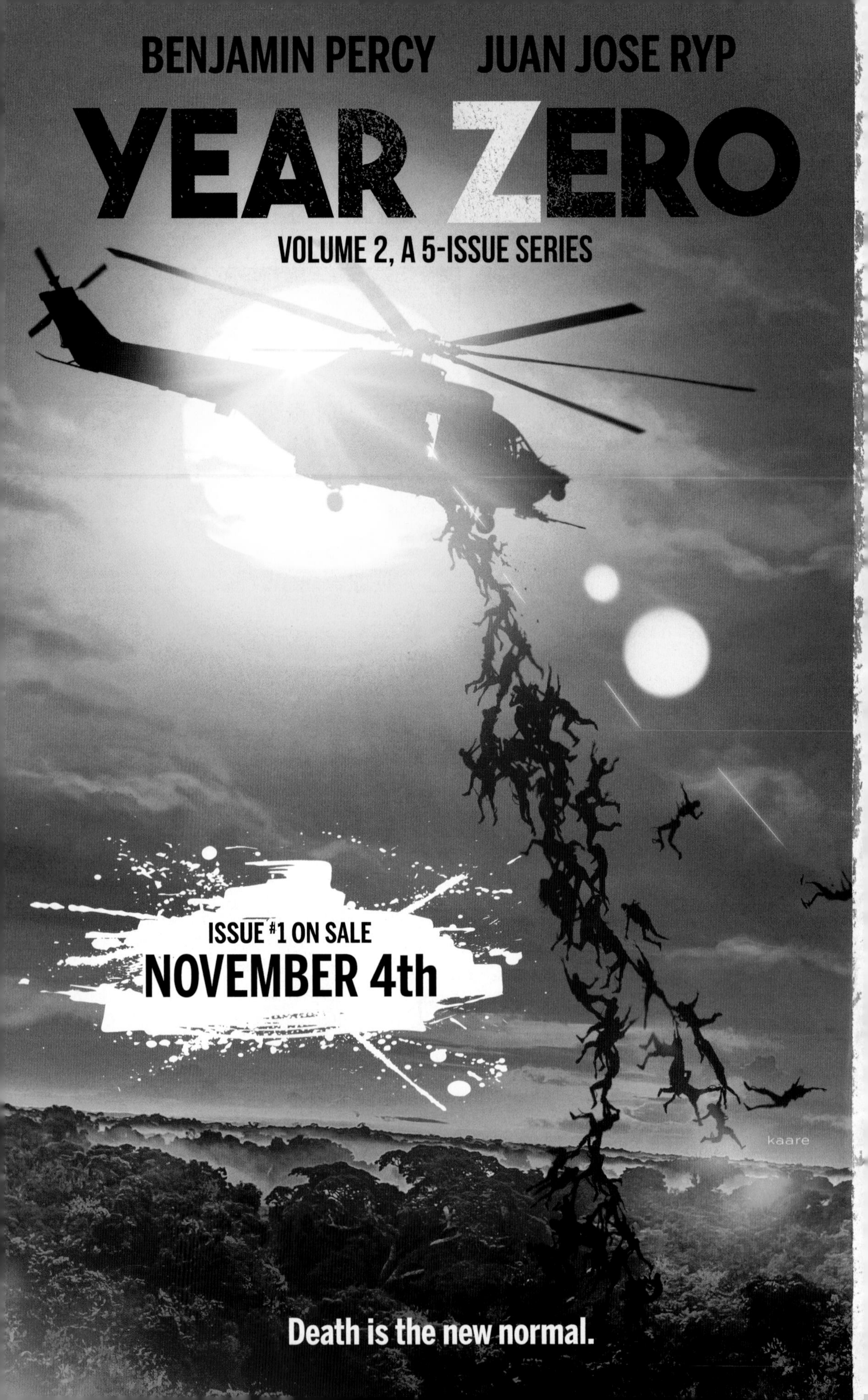
BENJAMIN PERCY JUAN JOSE RYP
YEAR ZERO
VOLUME 2, A 5-ISSUE SERIES
ISSUE #1 ON SALE
NOVEMBER 4th
kaare
Death is the new normal.